Commercial Bank Loan
and
Investment Behaviour

WILEY MONOGRAPHS IN APPLIED ECONOMETRICS

Editor

A. A. Walters, *Department of Economics, London School of Economics*

Commercial Bank Loan and Investment Behaviour
J. H. Wood,
University of Birmingham

Econometrics of Investment
J. C. R. Rowley,
Economic Council of Canada
and
P. K. Trivedi,
Australian National University

Further volumes in preparation

Commercial Bank Loan and Investment Behaviour

J. H. WOOD

University of Birmingham

JOHN WILEY & SONS

London · New York · Sydney · Toronto

Library of Congress Cataloging in Publication Data:

Wood, John Harold.
    Commercial bank loan and investment behaviour.
  Bibliography: p.
  1. Bank loans. 2. Bank loans—Mathematical models.
  3. Bank investments. 4. Monetary policy. I. Title.
HG1641.W65   332.1'753   75–1192

ISBN 0 471 95998 7

Photosetting by Thomson Press (India) Limited, New Delhi
and printed in Great Britain by the Pitman Press Ltd., Bath, Avon.

To Norma

Editor's Foreword

Economics is a body of principles and a way of thinking that enables the professional economist to unravel practical problems and to make predictions of the consequences of specified actions. Many of these statements are scientific in the sense that one can examine the consequences of such actions in the real world to see if the theory predicted correctly. Such tests are the essence of scientific credibility. Any theory that fails to predict correctly should be rejected and one should retain propositions and pursue research programmes that have not been clearly discredited by their failure to forecast the essential or key events of the real world.

The economist can rarely resort to the dramatic evidence derived from contrived experiment. Like the astro-physicist he must be content with observations of natural or market phenomena. Although such observed data are the product of market and social processes and so do not possess the cloistered purity of experimental evidence, they are at least real life events and are free from the antiseptic artificial and often misleading environment of the laboratory. Analysis of the workings of the markets of the real world is, however, difficult and elusive. Econometrics was developed in order to enable one to sift the evidence of market observations into a form such that the propositions of economics can be tested. Considerable strides have been made in applying such techniques to various economies and there are many hard lessons that have been learned.

In this series the authors attempt to give an account of the best econometric techniques now available in the context of some set of applied problems. The main focus is always on *practical* techniques that can be applied by virtually anyone with suitable computer access. In many problems, of course, it is still best to use simple methods of analysis; but it is one of the recurring themes of modern econometrics that however frequently simple methods may be usefully applied, in order to understand their subtleties one must be aware of the more complex and general methodology that underlies them.

The Series is devised for the practioner of econometrics — be he final year undergraduate, post-graduate student, thesis writer, civil servant, economic advisor, or any one of the many economists working in business and industry. We hope that the Series will have some effect in raising the standards of applied econometrics.

ALAN A. WALTERS
November 11, 1974

Preface

The research underlying this study was carried out at the Universities of Pennsylvania and Birmingham and at the Federal Reserve Bank of Philadelphia. It is a pleasure to acknowledge the generous support of the Federal Reserve Bank of Philadelphia. In addition to financial assistance, President David Eastburn and Directors of Research Mark Willes and Edward Boehne placed at my disposal the excellent secretarial, art, programming and computer facilities of the Bank. Judy Helmuth, Nancy Feldman, Bunny Jablon and Cindy Tyler managed my programming and computer needs at the Bank. I am also indebted to the Bank's research assistants—Kathy Holmes, Howard Keen, Pat Lipton and Saralyn Woods—for assistance in the collection of the data, to Ron Williams and Mary Cahill for drawing the figures and to Carol Jageman, Betty Meserve, Ginny Keiper and Claire Slowinski for typing early drafts of the text and tables.

I also wish to acknowledge a grant from the National Science Foundation and to express my appreciation to the Trustees of the Esmée Fairbairn Charitable Trust for their support.

My greatest intellectual debts are to Michael D. McCarthy, who was a continuing source of help and stimulus during my time at the University of Pennsylvania, and Donald R. Hodgman, who developed the customer relationship as a useful concept in the analysis of bank behaviour. Appendix A owes much to Professor McCarthy and to Maurice Dupre and Hirsh Tadman. Jack Guttentag's expert knowledge of institutional arrangements was of great assistance. Vincent Homolka read the entire study and made many helpful suggestions. David deCarlo wrote the programme for computing the data in Tables 2.2 and 4.2. John Morris wrote the programmes and supervised the computational work reported in Chapter 5. The substance and exposition of the study were improved by discussions with Edward Prescott, Duane Harris, Douglas Vickers, Dale Henderson, Gilbert Hebner, Mark Willes, Ira Kaminow,

George Oldfield, James Pierce, Rene Manes, Pat Hendershott, Richard Barrett, Tony Lancaster, David Sheppard, Gary Gillum, Don Patinkin, Albert Ando, Jacques Melitz, Edward Kane, Steve Littlechild, Chris Owen, Lance Davis, Ronald Sutherland, Carole Greenberg, Hans Stoll, Marshall Blume, Robert Edelstein, Phil Lewis, Uli Schlieper, James O'Brien, John Carlson, John Boyd, Frank Brechling and Richard Day.

I am grateful for the patience and help of graduate students at the University of Pennsylvania and to the members of seminars at the Federal Reserve Banks of Cleveland and Philadelphia and the Universities of Birmingham, Purdue, Essex, Hull, Odense, Aarhus and Pennsylvania, where portions of this study were presented. Comments by members of the Money Study Group Conference at Bournemouth in 1972 were also useful. An early version of portions of this study was published in the proceedings of that conference.

Portions of early drafts were typed by Pam Myers, Phyllis Hess, Ann Price, Susan Thompson and Sue Biggin. Finally, I wish to extend my thanks to Jennifer Saxby, who deciphered my handwriting to type the final draft in expert fashion.

Appreciation is expressed to the publishers of the following works for permission to use quotations appearing in this book:

The American Economic Association *for*

D. M. Jaffee and F. Modigliani, 'A Theory and Test of Credit Rationing', *American Economic Review*, December 1969.

The Bureau of Economic and Business Research of the University of Illinois at Urbana-Champaign *for*

Donald R. Hodgman, *Commercial Bank Loan and Investment Policy*, 1963.

Contents

CHAPTER 1

Introduction

The primary objective of this study is the development of a theoretical framework that will help to explain certain phenomena relating to American commercial banks. These phenomena are summarized below in Table 1.1, in which aggregate bank loans and security holdings are listed along with rates of return on loans and securities at post-World War II cyclical peaks and troughs as defined by the National Bureau of Economic Research[1]. The last date for which data were available when the table was compiled, April 1973, has been added. Perhaps the most striking features of Table 1.1 are the strong upward trends in interest rates and bank loans. However, it is the cyclical variation in these data to which I wish to draw the reader's attention. Note that both the loan rate, r, and the average yield on securities, y, rise during expansions and fall during recessions. But the cyclical variability of y exceeds that of r so that the difference $r - y$ tends to decrease in expansionary periods and increase during recessions. These movements in the rate differential during expansions, for example, would appear to cause securities, G, to become more attractive relative to loans, L, as bank investments. Yet bank holdings of securities relative to loans decline during expansions. Similarly, during recessions, bank holdings of loans relative to securities fall at the same time that rates of return on loans are rising relative to security yields. This inverse cyclical relation between $L/(L + G)$ and $r-y$ is not very sensitive to the NBER's choice of turning points[2] and is seen to hold even during the period November 1970 to April 1973 when, for the first time during a postwar expansion, loan rates fell.

The behaviour depicted in Table 1.1 cannot be called paradoxical because there exist several more-or-less plausible explanations of the data. One of these explanations has to do with the public-spiritedness of banks in meeting local credit needs. A sense of community responsibility impels them to accommodate the community's requirements during periods of rising credit demands. A closely related explanation of the data but one that does not necessarily assume the

1

same objectives on the part of banks is that 'banks play a fairly passive role in the lending process', that 'the initiative in the bank-loan market lies with the borrower, not with the banks'.[3] [Galbraith, 1963 p. 20]. A shortcoming of these explanations is that variations in the terms on which loans are extended, including interest rates, are given no role. Consequently, they can be of little assistance in explaining the empirical regularities in Table 1.1.

Table 1.1.   Interest rates and bank portfolios at postwar cyclical peaks and troughs

	Month	L	G	$\dfrac{L}{L+G}$	r	y	$r-y$
(P)	11–48	41·4	71·7	0·366	2·63	1·98	0·65
(T)	10–49	41·4	77·0	0·350	2·64	1·69	0·95
(P)	7–53	65·3	75·8	0·463	3·73	3·01	0·72
(T)	8–54	66·6	81·7	0·449	3·58	1·78	1·80
(P)	7–57	91·1	73·7	0·553	4·54	4·32	0·22
(T)	4–58	92·1	80·3	0·534	4·38	2·60	1·78
(P)	5–60	111·0	75·8	0·594	5·35	4·68	0·67
(T)	2–61	114·8	82·1	0·583	4·98	3·74	1·24
(P)	11–66	207·2	101·4	0·671	6·31	6·04	0·27
(T)	5–67	213·2	110·6	0·658	5·90	5·06	0·84
(P)	11–69	270·1	124·5	0·684	8·78	8·70	0·08
(T)	11–70	284·3	138·3	0·673	7·91	6·62	1·29
	4–73	400·2	177·1	0·693	7·26	7·12	0·14

L = Loans of all commercial banks in billions of dollars.
G = Security holdings of all commercial banks in billions of dollars.
r = Average rate of interest on short-term business loans, per cent per annum.
y = Weighted average of yields-to-maturity on securities, per cent per annum. The weights used are the average proportions of U.S. Government securities of different maturities and of state and local securities held by banks during the postwar period. If variable-weights had been used (the weights varying with proportions of bank security holdings) the values of y beginning in November 1948 would have been 1·76, 1·48, 2·79, 1·69, 4·11, 2·41, 4·57, 3·56, 6·39, 5·35, 9·68, 7·09, 7·68. The qualitative nature of the cyclical variation of $r-y$ discussed in the text is not changed by the use of variable weights.

Sources and detailed descriptions of the data are contained in Appendix B.

Another interpretation of the data takes into account the possibility that the observed rates r and y are not likely to be equal to expected rates of return on loans and securities, which we may denote $\bar{r}$ and $\bar{y}$. If the riskiness of loans as evaluated by bankers is inversely related to the level of economic activity, then observed variations in contract loan rates understate the variability of expected rates of return on loans. Another set of factors operating in the same direction is that loan terms other than the contract rate tend to become more stringent from the standpoint of borrowers and more attractive to banks during periods of rising economic activity and loan demand. Furthermore, if bankers expect recent changes in security yields to continue in the same direction, then the variability of $\bar{y}$ is less than that of y. Consequently, it is possible that the rate differential $\bar{r} - \bar{y}$ moves in the same direction as economic activity and as bank loans relative to total earning assets. On the other hand, if bankers formulate interest rate expectations such that movements away from a 'normal' rate are expected to be reversed, then observed cyclical variations in y understate those in $\bar{y}$.

An alternative explanation of the data may be described as follows. If, at times of economic expansion and upward pressures on interest rates, bank asset preferences tend to change such that their desire for loans increases at the expense of their demand for securities, we may observe loan rates rising less than security yields simultaneously with upward movements in bank loans relative to security holdings. Such a rationalization of the data, if it is to be complete, must include an explanation of why bank asset demands change in this manner. The theory of commercial bank behaviour developed below is an attempt at such an explanation. A theory is presented that takes as its point of departure the bank–customer relationship introduced to the literature on banking theory and practice by Hodgman [1961, 1963]. The objective is to determine whether the empirical regularities in Table 1.1 can be explained within the framework of a dynamic model of commercial bank asset choice built upon the customer relationship.

A model of individual bank behaviour is developed in Chapters 2–4. This model is based upon two related observations regarding differences between the markets for loans and securities as viewed by a bank: (i) The bank is a perfect competitor in the securities market but an imperfect competitor in the market for bank loans. (ii) Due to the nature of the bank–customer relationship, the loan demand confronting a bank currently is dependent not only upon current loan rates but also upon the quantities of loans extended by the bank in earlier periods. This is not true of the securities market—current yields on securities are independent of the bank's past investments in securities. As a consequence, in selecting its portfolio the profit-maximizing bank takes into account not only current loan demand but also the influence of current loans on future loan demands. A further dynamic consideration concerns deposits. A liberal loan policy may also induce increases in future deposit supplies. The principal implication of these dynamic loan and deposit aspects of the customer relationship is that banks raise loan rates less and increase the quantity of loans more during periods of economic expansion than would otherwise be the case. The parameters of the model developed in Chapters 2–4 are estimated in Chapter 5. The implications of these estimates are then discussed and the conditions under which the customer relationship is by itself sufficient to explain the data in Table 1.1 are derived.

No mention has been made of 'credit rationing' or the 'availability doctrine' as possible explanations of cyclical variations in commercial bank portfolios. To the extent that the proponents of these theories have had anything to say about bank portfolios in the aggregate it has usually been in connection with attempts to explain phenomena that are the reverse of those illustrated in Table 1.1, i.e. why banks might wish to move out of loans into securities during periods of rising interest rates.[4] Recently, however, Jaffee and Modigliani [1969] have built upon the early work in credit rationing by introducing loan demands, which most previous writers had neglected, thus making possible the explanation of observed bank behaviour within the framework of a theory of credit rationing.[5] The model developed in Chapters 2–4 is disaggregated in Chapter 6 in order that the significance of the customer relationship for the behaviour of large banks may be compared to that of small banks. Then the ability of the disaggregated customer relationship model to explain observed bank behaviour is compared with that of the Jaffee–Modigliani theory of credit rationing.

The customer relationship is often viewed as a substitute for variable deposit rates as a means of attracting deposits. To the extent that this is so the removal of prohibitions against interest payments on demand deposits should lead to a decline in the importance of the customer relationship. In Chapter 7 the efficacy of monetary policy in the presence of the customer relationship is compared to that in a regime in which the customer relationship is supplanted by variable deposit rates.

NOTES

1. For listings of the NBER's turning points see Moore and Shiskin [1967] and Fabricant [1971]. The dates of the 1966–67 mini-recession, which has not been accorded official recognition by the NBER, are those of Fabricant.
2. This may be seen in Chart 5.1.
3. Galbraith is here summarizing a view set forth in detail by Schumpeter [1939, pp. 641–43]. A special case of this passive approach to bank lending is the real bills doctrine' or 'commercial loan theory'. See Andersen and Burger [1969] for a comparison of the empirical implications of 'accommodation' and 'profit-maximizing' theories of bank behaviour.
4. For a critique of this literature see Kane and Malkiel [1965]. The 'lock-in effect' is also a rationalization of the unobserved, viz. why banks might be reluctant to sell securities in the face of rising interest rates. If the motives assumed by the lock-in effect have influenced commercial bank portfolio decisions it is apparent that they have been dominated by other forces. For discussions of the lock-in effect see Chase [1962], Kane and Malkiel [1965] and Kane [1968].
5. Guttentag [1960] has also advanced a model in which loan rates and various measures of credit availability are simultaneously determined by supply and demand forces.

CHAPTER 2

Dynamic Loan Demand: The Loan–Customer Relationship

2.1 INTRODUCTION AND ASSUMPTIONS

This chapter begins the development of a microeconomic model of commercial bank portfolio selection in a regime in which a bank's behaviour today influences its ability to earn profits tomorrow. Specifically, the current accommodation of prospective borrowers induces some of those customers to maintain recurrent or continuing loan and/or deposit relations with the bank. Hodgman and others have emphasized the intertemporal relation between current loans and future deposits, which will be treated in Chapter 3. This chapter deals exclusively with the intertemporal loan relationship.

The model presented here is exceedingly simple within any single period; all of the complications are of an intertemporal nature. The following simplifying assumptions are made:

(a) The sole objective of the bank is profit maximization and we abstract from all problems associated with risk and uncertainty. These assumptions, especially that of certainty, may be the cause of unhappiness to some readers. I do not question the usefulness of the considerable literature in which banks maximize expected profits. However, because of the difficulties associated with the simultaneous treatment of uncertainty and multi-period horizons, these studies have been limited to the analysis of single-period decision problems. The present study extends earlier analyses of bank behaviour by introducing intertemporal considerations and allowing the decision horizon to be of any length, although at the cost of imposing the certainty assumption. While a study encompassing both uncertainty and multi-period horizons would no doubt be very useful, the resultant model and its implications would be exceedingly complex. I believe that the simpler model presented below will be justified by its contribution to our understanding of certain intertemporal aspects of commercial bank behaviour. The empirical implications of this model will be compared with those of Jaffee and Modigliani's one-period expected-profit-maximization model in Chapter 6.

5

The assumption of profit maximization is, I think, easily defended. Although much of the traditional banking literature neglected to apply the standard tools of microeconomic analysis, it is not easy to understand how so many writers acquired the notion that the standard theory of the firm was peculiarly inapplicable to commercial banks. Certainly, the record does not support that view. The history of banking, at least in the United States and Great Britain, has been one of large scale shifts among assets in response to movements in differentials among rates of return. These shifts suggest a fairly regular pattern of bank behaviour based upon profit maximization and extrapolative expectations. The cycle of bank expansion, financial crisis, contraction and expansion again is familiar. Most proposals for the stricter regulation of banks have been firmly founded upon the assumption that banks will always subordinate the principles of 'sound and responsible banking' to those of profit maximization. Banking controversies have stemmed from differences about how, not whether, the profit maximizing proclivities of bankers are to be restrained. Of the several nineteenth century British bankers who committed themselves to print on the subject of how bankers ought to behave, all accepted, on the basis of a history of repeated financial panics and bank failures, the proneness of their colleagues to substitute profits for 'soundness'. (See Thornton [1802], Gilbart [1865] and Rae [1885]). A large and growing assemblage of laws and regulatory bodies has been instituted for the purpose of restraining the more extreme manifestations of the pursuit of profits by commercial banks. But there is no evidence that the profit motive is less important to banks now than it was a century ago, that banks have not persisted in maximizing profits subject to the constraints under which they operate even though those constraints apparently have become more restrictive. In fact, the available evidence indicates that banks have to a considerable extent been able to frustrate the purposes of regulations intended to reduce the risk associated with banking at the expense of bank profits. (See Peltzman [1970] and Mayne [1972].)

(b) Only two earning assets are available to the bank: homogeneous one-period securities and homogeneous one-period loans. No distinction is drawn between bond, bill, certificate or note obligations of the U.S. or state and local governments or between the various types of loans to firms and households. With respect to the assumption of homogeneous securities, Table 2.1 shows that the composition of commercial bank security portfolios has altered substantially in recent years. However, the increased bank holdings of state and local securities may be interpreted not so much as a shift in demand from one distinctive type of asset to another in response to changes in relative risk and return as a movement between highly substitutable assets due to a shift in relative supplies. This interpretation suggests that the assumption of homogeneous securities may not be unduly unrealistic. It is supported by the observation that the yields on these categories of securities have moved closely together over the postwar period despite substantial changes in relative quantities outstanding. The homogeneity assumption is also supported by the observation that the increase in state and local government securities in bank

Table 2.1.　End-of-year commercial bank loans and investments.[a] Billions of dollars and percentages ( ) of total

	1947		1960		1970	
Investments	76·7	(100)	81·9	(100)	147·9	(100)
U.S. Government (total)	67·9	(88)	61·0	(74)	61·7	(42)
0–1 year	18·6	(24)	16·5	(20)	23·3	(16)
1–5 years	37·0	(48)	35·5	(43)	32·2	(22)
5–10 years	6·8	(9)	6·4	(8)	5·5	(4)
over 10 years	5·5	(7)	2·6	(3)	0·7	(·5)
State and local government	5·1	(7)	17·6	(21)	69·6	(47)
Other investments[b]	3·6	(5)	3·3	(4)	16·5	(11)
Loans	37·6	(100)	120·0	(100)	314·1	(100)
Commercial and industrial	18·0	(48)	43·1	(36)	112·5	(36)
Agricultural	1·6	(4)	5·7	(5)	11·2	(4)
For purchasing and carrying securities	2·0	(5)	5·1	(4)	9·9	(3)
Real Estate	9·3	(25)	28·7	(24)	72·5	(23)
Other loans to individuals	5·6	(15)	26·4	(22)	65·8	(21)
Other loans[c]	1·0	(3)	11·0	(9)	42·3	(13)

[a]Total loans and investments in this table would differ from those in Table 1.1 even if the reporting dates were the same because, unlike Table 2.1, the data in Table 1.1 are seasonally adjusted, exclude interbank loans and have been adjusted to take account of revisions in the published series.
[b]Corporate bonds and stocks and obligations of Federal agencies.
[c]Mainly Federal funds sold and loans to financial institutions.

Source: *Federal Reserve Bulletin.*

portfolios has taken place largely at the expense of medium-term and long-term U.S. Government securities. As a result, there has been little change in the maturity structure of commercial bank security holdings. For example, the average maturity of U.S. securities held by commercial banks fell from 3.7 to 2.6 years from the end of 1947 to the end of 1970.[1] Since the average maturity of state and local government securities held by banks has also fallen slightly since 1947, it is probable that the average maturity of all bank security holdings has increased only slightly if at all.[2]

Changes have also taken place in the composition of commercial bank loan portfolios, although not as much as in the case of securities. The largest category of loans has remained those to commercial and industrial firms, although these have declined relatively to loans to individuals (mainly consumer credit) and to financial institutions (mainly Federal funds). The discussion in this study pertains principally to commercial and industrial loans, partly because these comprise the largest category of loans and also because the data on rates charged for these loans are superior to other loan-rate data. The average term to maturity of formal loan agreements has increased in recent years. However, both the tendency of short-term borrowers to borrow continuously from banks and the growing practice of letting loan rates vary over the life of loans serve to strengthen the substitutability between short-term and long-term loans from the standpoints of both banks and borrowers. These considerations mitigate but do not remove the problems arising from the aggregation of all loans into a single class. Aggregation problems will be alleviated somewhat in Chapter 6 when loans are disaggregated by size.

(c) Consistent with the assumption of homogeneous loans, it is assumed in Chapters 2–5 that borrowers are homogeneous. In particular, the form and parameters of the loan demands and deposit supplies confronted by a bank are identical for all borrowers and depositors. This allows us to deal with the aggregate loan demand and the aggregate deposit supply facing the bank. This assumption is relaxed in Chapter 6 when the behaviour of a bank that lends to different types of customers is examined.

(d) The only variable dimension of loans and securities is the rate of return. A large body of empirical evidence relating to the term structure of interest rates supports the assumption of equal expected returns on different types of securities, evidence that also supports our treatment of securities of different terms to maturity as perfect substitutes.[3] Our treatment of the rate of return as the only variable dimension of loans is a reasonable procedure if variations in other loan terms correspond closely to those in loan rates so that the average loan rate becomes an index of all loan terms. This approach has recently received empirical support from the work of Harris [1970, 1974]. The only systematic data on changes in loan dimensions are contained in the Federal Reserve Board's 'Quarterly Survey of Changes in Bank Lending Practices' as reported in the *Federal Reserve Bulletin*. An examination of these data by Harris has produced some interesting results that ought to be reassuring to those economists who have emphasized loan rates and neglected other loan terms: (i) Dimensions of the loan contract other than the contract rate of interest (such as compensating balance requirements, maturity and standards of credit worthiness) are highly correlated with the interest charge over time. (ii) The interest charge is the most volatile element in loan contracts. That is, bankers rely most heavily on interest rates as a device for rationing loans with other loan terms playing a supporting role in the rationing process.

(e) Rates of return are assumed to be net of taxes and operating costs. Problems arise immediately due to the differential tax treatment of capital gains and coupon income and because of the tax-exempt status of state and local government securities. However, if security markets operate in such a way that expected net one-period rates of return are equalized in the manner suggested by the expectations theory of the term structure of interest rates, if the expectations of commercial banks are consistent with those dominant in the market and if bank decision periods are shorter than one year, then Treasury bill rates are indicative of expected net rates of return on all classes of securities held by banks. This is the procedure adopted in the empirical work in Chapter 5.[4]

The average operating cost of extending loans is assumed to be constant and equal to the average operating cost of purchasing securities, where loans and securities are measured in dollars. That is, there are no economies due either to scale or to switching between securities and loans. Although the assumption of no economies of scale is an oversimplification,[5] its relaxation would alter the character of the study only by accentuating the results in Chapter 3; the bank would have an additional reason to charge a low loan rate currently in order to attract future deposits and thereby gain the advantages of a larger scale of operations.

(f) The individual bank is a price-taker in the securities market but an imperfect competitor in the market for loans. This competitive difference between the securities and loan markets as viewed by the individual bank is the first of two distinctions between these assets made in this study. The assumption of a perfectly competitive securities market is realistic even for state and local government securities, most of which are traded in centralized markets. The assumption of imperfectly competitive loan markets is especially applicable to small banks, which do business principally with small firms with limited alternative sources of credit, but may be less appropriate for those large banks that lend to firms with access to several banks as well as the money markets.

(g) The individual bank expects to lose all of the deposits that it creates in connection with loans; loans and security purchases deplete the bank's reserves in the same way. This is not inconsistent with assumption (f) in a monopolistically competitive regime in which many banks face downward sloping demand curves yet each bank is small relative to the markets for loans and deposits. This is a simplification but is not excessively unrealistic in a system of 13,000 banks. (See Chapter 4.1 for more about the assumption of monopolistic competition).

(h) We abstract until Chapter 4 from the effects on the individual bank of rates charged and loans extended by other banks.

(i) The bank's ratio of reserves to deposits is assumed fixed and it does not borrow from the Federal Reserve or other banks. These assumptions will be relaxed in Chapter 4.

(j) All items on the liability side of the bank's balance sheet are assumed fixed until Chapter 3 when deposit variation is introduced. This assumption requires that profits be paid to shareholders at the end of each period, which simplifies the arithmetic without having any qualitative effect on the results.

(k) Deposits are treated as homogeneous. This unrealistic assumption enables us to concentrate our attention on the asset side of the bank's balance sheet, which is the primary object of the study. Little damage is done if the bank's loan-security mix is independent of the relative quantities of time and demand deposits. We also abstract from the income and expenses associated with maintaining deposits.

(l) Consistent with the assumption of one-period assets and the additional assumption of rapid receipt, processing and application of new information, it is assumed that the allocation of the bank's portfolio between loans and securities in each period is optimal; there is no partial-adjustment process.

Clearly, a model based upon these highly restrictive assumptions, which exclude several important elements of bank behaviour, cannot approach a complete model of the commercial bank. I do not wish to argue that the development of a more general model is undesirable or potentially unfruitful, merely that the simple model made possible by these assumptions is capable of increasing our understanding of some interesting and important aspects of commercial bank behaviour.

2.2 THE TWO-PERIOD MODEL

Given the assumptions set forth above, if the bank's horizon is only one period or if future constraints are independent of current operations, the bank will set its loan rate such that loans are extended to the point at which the marginal revenue from loans equals the rate of return on securities. This point of one-period profit maximization occurs in Figure 2.1(a) at the loan rate r_1^0 and the quantity of loans l_1^0, where L_1A_1 and L_1M_1 are the loan demand and marginal revenue curves, respectively.[6]

This study, however, is founded upon the contention that the future constraints confronted by the bank, specifically loan demands, are not independent of the bank's current decisions. A large amount of evidence indicates that banks and their borrowers tend to maintain continuous relationships and that both groups are keenly conscious of the need to keep those relationships unimpaired. For example, a Federal Reserve survey of business loans outstanding at member banks in October 1955 showed that

'the majority of business loans, although nominally of short maturities, have been converted into longer-term credit in effect through the practice of continuous renewals. Thus, one-half of the volume of commercial and industrial loans was outstanding to borrowers who had been continuously in debt to the same bank for 2 years or more, while one-fourth of the loan volume represented continuous borrowers of 5 years or longer ....

'The business loan survey disclosed that while only one-third of the amount of notes was over one year old, nearly two-thirds of the dollar volume of commercial and industrial loans was outstanding to borrowers who had been continuously in debt on such loans to the same banks for one year or more. Similarly, while only 22 per cent of the amount of notes was 2 years or more, half of the amount of notes represented borrowers continuously in debt for 2 years or longer.

'At the extremes of "age", although over one-third of the dollar amount of notes was less than 3 months old, only 8 per cent of the dollar volume represented borrowers who had been in debt to the same banks for as little as 3 months. At the opposite extremes, while only 6 per cent of the amount of notes showed an age of 5 years or more, no less than 25 per cent of the dollar volume of loans was outstanding to borrowers who had been continuously in debt to the same banks for five years or longer.

'Not only notes recently made, but notes of all ages showed evidence of having been renewed often.'

[Federal Reserve Bank of Cleveland, 1956][7]

The repeated renewal of loans is not a new phenomenon but has been the subject of comment by numerous writers in reference to a variety of times and places; for example, by Mints [1945, p. 20] for seventeenth century England and Hammond [1957, pp. 680–84] and Payne and Davis [1956, pp. 134–37] for the United States in the nineteenth century. Of the many interesting implications of the bank-borrower relationship suggested by these observations, the one to be explored here is that the current accommodation of prospective borrowers by a bank influences future demands for credit from that bank. This effect is due to search costs and other costs to borrowers of transferring business from one bank to another. We have thus introduced the second distinction between loans and securities—the loan-customer relationship. Not only is there an inverse relation between the quantity of loans and the loan rate in the current period, the current quantity of loans extended affects the strength of future loan demands. Neither of these characteristics applies to a bank's operations in securities. The profitability of future security transactions is not altered by a bank's failure to buy another bond today. However, by a decision not to accommodate a prospective borrower on favourable terms a bank not only foregoes the revenue from that loan, the dissatisfied borrower may take his business elsewhere in the future. The bank has missed an opportunity to strengthen future loan demands. The imposition of stringent loan terms by the bank will induce larger and more rapid declines in future loan demands the greater is the access of borrowers to alternative sources of credit on terms competitive with those required by the bank.

Consider a bank whose balance sheet in the tth period may be expressed as follows:

$$L_t + G_t = (1 - k)Q_t + K \tag{2.1}$$

where L_t, G_t and Q_t are dollar values of loans, securities and deposits, respectively. The capital account, K, which is also expressed in dollars, and the reserve ratio, k, are assumed to be invariant over time. Deposits are also assumed to be constant in this chapter but are allowed to vary beginning with Chapter 3.

The quotation and argument at the beginning of this section suggest that the loan demand confronting the bank in the tth period may be written

$$L_t = L(r_t, y_t, z_t, L_{t-1}, L_{t-2}, \ldots, L_{t-n}) \tag{2.2}$$

where current loan demand is dependent upon the quantities of loans extended over the previous n periods. An index of economic activity, z_t, is assumed to be an indicator of the strength of loan demand. Current and future economic activity are assumed to be unaffected by the policies of the individual bank; i.e. z_t, like the rate of return on securities, is given exogenously to the bank. The demand for loans in the tth period responds negatively to the loan rate,

r_t, and positively to the security rate, y_t, in that period. A higher y_t increases the possibility that those requiring funds will seek loans rather than sell securities.

One can easily imagine circumstances in which some of the derivatives $\partial L_t / \partial L_{t-i}$ ($i = 1, 2, ..., n$) are either less than zero or greater than unity. For example, additional customers may be attracted if a liberal loan policy by the bank becomes widely known, in which case some of the $\partial L_t / \partial L_{t-i}$ might exceed unity. On the other hand, if the bank is large relative to the size of the community, a liberal loan policy might reduce future loan demands by satiating the demand for funds.[8] Although the model admits these circumstances as special cases, the discussion will in general be based on the assumption that all $\partial L_t / \partial L_{t-i}$ lie between zero and unity; i.e., for constant r_t, y_t and z_t, some of the loan demands accommodated by the bank in earlier periods, but not all, will be repeated in the tth period.

We wish to determine the optimal proportions of loans and securities in the bank's portfolio of earning assets. Therefore, it will be useful to divide (2.1) by the fixed quantity $L_t + G_t = (1 - k)Q_t + K = F$ in order to express the balance sheet as follows:

$$l_t + g_t = 1 \qquad (2.3)$$

where l_t and g_t are loans and securities, respectively, as proportions of total earning assets, F. The demand for loans can also be expressed as a proportion of F by substituting Fl_{t-i} for L_{t-i} ($i = 0, 1, ..., n$) in (2.2) and dividing through by F:

$$l_t = l(r_t, y_t, z_t, l_{t-1}, l_{t-2}, ..., l_{t-n}; F) \qquad (2.4)$$

Assume that the bank desires to maximize the sum of discounted profits, π, which is expressed in equation (2.5) as a proportion of total earning assets:

$$\pi = \sum_{t=1}^{T} \beta^{t-1}(r_t l_t + y_t g_t) \qquad 0 \le \beta \le 1 \qquad (2.5)$$

where T is the bank's decision-making horizon. The discount factor, β, depends upon rates of return on investments alternative to bank capital and may be regarded as an independent variable from the standpoint of the bank.

Let us assume for the remainder of this section that the bank's horizon is two periods ($T = 2$). In such a case the bank will select r_t, l_t and g_t for $t = 1, 2$ so as to maximize the objective function (2.5) subject to the balance sheet and market restraints (2.3) and (2.4). This constrained maximization procedure yields the following marginal conditions:

$$\left(r_1 + \frac{\dfrac{l_1}{\partial l_1}}{\partial r_1} \right) - \frac{\beta l_2}{\dfrac{\partial l_2}{\partial r_2}} \frac{\partial l_2}{\partial l_1} = y_1 \qquad (2.6)$$

$$r_2 + \frac{l_2}{\dfrac{\partial l_2}{\partial r_2}} = y_2 \qquad (2.7)$$

The left-hand side of (2.7) is marginal revenue from loans in the second period. Since y_2 is marginal revenue from second-period security purchases, equation (2.7) merely states that the bank plans to extend loans in the second period (select r_2) such that the marginal returns from loans and securities will be equalized. Because the bank's horizon ends with the second period in the present example, there are no additional factors influencing the bank's plans for that period.

But we see from (2.6) that, where $\partial l_2/\partial r_2 < 0$ and $\partial l_2/\partial l_1 > 0$ so that the term outside the parentheses on the left-hand side of (2.6) is positive, the bank maximizes profit by arranging its first-period portfolio such that first period marginal revenue from loans [the term in parentheses in (2.6)] is less than that from securities (y_1). That is, the bank extends more loans in the first period than would be the case if it considered only first-period profit. It does this because by thus expanding loans it induces an increase in loan demand and therefore profit in the second period. In an analysis similar in many respects to that presented here, Phelps and Winter refer to their version of the inter-temporal term in (2.6) as the 'imputed value of patronage'. It is 'a value whose economic rationale is that the patronage costs something to acquire (through temporary price concessions) and can be reconverted to cash (through price increases)'. [1970, p. 316]. That patronage is more valuable and the bank has more incentive to extend loans beyond the single-period optimum the greater is the strength of the loan-customer relationship, $\partial l_2/\partial l_1$, the greater is the present value of a dollar earned in the second period, β, and the less elastic is second-period loan demand. The elasticity of second-period loan demand is important because of the upward influence of the increased loan demand on r_2. The less elastic (in absolute value) is second-period loan demand $(\partial l_2/\partial r_2)(r_2/l_2)$ the greater will be the addition to second-period revenue resulting from the higher value of r_2. The effect of an increase in l_1 on second-period revenue is due partly to the shift in l_2 and partly to the movement along the new demand curve to the higher r_2.

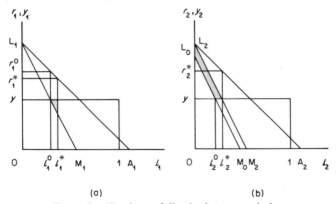

Figure 2.1. Bank portfolios in the two-period case

These results are illustrated in Figure 2.1. $L_1 A_1$ is the loan demand confronting the bank in the first period and $L_1 M_1$ is the corresponding marginal revenue curve. The marginal revenue ($=$ average revenue) from bond purchases is perfectly elastic at y ($= y_1 = y_2$), where for simplicity it is assumed that the bank expects the bond rate in the second period to be equal to the rate currently prevailing. If the bank were interested only in first period profit ($\beta = 0$) or if future loan demand were independent of current loans extended ($\partial l_2 / \partial l_1 = 0$), the bank would set a loan rate r_1^0 and extend a quantity of loans l_1^0 (as a proportion of its earning assets) at which the marginal revenue from loans equals that from securities. But, as seen from equation (2.6), the bank increases loans beyond l_1^0 when dynamic considerations are introduced. In Figure 2.1 maximization of the sum of discounted profits implies a first-period loan rate $r_1^* < r_1^0$ and first-period loans $l_1^* > l_1^0$. This increase in loans in the amount $l_1^* - l_1^0$ reduces first-period profit below the maximum attainable by the amount indicated by the shaded area in Figure 2.1(a). The number 1 on the horizontal axis indicates the maximum possible value of l_t as a proportion of the bank's investment fund. Thus, $1 - l_1^* = g_1^*$ is the optimal first-period investment in securities.

The loan demand facing the bank in the second period is $L_2 A_2$ and the corresponding marginal revenue curve is $L_2 M_2$. If the bank had maximized first-period profit by setting $r_1 = r_1^0$ and $l_1 = l_1^0$, second-period marginal revenue would have been $L_0 M_0$ ($L_0 A_0$ is not shown). The increment in second-period profit resulting from the bank's policy of setting l_1 at l_1^* rather than l_1^0 is indicated by the shaded area in Figure 2.1(b). The additional revenue from second-period loans is the shaded area plus the rectangle with height Oy and base $l_2^0 l_2^*$. Since the introduction of the dynamic element into loan demand has reduced the optimal g_2 from $1 - l_2^0$ to $1 - l_2^*$, the decrease in second-period revenue from securities is measured by the same rectangle. The second-period revenue pertinent to the bank's decision is that shown in Figure 2.1(b) times the discount factor β.

Equation (2.6) indicates that the extent to which the bank is able to increase total profit by reducing first-period profit depends upon, among other factors, the discount factor β and the strength of the dynamic relation $\partial l_2 / \partial l_1$. If these factors are sufficiently strong it will pay the bank to put all of its funds into loans: we will have a corner solution at $l_1^* = 1$. On the other hand, if $\partial l_2 / \partial l_1$ were negative and large in absolute value, we would obtain a corner solution at $l_1^* = 0$. Thus, if the first-order conditions (2.6) and (2.7) are to be consistent with a maximum, β and $\partial l_2 / \partial l_1$ must not be overly large in absolute value. It will be seen in the linear two-period case that an interior maximum requires $\beta(\partial l_2 / \partial l_1)^2 < 4$. This is a necessary but not a sufficient condition for an interior maximum; the bank might choose an undiversified portfolio for either very strong or very weak demand functions even if $\partial l_2 / \partial l_1$ and β satisfy the above restriction. In this study we will consider only those demand functions that yield interior solutions; i.e. we will assume the inequality restraints $0 < l_t, g_t < 1$ always to be satisfied.

It will be remembered from the discussion in Chapter 1 that the motivation of this study was the desire to explain cyclical variations in loans as a proportion of bank earning assets, l_t, in relation to the differential between loan and security rates, $r_t - y_t$. On the basis of the groundwork developed above, we are now able to bring the model to bear on this problem. Linear loan demands will be used for reasons of simplicity. The loan demand function (2.4) may be written in linear form as follows:

$$l_t = a - br_t + cz_t + uy_t + \gamma \sum_{i=1}^{n} d^i l_{t-i} \quad 0 \le d < 1 \tag{2.8}$$

where $b, c, u, \gamma, d \ge 0$. The coefficients a, b, c and u, like l, are proportions of earning assets, F. A dynamic loan relation in the form of a distributed lag with geometrically declining weights has been used partly because the calculation and interpretation of results is simplest for this type of lag distribution and also because it seems reasonable to suppose that the loan-customer relationship is strongest for those customers that have most recently borrowed from the bank. This is consistent with the Federal Reserve survey quoted above.

In order to be able to predict the bank's cyclical behaviour we must know how it formulates expectations of future events. Specifically, we must state the manner in which the bank revises its expectations of future levels of economic activity and security yields in response to observed changes in z_t and y_t. Extending a procedure used by Metzler [1941] and Enthoven [1956], assume that the level of economic activity expected by the bank to prevail next period, z_{t+1}, is equal to the current level, z_t, plus some fraction, w, of the most recent change in economic activity, $z_t - z_{t-1}$:

$$z_{t+1} = z_t + w(z_t - z_{t-1}) \tag{2.9}$$

Using Enthoven's terminology, expectations are 'static' when $w = 0$ and the current level of economic activity is expected to persist. Expectations are 'extrapolative' when $w > 0$; i.e. the expected value of z_{t+1} is an extrapolation of the movement in observed levels of economic activity. Equation (2.9) has desirable steady-state properties—no change in economic activity between periods $t - 1$ and t implies that no change is expected to occur between periods t and $t + 1$.

If we assume that w is non-negative but less than unity and let the current period be denoted by $t = 1$, equation (2.10) may be derived from (2.9) by repeated substitution:

$$z_t = \left(\frac{1 - w^t}{1 - w}\right) z_1 - \left(\frac{w - w^t}{1 - w}\right) z_0 \quad (0 \le w < 1)\,(t = 1, 2, ..., T) \tag{2.10}$$

Consequently, induced changes in expected levels of economic activity are governed by the relationship

$$\frac{\partial z_t}{\partial z_1} = \frac{1 - w^t}{1 - w} \tag{2.11}$$

Because of the extrapolative nature of expectations when w exceeds zero, the bank revises expectations of z_t by larger amounts the greater is t. Revisions of expectations in the distant future approach $1/(1 - w)$ as the bank's horizon approaches an infinite length.

Assume that the bank revises its expectations of security yields in the same manner as for economic activity so that

$$\frac{\partial y_t}{\partial y_1} = \frac{1 - w^t}{1 - w} \tag{2.12}$$

Under the conditions set forth in equations (2.1)–(2.12), the bank's response to increases in economic activity and the rate of return on securities will be as follows: First, in the absence of dynamic elements (γ, d or β equal to zero) there will be increases in the loan rate, r_1, and in bank loans as a proportion of total earning assets, l_1.[9] Let these variables take initial values of r_1' and l_1' and rise to $r_1'' > r_1'$ and $l_1'' > l_1'$ after the increases in z_1 and y_1 (from z_1' to z_1'' and y_1' to y_1'') but before the introduction of dynamic considerations. When future profits and the dynamic aspects of loan demand are considered the bank has an additional reason to extend more loans. The rise in economic activity has confronted the bank with increased demands for credit from present and prospective customers. As a result, each increase in the loan rate means a greater number of disappointed borrowers than formerly and, therefore, a greater cost to the bank in the form of weaker future loan demands than might have been achieved by a liberal lending policy. This cost is positively related to γ and d, which determine the response of future loan demands to current loans extended, and β, the rate of discount against future profits. Consequently, the increase in the loan rate will be less and the increase in loans will be greater for high than for low values of γ, d and β. Because of these intertemporal elements, the optimal levels of r_1 and l_1 following the rise in economic activity will be $r_1''' < r_1''$ and $l_1''' > l_1''$. If γ, d and β are sufficiently large, the increase in r_1 from its initial position, $r_1''' - r_1'$, will be less than the increase in the rate of return on securities, $y_1'' - y_1'$. If this is the case, we will observe a movement by the bank out of securities into loans at the same time that the rate of return on loans declines relatively to that on securities. Thus, the customer relationship as embodied in the parameters γ, d and β is at least in principle capable of explaining the cyclical variations in bank behaviour observed in Table 1.1.

The effects of changes in economic activity on loans and relative rates described above may occur even in the presence of 'static' expectations ($w = 0$), i.e. where induced expectations are zero and the new level of z is expected to persist. But if expectations are 'extrapolative' ($w > 0$) the bank has further reason to hold r_1 at a relatively low level in order to increase l_1. This is because an increase in future economic activity and therefore loan demand will enable the bank to charge higher rates than otherwise on the future loans attracted by a current liberal lending policy.

Let us examine more closely the bank's response to economic activity in the linear two-period case. The purpose is to determine those values of γ, d, β and

w that are consistent with alternative patterns of commercial bank interest rate and portfolio behaviour. The following calculations are performed: First maximize (2.5) subject to (2.3) and (2.8) with respect to l_t, r_t, g_t $(t = 1, 2)$; then solve for the optimal values of the bank's decision variables—l_t^*, r_t^*, g_t^*; finally, substitute (2.11) into this solution and partially differentiate with respect to z_1. As in any intertemporal model, while current decisions and future plans are simultaneously determined in such a way as to maximize the objective function, only current decision variables (l_1^*, r_1^*, g_1^*) are sure of being implemented. Future portfolios and loan rates may or may not assume the values chosen in the first (current) period, depending upon whether or not the bank's expectations are realized. The decision process is repeated each period based upon new information and revised expectations. The portfolio that is implemented in any period is always that which corresponds to $t = 1$. The results are as follows, where the derivative of g_1^* is not shown because it is simply $\partial g_1^*/\partial z_1 = -\partial l_1^*/\partial z_1$:

$$\left(\frac{\partial l_1^*}{\partial z_1}\right)_y = \frac{c[2 + \beta\gamma d(1 + w)]}{4 - \beta\gamma^2 d^2} > 0; \quad \left(\frac{\partial^2 l_1^*}{\partial z_1 \partial d}\right)_y > 0 \qquad (2.13)$$

$$\left(\frac{\partial r_1^*}{\partial z_1}\right)_y = \frac{c[2 - \beta\gamma^2 d^2 - \beta\gamma d(1 + w)]}{b(4 - \beta\gamma^2 d^2)} \gtreqless 0; \quad \left(\frac{\partial^2 r_1^*}{\partial z_1 \partial d}\right)_y < 0 \qquad (2.14)$$

These partial derivatives take into account revisions in the expected value of z_2 induced by variations in z_1. The subscript y is used to indicate that current and expected values of y_t are held constant. Consistent with the preceding discussion, equations (2.13) and (2.14) show that the customer relationship reinforces the response of l_1^* and reduces or reverses the response of r_1^* to changes in z_1. For example, if β, γ, d and w are large, an increase in the demand for loans resulting from an increase in economic activity may lead to a reduction in the loan rate. The signs of the second partial derivatives indicate the direction of impact of the customer relationship on the decision variables and would not be affected if d were replaced by γ, β or w.

The results in (2.13) and (2.14), as well as those to be presented below, depend upon the satisfaction of the second-order conditions for a profit maximum. In the two-period case these conditions are

$$b, \ (4 - \beta\gamma^2 d^2) > 0 \qquad (2.15)$$

The condition $(4 - \beta\gamma^2 d^2) > 0$ was discussed above. The condition $b > 0$ requires that the loan demand function be downward sloping.

Replacing (2.11) by (2.12) in the procedure outlined above and partially differentiating with respect to y_1, we obtain the responses of the bank's current decision variables to variations in rates of return on securities when expected y_2 is revised in response to changes in y_1 but current and expected levels of economic activity are held constant:

$$\left(\frac{\partial l_1^*}{\partial y_1}\right)_z = \frac{-(b - u)[2 + \beta\gamma d(1 + w)]}{4 - \beta\gamma^2 d^2} < 0; \quad \left(\frac{\partial^2 l_1^*}{\partial y_1 \partial d}\right)_z < 0 \qquad (2.16)$$

$$\left(\frac{\partial r_1^*}{\partial y_1}\right)_z = \frac{(b+u)}{2b} + \frac{(b-u)\beta\gamma d[\gamma d + 2(1+w)]}{2b(4-\beta\gamma^2 d^2)} > 0 ; \left(\frac{\partial^2 r_1^*}{\partial y_1 \partial d}\right)_z > 0 \quad (2.17)$$

The indicated signs of (2.16) and (2.17) depend upon the assumption that $b > u$; i.e. the response of loan demand to r, the own-rate, exceeds the response to y, the rate of return on the substitute asset. We see that the customer relationship accentuates the upward movement in the loan rate and the downward movement in loans caused by an increase in security yields. This is due partly to the extrapolative nature of expectations. A rise in y_1 and the induced upward revision in expected y_2 increase the opportunity costs of both current and future loans, including those future loans elicited by the extension of current loans beyond the one-period optimum. The rise in expected security yields has reduced the value of patronage as measured by the shaded area in Figure 2.1(b). Consequently, the bank will reduce the amount by which it extends loans beyond the one-period optimum, the extent of the reduction being positively related to the difference $l_1^* - l_1^0$ in Figure 2.1(a), which in turn depends upon the strength of the customer relationship.

But economic activity and security yields do not move independently over time. Rather, as Table 1.1 shows, they tend to be strongly positively correlated, an association that is important to the analysis of the cyclical behaviour of commercial banks. We shall incorporate this relationship into the model by means of the simplifying assumption that banks expect y_t and z_t to be linearly related such that

$$\frac{\partial y_t}{\partial z_t} = f > 0 \quad (2.18)$$

From this point, the analysis of the responses of loan and loan-rate decisions to variations in economic activity and security yields will be based on the assumption of concurrent movements in these determinants of commercial bank behaviour. That is, all derivatives with respect to z_1 will take account of corresponding movements in y_1 as well as induced revisions in expected levels of z_t and y_t.[10] In the two-period case these derivatives are

$$\frac{\partial l_1^*}{\partial z_1} = \frac{(c + uf - bf)}{2} \frac{[4 + 2\beta\gamma d(1+w)]}{(4-\beta\gamma^2 d^2)} > 0 ; \quad \frac{\partial^2 l_1^*}{\partial z_1 \partial d} > 0 \quad (2.19)$$

$$\frac{\partial r_1^*}{\partial z_1} = \frac{(c+uf+bf)}{2b} - \frac{(c+uf-bf)\beta\gamma d[\gamma d + 2(1+w)]}{2b(4-\beta\gamma^2 d^2)} \gtreqless 0 ; \quad \frac{\partial^2 r_1^*}{\partial z_1 \partial d} < 0 \quad (2.20)$$

We see from (2.20) that the model is capable of explaining why loan rates may decline during economic expansions, as was the case during 1971–73. But we are interested not so much in variations in r_1^* as in the difference $r_1^* - y_1$, which is obtained from (2.18) and (2.20).

$$\frac{\partial r_1^*}{\partial z_1} - \frac{\partial y_1}{\partial z_1} = \frac{\partial r_1^*}{\partial z_1} - f = \frac{(c+uf-bf)}{2b} \frac{[4 - 2\beta\gamma^2 d^2 - 2\beta\gamma d(1+w)]}{(4-\beta\gamma^2 d^2)} \gtreqless 0 ;$$

$$\frac{\partial^2 (r_1^* - y_1)}{\partial z_1 \partial d} < 0 \tag{2.21}$$

The indicated signs of (2.19) and (2.21) depend upon the assumption that $(c + uf - bf) > 0$, which is the case if the shift in the marginal revenue curve for loans in period t as the result of a movement in z_t exceeds the shift in the marginal revenue from securities. This may be shown as follows: The tth period discounted marginal revenues from loans and securities are

$$\frac{\partial \pi}{\partial l_t} = \frac{\beta^{t-1}}{b} (a + cz_t + uy_t + \gamma dl_{t-1} + \gamma d^2 l_{t-2} - 2l_t) \tag{2.22}$$

$$\frac{\partial \pi}{\partial g_t} = \beta^{t-1} y_t \tag{2.23}$$

For given l_t and g_t a change in z_t has the following effects on marginal revenues:

$$\frac{\partial^2 \pi}{\partial l_t \partial z_t} = \frac{\beta^{t-1}}{b} (c + uf); \frac{\partial^2 \pi}{\partial g_t \partial z_t} = \beta^{t-1} f \tag{2.24}$$

If an increase in current or expected z_t induces an upward shift in $\partial \pi / \partial l_t$ by an amount exceeding the discounted value of the current or expected increase in y_t—i.e. if $\beta^{t-1} (c + uf)/b > \beta^{t-1} f$ or $(c + uf - bf) > 0$—the marginal revenue curves will intersect at a greater value of l_t than was the case prior to the disturbance, inducing a rise in the optimal l_t. Such a case is depicted in Figure 2.2, where $L'A'$ and $L''A''$ are loan demands before and after the increase in z, $L'M'$ and $L''M''$ are the corresponding marginal revenues, l', r' and y' denote initial values and l'', r'' and y'' denote optimal values after the increase in z. Time subscripts have been omitted because all values pertain to the same period. This result holds both when the bank equates current marginal revenues, as in Figure 2.2, and when $\partial \pi / \partial l_t$ is less than y_t, as in the case $l_1 = l_1^*$ in Figure 2.1.

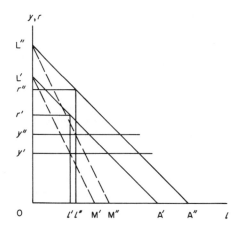

Figure 2.2. Effects of a change in z on r, y and l

The assumption that $(c + uf - bf) > 0$ is supported by the regression estimates in Chapter 5 and the implications of the model will be interpreted in this light.

The importance of the customer relationship to the bank's responses to economic activity and security yields is indicated by the second terms on the right-hand sides of (2.19) and (2.21). Each is equal to unity when γ, d, or β is zero, in which case we have the one-period result and $\partial l_1^*/\partial z_1$ and $\partial(r_1^* - y_1)/\partial z_1$ have the same sign. Thus the model is not capable of explaining the data in Table 1.1 in the absence of the customer relationship.[11] When γ, d, β and w are introduced, the responses of l_1^* and $r_1^* - y_1$ to movements in z_1 are respectively increased and either reduced or reversed. The derivative $\partial l_1^*/\partial z_1$ is always positive under our assumptions while $\partial(r_1^* - y_1)/\partial z_1$ may be negative and the model is capable of rationalizing the data in Table 1.1 if γ, d, β and w are large. For example, as β and w approach unity, their common upper limit, equation (2.21) exceeds, equals or is less than zero as γd is less than, equal to or greater than (approximately) 0.73. Since (2.15) requires that $\gamma d < 2$ under these conditions, the two-period model may be consistent with the empirical regularities observed in Table 1.1, for $0.73 < d < 2$. Smaller values of β and w imply higher ranges of γd if $\partial(r_1^* - y_1)/\partial z_1$ is to be negative. These are high values of γd but it will be shown in the next section that longer horizons reduce the levels of γ, d, β and w necessary to explain the data.

Before discussing horizons longer than two periods it may be useful to illustrate the importance of extrapolative expectations to the results presented above. This may be done by showing that these results can be reversed by 'reactionary' expectations. Suppose that expectations, instead of being governed by (2.11), are revised such that $\partial z_t/\partial z_1 < 0$ $(t = 2, 3, ...)$. Such a negative response means that the bank expects the economy to react to increases in economic activity by falling to levels lower than those preceding the rise. An expectations model with this property may be derived for the two-period case by letting $t = 1$ and substituting $-(1 + w')$, $w' > 0$, for w in (2.9) to get $z_2 = z_0 - w'(z_1 - z_0)$. The value of the customer relationship is considerably reduced by reactionary expectations. The bank will not wish to forego current profits in order to build relationships with customers if future levels of economic activity and, therefore, loan rates are expected to be low. If w' is sufficiently large, an economic expansion may even induce a reduction in loans as banks reassess the future value of current loans in the light of the expected recession. Extrapolative expectations are used throughout this study but it should be remembered that the implications of the models to be presented below should be substantially modified in circumstances where reactionary expectations seem appropriate.

2.3 THE THREE-PERIOD AND INFINITE-HORIZON MODELS

If the bank's decision horizon and the time span over which current loans influence future loan demands are both three periods long $(T = n = 3)$, the responses of l_1^* and $r_1^* - y_1$ to variations in economic activity and security yields may be expressed as follows:

$$\frac{\partial l_1^*}{\partial z_1} = \frac{(c + uf - bf)}{2} \frac{[4 - \gamma^2 d^2 \beta + \gamma d \beta (2 + \gamma d^2 \beta)(1 + w) + \gamma d^2 \beta^2 (2 + \gamma)(1 + w + w^2)]}{[4 - 2\gamma^2 d^2 \beta - (1 + \gamma)\gamma^2 d^4 \beta^2]}$$

(2.25)

$$\frac{\partial r_1^*}{\partial z_1} - \frac{\partial y_1}{\partial z_1} = \frac{(c + uf - bf)}{2b} \cdot$$

$$\frac{[4 - 3\gamma^2 d^2 \beta - 2(1 + \gamma)\gamma^2 d^4 \beta^2 - \gamma d \beta (2 + \gamma d^2 \beta)(1 + w) - \gamma d^2 \beta^2 (\gamma + 2)(1 + w + w^2)]}{[4 - 2\gamma^2 d^2 \beta - (1 + \gamma)\gamma^2 d^4 \beta^2]}$$

(2.26)

where, from (2.11) and (2.12), $\partial z_3 / \partial z_1 = \partial y_3 / \partial y_1 = (1 + w + w^2)$. The second-order conditions for a profit maximum are

$$b, [4 - 2\gamma^2 d^2 \beta - (1 + \gamma)\gamma^2 d^4 \beta^2] > 0 \qquad (2.27)$$

In the extreme case in which β and w approach unity and if γ also equals unity, $\partial(r_1^* - y_1)/\partial z_1 < 0$ and the second-order conditions are satisfied for $0.42 < d < 1$. Compared with the two-period case, this is a considerable reduction in the strength of the customer relationship necessary to explain the data in Table 1.1.

The effects of changes in economic activity on l_1^* and $r_1^* - y_1$ for horizons of any length ($n = T = 1, 2, \ldots$) are given in equations (A.43)–(A.44) in Appendix A.[12] Letting the horizon and the duration over which current loans influence future loan demands both approach infinity, the limits of $\partial l_1^*/\partial z_1$ and $\partial(r_1^* - y_1)/\partial z_1$ are stated in equations (A.45) and (A.46) and the second-order conditions in (A.40). In the case in which $\gamma = \beta = w \to 1$, $\partial(r_1^* - y_1)/\partial z_1 < 0$ and the second-order conditions are satisfied for $0.31 < d < 0.50$. Smaller values of γ, β and w imply higher ranges of d if the customer relationship is to be sufficiently important to explain the data in Table 1.1.

In comparing the results of the two-, three- and infinite-horizon cases, it is seen that the values of γ, d, β and w that (i) enable the model to explain observed bank behaviour and (ii) are consistent with the second-order conditions are inversely related to the length of the bank's horizon. This is because the more future periods for which (i) profits enter the objective function and (ii) current loans influence future loan demands, the more reason will the bank have to accommodate increases in current loan demand. A liberal lending response currently, although perhaps not conducive to short-term profit maximization, will induce repercussions favourable for bank profits in the near and distant future, these repercussions being stronger or weaker as γ, d and w are large or small and being more or less important to the bank as β is large or small. The strength of the customer relationship is best expressed in terms of the magnitudes of L_T and R_T ($T = 1, 2, \ldots$), where, for example, L_T ($T = 2, 3, \infty$) represents the terms in γ, d, β and w in (2.19), (2.25) and (A.45) and R_T ($T = 2, 3, \infty$)

Table 2.2. Impact of the loan–customer relationship on $\partial(r_1^* - y_1)/\partial z_1$ for selected β, w, d ($\gamma = 1$)

	$\beta = 0.5$; $w = 0$			$\beta = 0.5$; $w = 0.5$			$\beta = 0.5$; $w = 0.9$		
d	R_2	R_3	R_∞	R_2	R_3	R_∞	R_2	R_3	R_∞
0	1·0000	1·0000	1·0000	1·0000	1·0000	1·0000	1·0000	1·0000	1·0000
0·1	0·9737	0·9717	0·9716	0·9612	0·9578	0·9575	0·9512	0·9459	0·9453
0·2	0·9447	0·9361	0·9346	0·9196	0·9050	0·9021	0·8995	0·8773	0·8720
0·3	0·9128	0·8916	0·8852	0·8748	0·8394	0·8276	0·8445	0·7914	0·7696
0·4	0·8776	0·8357	0·8156	0·8265	0·7578	0·7216	0·7857	0·6843	0·6175
0·5	0·8387	0·7647	0·7085	0·7742	0·6555	0·5560	0·7226	0·5499	0·3674
0·6	0·7958	0·6731	0·5093	0·7173	0·5250	0·2424	0·6544	0·3793	−0·1392
0·7	0·7483	0·5521	−0·3095	0·6551	0·3549	−1·1024	0·5806	0·1581	−2·6340
0·8	0·6957	0·3874	—	0·5870	0·1263	—	0·5000	−0·1374	—
0·9	0·6370	0·1534	—	0·5118	−0·1948	—	0·4117	−0·5499	—
1·0	0·5714	−0·2000	—	0·4286	−0·6750	—	0·3143	−1·1630	—

	$\beta = 0.9$; $w = 0$			$\beta = 0.9$; $w = 0.5$			$\beta = 0.9$; $w = 0.9$		
d	R_2	R_3	R_∞	R_2	R_3	R_∞	R_2	R_3	R_∞
0	1·0000	1·0000	1·0000	1·0000	1·0000	1·0000	1·0000	1·0000	1·0000
0·1	0·9526	0·9462	0·9452	0·9301	0·9189	0·9170	0·9121	0·8949	0·8914
0·2	0·9001	0·8720	0·8614	0·8547	0·8068	0·7869	0·8184	0·7457	0·7080
0·3	0·8415	0·7713	0·7195	0·7726	0·6550	0·5586	0·7175	0·5413	0·3531
0·4	0·7759	0·6333	0·4206	0·6826	0·4487	0·0557	0·6079	0·2629	−0·5453
0·5	0·7020	0·4389	−0·9071	0·5828	0·1617	−2·3427	0·4874	−0·1236	−6·2091
0·6	0·6181	0·1522	—	0·4712	−0·2563	—	0·3536	−0·6833	—
0·7	0·5221	−0·3039	—	0·3450	−0·9129	—	0·2034	−1·5572	—
0·8	0·4112	−1·1284	—	0·2009	−2·0869	—	0·0327	−3·1100	—
0·9	0·2819	−3·0366	—	0·0342	−4·7819	—	−0·1639	−6·6572	—
1·0	0·1290	−12·0345	—	−0·1613	−17·4267	—	−0·3935	−23·2487	—

	$\beta = 0.98$; $w = 0$			$\beta = 0.98$; $w = 0.5$			$\beta = 0.98$; $w = 0.9$		
d	R_2	R_3	R_∞	R_2	R_3	R_∞	R_2	R_3	R_∞
0	1·0000	1·0000	1·0000	1·0000	1·0000	1·0000	1·0000	1·0000	1·0000
0·1	0·9484	0·9408	0·9394	0·9239	0·9106	0·9081	0·9042	0·8839	0·8792
0·2	0·8911	0·8578	0·8436	0·8416	0·7847	0·7581	0·8021	0·7157	0·6647
0·3	0·8271	0·7434	0·6712	0·7520	0·6118	0·4770	0·6919	0·4819	0·2144
0·4	0·7552	0·5842	0·2585	0·6532	0·3729	−0·2329	0·5716	0·1582	−1·1358
0·5	0·6738	0·3553	−5·1384	0·5433	0·0337	−10·5568	0·4389	−0·3001	−34·6741
0·6	0·5808	0·0076	—	0·4196	−0·4750	—	0·2906	−0·9837	—
0·7	0·4738	−0·5725	—	0·2789	−1·3131	—	0·1230	−2·1027	—
0·8	0·3491	−1·7147	—	0·1167	−2·9465	—	−0·0693	−4·2708	—
0·9	0·2022	−4·9470	—	−0·0729	−7·5355	—	−0·2929	−10·3355	—
1·0	0·0265	−72·0057	—	−0·2980	−102·3836	—	−0·5576	−135·3874	—

	$\beta = 1$; $w = 0$			$\beta = 1$; $w = 0.5$			$\beta = 1$; $w = 0.9$		
d	R_2	R_3	R_∞	R_2	R_3	R_∞	R_2	R_3	R_∞
0	1·0000	1·0000	1·0000	1·0000	1·0000	1·0000	1·0000	1·0000	1·0000
0·1	0·9474	0·9394	0·9380	0·9223	0·9085	0·9058	0·9023	0·8810	0·8761
0·2	0·8889	0·8542	0·8389	0·8384	0·7791	0·7505	0·7980	0·7080	0·6532
0·3	0·8235	0·7363	0·6579	0·7468	0·6006	0·4544	0·6854	0·4665	0·1751
0·4	0·7500	0·5714	0·2087	0·6458	0·3532	−0·3226	0·5625	0·1310	−1·3289
0·5	0·6667	0·3333	—	0·5333	0·0	—	0·4267	−0·3467	—
0·6	0·5714	−0·0312	—	0·4066	−0·5338	—	0·2747	−1·0645	—
0·7	0·4615	−0·6471	—	0·2621	−1·4243	—	0·1026	−2·2544	—
0·8	0·3333	−1·8889	—	0·0952	−3·2020	—	−0·0952	−4·6162	—
0·9	0·1818	−5·6316	—	−0·1003	−8·5226	—	−0·3260	−11·6546	—
1·0	0·0	—	—	−0·3333	—	—	−0·6000	—	—

represents the analogous terms in (2.21), (2.26) and (A.46).[13] Thus our results may in general be expressed as follows:

$$\frac{\partial l_1^*}{\partial z_1} = \frac{(c + uf - bf)}{2} L_T \tag{2.28}$$

$$(T = 1, 2, \ldots)$$

$$\frac{\partial r_1^*}{\partial z_1} - \frac{\partial y_1}{\partial z_1} = \frac{(c + uf - bf)}{2b} R_T \tag{2.29}$$

All of the dynamic or intertemporal properties of the model are incorporated in L_T and R_T, which are both equal to unity for $\beta \gamma d = 0$ or $T = 1$. L_T is a monotonically increasing function and R_T is a monotonically decreasing function of γ, d, β, w and T provided that γ, d, $\beta > 0$, $0 \le w < 1$ and $T > 1$. Table 2.2 lists values of R_T for $\gamma = 1$ and selected values of d, β and w for $T = 2, 3, \infty$. L_T may be calculated from the table since $L_T + R_T = 2$ in all cases consistent with the second-order conditions. No figures are listed for those combinations of parameters that violate the second-order conditions. We see from Table 2.2 that R_3 and R_∞ are close approximations of R_2 if β, d and w are small. However, if these parameters are large and if the bank's decision period is longer than two periods, the two-period model yields results very different from the optimal values of the bank's decision variables.

Table 2.3, which is based on the computations underlying Table 2.2, lists approximate minimum values of d for which R_T and, therefore, $\partial (r_1^* - y_1)/\partial z_1 \le 0$

Table 2.3. Values of d for selected β and w ($\gamma = 1$) above which $\partial(r_1^* - y_1)/\partial z_1 < 0$

β	w	$T = 2$	$T = 3$	$T \to \infty$
0·5	0	1·57	0·95	0·69
0·5	0·1	1·53	0·93	0·68
0·5	0·5	1·39	0·85	0·65
0·5	0·8	1·30	0·78	0·60
0·5	0·9	1·27	0·76	0·59
0·9	0	1·08	0·64	0·46
0·9	0·1	1·04	0·63	0·45
0·9	0·5	0·92	0·55	0·41
0·9	0·8	0·85	0·49	0·37
0·9	0·9	0·82	0·48	0·36
0·98	0	1·02	0·61	0·43
0·98	0·1	0·99	0·59	0·43
0·98	0·5	0·87	0·51	0·38
0·98	0·8	0·79	0·46	0·35
0·98	0·9	0·77	0·44	0·33
1·00	0	1·00	0·60	0·43
1·00	0·1	0·97	0·58	0·42
1·00	0·5	0·86	0·50	0·38
1·00	0·8	0·78	0·45	0·34
1·00	0·9	0·76	0·44	0·33

for $\gamma = 1$ and selected β and w. This table illustrates the property of the model that for every $T > 1$ there is some combination of γ, d, β and w such that the second-order conditions are satisfied and $R_T < 0$. Many of these combinations include what appear to be plausible values of the parameters, especially when T is large. If the customer relationship is in fact an important influence on commercial bank behaviour it is easy to understand why, in view of these implications of the model, (i) loan rates have been characterized as 'sticky' and (ii) banks have often been anxious to obtain funds at higher interest rates than those earned on loans to their better customers. The results presented above show that both of these aspects of bank behaviour may be consistent with long-run profit maximization.

2.4 THE LONG RUN

Few of the characteristics of the model presented above are peculiar to commercial banks. It must be true of many imperfectly-competitive firms with multi-period horizons that customer relationships exist such that future demands depend not only upon future prices and incomes but also upon current sales and, hence, current prices. Consequently, our model should be applicable, with modifications, to a wide variety of firms. For example, the form and rationale of the loan demand functions (2.2) and (2.8) are similar in several respects to the dynamic demands based on habit formation discussed by Houthakker and Taylor [1966], Pollak [1970] and others.[14] And the response of our bank to such demands has much in common with the optimal price policies of firms confronted by dynamic demands set forth by Stigler [1952, pp. 210–13] and Phelps and Winter [1970]. Therefore, while this section is devoted to an analysis of a bank's optimal decisions over time and in long-run equilibrium, it should be remembered that the same kind of analysis may also be applicable to other types of firms.

The following discussion will be confined to the two-period case introduced in Section 2.2. (The general and infinite-horizon cases are presented in Appendix A.5.) The optimal quantity of loans and loan rate selected by the bank in the tth period are given in (2.30) and (2.31). All l_t and r_t correspond to the first-period profit-maximizing values discussed in Section 2.2.

$$l_t = \frac{\begin{array}{c}(2 + \beta\gamma d)a + 2cz_t + \beta\gamma dcz_{t+1} - 2(b - u)y_t - \beta\gamma d(b - u)y_{t+1} \\ + (2\gamma d + \beta\gamma^2 d^3)l_{t-1} + 2\gamma d^2 l_{t-2}\end{array}}{4 - \beta\gamma^2 d^2} \quad (2.30)$$

$$r_t = \frac{\begin{array}{c}(2 - \beta\gamma d - \beta\gamma^2 d^2)a + c(2 - \beta\gamma^2 d^2)z_t - \beta\gamma dcz_{t+1} + [2b + u(2 - \beta\gamma^2 d^2)]y_t \\ + \beta\gamma d(b - u)y_{t+1} + (2\gamma d - \beta\gamma^2 d^3 - \beta\gamma^3 d^3)l_{t-1} + (2\gamma d^2 - \beta\gamma^3 d^4)l_{t-2}\end{array}}{b(4 - \beta\gamma^2 d^2)} \quad (2.31)$$

The partial derivatives of (2.30) and (2.31) with respect to $z_t = z_1$ subject to (2.11), (2.12) and (2.18) were shown in (2.19) and (2.20). Those partial derivatives indicated the first-period impacts of a change in the level of economic activity. This section is concerned with the long-run effects of such a change, particularly the time paths of movements between long-run equilibria. Assume an equilibrium situation in which economic activity and security yields are constant $(y_t = y_{t+1} = y_{t+2} = \ldots = y; z_t = z_{t+1} = z_{t+2} = \ldots = z)$ so that (2.30) may be expressed as the following second-order difference equation:

$$l_t = Al_{t-1} + Bl_{t-2} + C \tag{2.32}$$

where

$$A = \frac{(2\gamma d + \beta\gamma^2 d^3)}{4 - \beta\gamma^2 d^2}; B = \frac{2\gamma d^2}{4 - \beta\gamma^2 d^2}; C = \frac{(2 + \beta\gamma d)[a + cz - (b - u)y]}{4 - \beta\gamma^2 d^2}$$

Given initial conditions l_0 and l_1, the solution of equation (2.32) is

$$l_t = k_1 x_1^t + k_2 x_2^t + l_e \tag{2.33}$$

where the long-run equilibrium value of l_t is

$$l_e = \frac{C}{1 - A - B} = \frac{(2 + \beta\gamma d)[a + cz - (b - u)y]}{4 - \beta\gamma^2 d^2 - 2\gamma d - \beta\gamma^2 d^3 - 2\gamma d^2}; \frac{\partial l_e}{\partial d} > 0 \tag{2.34}$$

and

$$x_1 = \frac{A + \sqrt{A^2 + 4B}}{2}; x_2 = \frac{A - \sqrt{A^2 + 4B}}{2}; k_1 = \frac{l_1 - l_e + (l_e - l_0)x_2}{\sqrt{A^2 + 4B}}$$

$$k_2 = \frac{l_e - l_1 + (l_0 - l_e)x_1}{\sqrt{A^2 + 4B}}$$

Long-run equilibrium is stable if $\lim_{t \to \infty} l_t = l_e$, which requires that $|x_1|, |x_2| < 0$. This necessary condition for stability is satisfied if

$$(4 - \beta\gamma^2 d^2)(4 - \beta\gamma^2 d^2 - 2\gamma d - \beta\gamma^2 d^3 - 2\gamma d^2) > 0 \tag{2.35}$$

We see from (2.15) that the first of the two terms in (2.35) is positive if the second-order conditions for a profit maximum are satisfied. Therefore, the stability of long-run equilibrium requires that the second term be positive, which is the case if the sum of the coefficients of l_{t-1} and l_{t-2} in (2.32) is less than unity.

The time path of r_t is found by substituting equation (2.33) for l_{t-1} and l_{t-2} in (2.31) and letting $z_t = z_{t+1} = z$ and $y_t = y_{t+1} = y$. The long-run equilibrium loan rate is

$$r_e = \frac{(2 - \beta\gamma d)(a + cz + uy) + (2 + \beta\gamma d)(1 - \gamma d - \gamma d^2)by}{b(4 - \beta\gamma^2 d^2 - 2\gamma d - 2\gamma d^2 - \beta\gamma^2 d^3)}; \frac{\partial r_e}{\partial d} > 0 \tag{2.36}$$

It will be remembered from the discussion of Figure 2.1 above that, given past loans and current and expected economic activity and security yields, the customer relationship leads the bank to charge a lower interest rate on loans than would otherwise be the case. However, as indicated by the derivative to the right of equation (2.36), the customer relationship implies a higher long-run equilibrium loan rate than would prevail in the absence of dynamic considerations. These short-run and long-run effects of the customer relationship are easily reconciled. By charging a low interest rate initially, the bank fosters the customer relationship, stimulating increases in future loan demands until eventually it enjoys the profits arising from a large quantity of loans combined with a high loan rate.

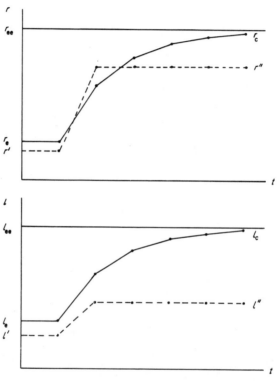

Figure 2.3. Long-run and short-run effects of a rise
in z

The long-run effects of the customer relationship are illustrated in Figure 2.3 in which the effects of a jump in z and the associated rise in y on l_e and r_e are compared with the effects on l and r in the absence of the customer relationship. Let r_e and l_e be the optimal loan rate and quantity of loans in the initial long-run equilibrium and let r_{ee} and l_{ee} be the long-run equilibrium values following the increases in z and y. Let l' and r' be the optimal values of l and r corresponding to the initial levels of z and y in the absence of the customer relationship, i.e. in the one-period case that is derived by setting β, γ or d equal to zero in equations (2.34) and (2.36). The optimal values of l and r in the one-period case following the increases in z and y are denoted l'' and r''. If z and y move to their new equilibrium values within a single period l' and r' will also move directly to l'' and r'' as shown in the figure. In the presence of the customer relationship, however, the profit-maximizing l and r approach l_{ee} and r_{ee} asymptotically in the manner dictated by the solution of the difference equation (2.33) along the paths denoted $r_e r_c$ and $l_e l_c$. In the first period following the disturbance the rise in r_c is less than the increase from r' to r''. It may even happen that r'' will exceed r_c as shown in the figure but this will not always be the case. The relatively small increase in r_c brings forth an upward movement in l_c exceeding the rise from l' to l''. Because the large first-period increase in l_c induces higher future loan demands via the customer relationship, r_c will at some point rise above r''. The time paths in Figure 2.3 correspond to a very simple case and would be substantially changed if, for example, (i) z and y moved gradually to their new equilibrium levels instead of in a single jump, in which case the movements between r' and r'' and between l' and l'' would also be gradual and the slopes of $r_e r_c$ and $l_e l_c$ would be less steep than shown in Figure 2.3, or (ii) β, γ, d and w were sufficiently large to cause r_c to fall below r_e or to cause l_c to rise above l_{ee} in the short run.[15] However, in these as in all other cases for which the stability conditions are satisfied, the stronger is the customer relationship the less will be the first-period rise in r, the greater will be the long-run rise in r and the greater will be the increases in l in both the first period and the long run.

As may be seen from (2.15) and (2.35), the values of β, γ and d consistent with the stability of long-run equilibrium are considerably less than those values consistent with the second-order conditions for a profit maximum. For example, it will be remembered that in the two-period case in which $\beta = \gamma = w \to 1$ the second-order conditions are satisfied and $\partial(r_1^* - y_1)/\partial z_1 < 0$ for $0.73 < d < 2$. However, when $\beta = \gamma = 1$ the second-term in (2.35) requires that $d < 0.79$. Hence, the range of d that is consistent with the empirical phenomena that we have set out to explain is narrowed considerably in the two-period model by the introduction of stability conditions; in the present example that range is $0.73 < d < 0.79$. However, the amounts by which the upper limits of β, γ and d consistent with the second-order conditions exceed the maximum values consistent with long-run stability declines as T increases. For example, in the infinite-horizon case in which $\beta = \gamma = 1$, each condition is satisfied if and only if $d < 0.50$.

The long run is not discussed in Chapters 3 and 4. But Tth-order difference equations and long-run equilibrium solutions that take account of all of the complications introduced in Chapters 2–4 are presented in Appendix A.5.

NOTES

1. Calculated from the 'Survey of Ownership' reported in the *Treasury Bulletin*.
2. If the 1947 data of Robinson [1960, p. 88] and the 1965 data of Rothwell [1966] are consistent, the proportion of commercial bank holdings of state and local government securities maturing in one year or less rose from 0.17 to 0.20 while the proportion

maturing in over ten years declined from 0·28 to 0·25. The proportions in the 1–5 and 5–10 year groups were virtually unchanged.

3. See Telser [1967] for a survey of empirical work on the term structure of interest rates.

4. As may be seen from a comparison of Tables 1.1 and 5.1, the cyclical variation in $r - y$ discussed in Chapter 1 continues to hold for all but one observation when the three-month Treasury bill rate is substituted for the average yield on securities used in Table 1.1.

5. See the work of Benston [1965] and others reviewed in Guttentag and Herman [1967] for evidence of economies of scale in banking.

6. The one-period model described here is very much in the spirit of Galbraith [1963, pp. 96–121] and Moore [1968, p. 179–83].

7. The article in the Federal Reserve Bank of Cleveland's *Monthly Business Review* applied these data to a different purpose than does the present study. According to that article these data imply that banks do not extend loans according to the principles of the real bills doctrine. On the contrary, while it is probably true that banks have in fact ignored the prescriptions of the real bills doctrine, the data discussed in the above quotation cast no light on that particular issue. Many firms rely upon bank credit on a continuous basis for the financing of inventories. The accommodation of those requirements by banks is consistent with the real bills doctrine.

8. The second example conflicts with assumption (g) unless we impose the additional assumption that all funds obtained from the bank are spent outside the bank's marketing area.

9. The increase in l_1 depends upon the assumption that the upward shift in the marginal revenue curve for loans due to the rise in z exceeds the increase in y, which is the marginal revenue from securities. See the discussion pertaining to equations (2.22)–(2.24) and Figure 2.2 below.

10. Although one would expect the bank's rate of discount to be positively related and therefore β to be negatively related to market rates of return, I have let β be constant because a variable β would very much increase the complexity of the algebraic statements presented below. A β that varied positively with z and y would moderate the effects of the customer relationship discussed in this study. This is so because, for example, a reduction in β associated with increases in z_1 and y_1 would cause future profits and therefore the customer relationship to be less valuable to the bank.

11. This is a property of our linear model and will not be true for all possible loan demand functions. That is, $\partial(r_1^* - y_1)/\partial z_1$ may be negative in the presence of some non-linear demands even in the one-period case or when β or $\partial l_2/\partial l_1$ is zero.

12. The results in Appendix A include the effects of the deposit relationship and interbank competition to be introduced in Chapters 3 and 4. The statements in Appendix A should be simplified by setting $b_0 = \gamma_0 = h = \alpha = 0$ in order to obtain the results pertinent to the loan-customer relationship discussed in this chapter.

13. L_T and R_T do not include the terms in h in (A.45) and (A.46).

14. See the references in Pollak's article.

15. The parameter w, which indicates the extent to which expectations are revised in response to changes in z and y, does not enter long-run equilibrium solutions because z and y are assumed fixed in equilibrium. However, w may figure prominently in the determination of paths between long-run equilibria arising from changes in z and y. The examples in this section have been simplified by letting $w = 0$.

CHAPTER 3

Dynamic Deposit Supply: The Deposit Relationship

3.1 INTRODUCTION AND ASSUMPTIONS

As pointed out in Chapter 2, banks are not unique in possessing the characteristic that future demands for their products are dependent upon current pricing decisions. It is probably less common for future supplies of inputs to be related to current output prices. Yet some writers have contended that such an intertemporal connection between output demands and input supplies is one of the principal distinguishing features of commercial banks.[1] In fact, the term 'customer relationship' as used by economists and bankers is often restricted to the relationship between current loans and future deposits. This intertemporal loan-deposit connection is designated the 'deposit relationship' in the present study in order to distinguish it from the 'loan-customer relationship' discussed in Chapter 2.

In his important book Hodgman discusses the results of a series of interviews with bankers. One of the questions asked by Hodgman was: 'What criteria do bankers apply in deciding whether or not to make a loan which has been requested?' [1963, p. 24] The response indicated that the 'criterion with highest priority is that of the deposit relationship'. The deposit relationship involves more than compensating balances, which have been 'interpreted simply as a device to secure a higher effective rate of interest on the specific loan'. The dominant consideration with respect to deposits in the evaluation of loan requests by banks is not 'the current ratio of deposit to loan'. Rather, banks want 'long-term deposit relationships'. The 'significance of the deposit criterion stems from the importance of deposits as the primary determinant of the individual bank's lending capacity'. [pp. 24–25] In short, banks prefer to lend to those applicants who are most likely to maintain long-term deposit relationships with the bank, relationships extending beyond the maturities of loan agreements and which cannot be guaranteed by compensating balance requirements.

As with the loan–customer relationship, the deposit relationship influences

29

both bank and customer behaviour. Banks extend more loans, especially to commercial and industrial borrowers, than would otherwise be the case because of the possibility of developing long-term deposit relationships with these customers. In fact, according to Hodgman, in the absence of the deposit relationship and in terms of other important criteria for loan selection — net rate of return, risk and liquidity — commercial and industrial loans would be far down the list of loans preferred by banks.[2] There is little doubt that the deposit relationship is an important influence on commercial bank decisions. In addition to Hodgman's survey, the importance of the customer relationship has been emphasized by many business economists,[3] it is often discussed at length in bank publications[4] and Hester's [1962] empirical results indicate that, holding other factors constant, the terms of loan contracts are more favourable for those borrowers with large and long-standing deposit balances with the lending bank than for other borrowers. The other side of the deposit relationship is that firms keep more deposits with their banks than they would in the absence of the intertemporal relationship between deposits and the granting of loan requests by banks. By maintaining a sizable deposit balance with its bank, a firm hopes to improve its ability to obtain loans in the future at favourable rates and, perhaps more importantly, hopes to enjoy a preferred status during periods of tight money.

While the model presented in this study owes a large debt to Hodgman's work, the approach developed here differs from Hodgman's in several respects, the most important of which are the following: First, the effect of current loans upon future loan demands, as well as upon future deposits, is considered. This loan–customer relationship was introduced in Chapter 2 and will be retained throughout the study. Second, time is treated explicitly in the present model by means of intertemporal profit, demand and supply functions.[5] Third, whereas Hodgman was concerned primarily with the effect of the deposit relationship upon bank preferences among loans, the present study emphasizes the choice between loans in the aggregate and the bank's total security holdings.[6] We are able to alter the focus of the customer relationship in this way because of our fourth departure from Hodgman's approach — a concentration upon marginal rather than average relationships.[7] Hodgman's emphasis on average costs and revenues is most apparent in his table and discussion of 'rank order of loans by various criteria .... Loan categories in order of overall desirability are as follows: (1) commercial and industrial loans, (2–3) loans to brokers and dealers; retail automobile instalment paper, ..., and (10) real estate loans secured by non-farm, non-residential properties'. [1963, pp. 18–19] As indicated previously, commercial and industrial loans are ranked first because of the customer relationship, specifically the deposit relationship. But it is not clear that loan rankings are consistent with optimizing behaviour. If the bank maximizes an objective function (profits in our model) subject to a variety of constraints, it will choose values for the instruments at its disposal, corner solutions apart, such that the marginal contributions of all assets to the value of the objective function are the same. All assets are equally desirable at the margin and no rank order exists, a state of affairs implied by the results of the present study.[8] Such a rank order may exist when the bank is not at its optimal position. But this is not the meaning of Hodgman's rank order, which is independent of time, interest rates and the composition of the bank's portfolio. It is not possible to attach precise meaning to Hodgman's ranking since no objective function is specified and the means used by banks to ration loans are not made explicit. A fifth difference between the present study and Hodgman's is that here loans are rationed by means of the price mechanism, i.e. by the rate of interest. This assumption is disputed by Hodgman on the basis of his interviews [1963, pp. 29–33] but has received substantial empirical support from the work of Harris [1970, 1974] discussed in Chapter 2.1.

3.2 THE TWO-PERIOD MODEL

The model presented in Chapter 2 will now be complicated by the introduction of variable deposits. As before, deposits are homogeneous and there is no net gain or loss accruing from service charges and interest payments on deposits; the bank is interested in deposits only as a source of loanable funds.[9] The supply of deposits to a bank, Q_t, is assumed to be a function of its past loans. That is, the choice of a particular bank as a depository by households and firms depends partly upon the extent to which that bank has in the past accommodated borrowers on favourable terms, some of whom have as a consequence been induced to keep their deposits with the bank. The level of deposits in an individual bank will also be positively related to total deposits in the banking system, $Q_t + Q_t^0$, where Q_t^0 is the sum of deposits in other banks. Those factors other than past loans that influence a bank's share of total deposits are assumed to be constant. Such factors include advertising, relative income levels among different banking markets, competition from non-bank lenders and the size, number and convenience of location of offices. Under these assumptions the supply of deposits to the bank in the tth period may be written as follows, where loans and deposits are expressed as proportions of first-period earning assets of the bank, F_1:

$$q_t = q(q_t + q_t^0, l_{t-1}, l_{t-2}, ..., l_{t-n}; F_1) \tag{3.1}$$

Equation (3.1) is obtained from a deposit-supply equation valued in dollars by substituting $F_1 q_t$, $F_1 q_t^0$ and $F_1 l_{t-i}$ for Q_t, Q_t^0 and L_{t-i}, respectively, and dividing through by F_1. Unlike the analysis in Chapter 2, the value of earning assets, $L_t + G_t = (1 - k)Q_t + K = F_t$, may change over time due to variations in deposits. But this presents no problems since we are interested primarily in first-period proportions, l_1 and g_1, and the first-period level of deposits is assumed to be a function only of past loans and total deposits in the system and is therefore predetermined from the standpoint of the individual bank. Consequently, retaining the assumptions that the capital account, K, and the reserve ratio, k, are constant, the level of first-period earning assets, F_1, is also predetermined. All of the values of l_t, g_t and q_t discussed below are proportions of F_1. This includes l_t and g_t in the objective function (2.5) and the loan-demand equation (2.4), in which F is replaced by F_1. The balance sheet equation (2.1) may also be expressed in terms of proportions of F_1 as follows:

$$l_t + g_t = (1 - k)q_t + \kappa \tag{3.2}$$

where $\kappa = K/F_1$ and $l_1 + g_1 = (1 - k)q_1 + \kappa = 1$.

Considering the two-period case ($T = n = 2$), let the bank maximize profit (2.5) given past, current and expected future values of the predetermined variables—l_{t-i}, $q_t + q_t^0$, z_t, y_t—subject to the market and balance sheet restraints—(2.4), (3.1), (3.2). The resulting marginal conditions are

$$\left(r_1 + \frac{l_1}{\frac{\partial l_1}{\partial r_1}}\right) - \frac{\beta l_2}{\frac{\partial l_2}{\partial r_2}}\frac{\partial l_2}{\partial l_1} + \beta(1 - k)y_2\frac{\partial q_2}{\partial l_1} = y_1 \tag{3.3}$$

$$r_2 + \frac{l_2}{\frac{\partial l_2}{\partial r_2}} = y_2 \tag{3.4}$$

Equation (3.4) is identical to (2.7); the decision in the second period is equivalent to that for the one-period model because the bank's horizon in the present example ends with the second-period. Equation (3.3) differs from (2.6) by the addition of the last term on the left-hand side of (3.3). This term is the present value of the added revenue from second-period security investments due to a marginal increase in first-period loans. The magnitude of this term is a measure of the effect of the intertemporal loan-deposit relationship on the bank's current behaviour. The greater is this term the more incentive will the bank have to extend first-period loans beyond that point at which first-period profit would be maximized. The derivative $\partial q_2/\partial l_1$ is the increase in second-period deposits in response to an increase in first-period loans, $(1 - k)$ is the proportion of the deposit increase that is invested, y_2 is the rate of return on those investments and β is the factor by which second-period earnings are discounted.

The bank now has two reasons to extend loans beyond the single-period optimum—the loan–customer relationship and the deposit relationship, the magnitudes of which are measured by the second and third terms, respectively, on the left-hand side of (3.3). The effects of these intertemporal considerations on the bank's first-period decisions are illustrated in Figure 3.1(a). Comparing this figure with Figure 2.1(a), we see that the addition of the deposit relationship has induced an increase in the optimal first-period quantity of loans, l_1^*, beyond that point at which the loan–customer relationship was the only dynamic element in the model.[10]

While our main concern is with the bank's first-period behaviour, the effect of that behaviour on the size and composition of its portfolio in the second period is also of interest. This effect is illustrated in Figure 3.1(b). As in Figure 2.1(b), L_0M_0 denotes the second-period marginal revenue from loans that

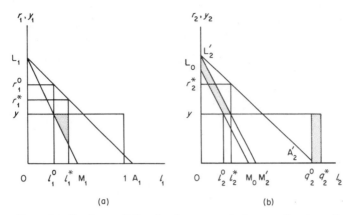

Figure 3.1. Bank portfolios in the two-period case: the deposit relationship

would have existed if the bank had maximized first-period profit by extending a quantity of first-period loans, l_1^0. The second-period marginal and average revenues that prevail as a result of the quantity of first-period loans l_1^* are $L_2'M_2'$ and $L_2'A_2'$, which lie to the right of L_2M_2 and L_2A_2, respectively, in Figure 2.1(b) because of the addition of the deposit relationship. The net addition to second-period revenue resulting from the increased loan demand is indicated by the shaded area between L_0M_0 and $L_2'M_2'$. There has also been an increase in deposits in the amount $q_2^* - q_2^0$ because $\partial q_2/\partial l_1 > 0$. The increase in second-period revenue due to this increase in deposits is equal to $(1-k)$ times the increase in deposits times the second-period rate of return on securities, y_2, i.e. $(1-k)$ times the shaded area between q_2^0 and q_2^*.

It is interesting to compare the choice between total loans and securities in the present model with the more realistic case in which loans to both prime and non-prime customers are taken into account, i.e. when the assumption of homogeneous borrowers is relaxed. A prime borrower is 'one who is aware of alternative sources of bank credit and whose business a bank will lose if it fails to offer him as generous terms on loans and routine banking services as competing banks offer'. [Hodgman, 1963, p. 120] It is sometimes argued that banks extend loans to prime customers at a favourable rate (the prime rate) mainly for the purpose of attracting their deposits which may then be lent at higher rates to non-prime customers, customers whose alternative sources of credit are limited and who are therefore unlikely to terminate their loan and deposit relationships upon being charged high rates of interest. In the model presented above, banks extend some loans, the difference between l_1^* in Figure 2.1(a) and l_1^* in Figure 3.1(a), in order to attract deposits which are then invested in securities, which may be compared to loans to non-prime customers. The shortcoming of this analogy is that in the present model the optimal loan rate will usually exceed the yield on securities while the prime rate is in fact less than rates charged to non-prime customers. On the other hand, the analogy is true in the sense that in our model the current marginal revenue from securities (non-prime customers) exceeds that from loans. Differences between the loan demands and deposit supplies of prime and non-prime customers will be considered explicitly in Chapter 6. In the meantime, the analysis will be focused on the simpler case of homogeneous borrowers.

Let us now examine the effects of variations in economic activity on first-period loans and interest rates. As in Chapter 2 we linearize the model for reasons of simplicity. Thus we again utilize the linear loan demand and expectations equations—(2.8), (2.11), (2.12), (2.18)—and rewrite (3.1) as follows:

$$q_t = a_1 + \alpha \sum_{i=1}^{n} h^i l_{t-i} + s(q_t + q_t^0) \qquad 0 \le h < 1 \qquad (3.5)$$

As with y and d in the intertemporal loan demand function (2.8), α and h indicate both the strength of the influence of past actions on current conditions and the speed with which this influence declines in importance as the periods to which the weights apply recede into the past. It is reasonable to suppose that $0 \le h < 1$, i.e. that the deposit relationship is strongest for those customers who have most recently obtained loans from the bank. It is assumed that $s > 0$ but no restriction is placed on the sign of a_1.

Before analysing the response of the bank to variations in economic activity and security yields we must consider the relation between total deposits, $Q_t + Q_t^0$, and current events. We will make the simplifying assumption that the Federal Reserve fixes total deposits in response to economic activity with a one-period lag. This implies that $Q_t + Q_t^0$ is independent of current income and interest rates even though the public's demand for deposits depends upon these variables. The Federal Reserve offsets the effects of current influences on the quantity of deposits in its efforts to bring deposits—a proximate objective—to the level that it considers conducive to the attainment of its ultimate objectives, always responding to events with a one-period lag.[11] The aggregate supply of deposits may therefore be written as follows, where we continue to assume linearity and to express dollar values as proportions of F_1:

$$q_t + q_t^0 = a_2 + \sigma z_{t-1} \qquad (3.6)$$

No restrictions are placed on a_2 and σ except that they must take values such that $q_t + q_t^0 > 0$. It might be considered more reasonable to suppose that the Federal Reserve, instead of being concerned with levels, controls changes in deposits in response to lagged changes in economic activity. Such an assumption would not alter the results discussed below, the key requirement for our purposes being that current q is independent of current z.

Differentiating the bank's optimal first-period loan rate and quantity of loans with respect to z_1 subject to the expectations equations (2.11) and (2.12) and the correspondence between y_t and z_t indicated by (2.18), we obtain the following results where $\partial y_1 / \partial z_1$ is subtracted from $\partial r_1^* / \partial z_1$:

$$\frac{\partial l_1^*}{\partial z_1} = \frac{(c + uf - bf)}{2} L_2 + \frac{2bf\alpha h\beta(1 - k)(1 + w)}{(4 - \beta\gamma^2 d^2)} \tag{3.7}$$

$$\frac{\partial r_1^*}{\partial z_1} - \frac{\partial y_1}{\partial z_1} = \frac{(c + uf - bf)}{2b} R_2 - \frac{2f\alpha h\beta(1 - k)(1 + w)}{(4 - \beta\gamma^2 d^2)} \tag{3.8}$$

where L_T and R_T, which were defined in connection with (2.28) and (2.29), indicate the strength of the loan–customer relationship while the last terms in (3.7) and (3.8) measure the influence of the deposit relationship.

Comparing (3.7) and (3.8) with (2.19) and (2.21), we see that the introduction of the deposit relationship strengthens the results obtained in Chapter 2 by further moderating changes in the loan rate and thereby accentuating changes in loans in response to variations in economic activity. Let us consider the influence of the deposit relationship in the absence of the loan–customer relationship, i.e. when $\alpha h > 0$, $\gamma d = 0$. In such a case an increase in loans extended in response to a rise in economic activity will not cause increases in future loan demands but will induce higher future levels of deposits. This will not lead to an increase in the optimal quantity of loans, however, unless expectations of rates of return on securities have also been affected. The value of the deposit relationship as indicated by the last term on the left-hand side of (3.3) is independent of shifts in loan demand in the linear case but depends only upon the constants β, $(1 - k)$ and $\partial q_t/\partial l_1$ and expected values of y_t $(t = 2, 3, ..., T)$. Therefore, the bank will increase current loans and so reduce current profit only if the rise in z_1 is associated with increases in expected y_t, for example, if $\partial y_2/\partial z_1 = f(1 + w) > 0$ in the two-period case. Thus, while revisions of expectations contribute to the impact of the loan–customer relationship on the cyclical behaviour of commercial banks, such revisions are essential to the influence of the deposit relationship.

It is seen from (3.7) and (3.8) that the loan–customer and deposit relationships interact. Specifically, an increase in the strength of one relationship reinforces the influence of the other. For example, an increase in the strength of the deposit relationship (i.e. an increase in αh) that causes a bank to extend more loans in order to attract deposits in the future will have the additional effect of inducing increases in future loan demands via the loan–customer relationship (γd). Consequently, an increase in αh is more profitable and has a greater influence on bank behaviour the greater is γd.

The addition of the deposit relationship has not changed the second-order conditions from those given in Chapter 2, equation (2.15) in the two-period case. That is, unlike $\partial l_2/\partial l_1 = \gamma d$, $\partial q_2/\partial l_1 = \alpha h$ does not enter the second-order conditions. As may be seen in Figure 3.1, equal increments in l_1 beyond l_1^0 cause first-period profit, π_1, to decrease at an increasing rate. This is because the marginal revenue from loans is a decreasing function of loans while the opportunity cost of loans, the rate of return on securities, is constant. Furthermore, because of the upward influence of l_1 on future optimal values of both l_t and r_t, increments in l_1 induce increases in future π_t at increasing rates. For example, letting $T = 2$ and assuming that π_2 is maximized for given l_1, we can express both π_1 and $\beta\pi_2$ as functions of l_1 with the following first and second derivatives:

$$\frac{\partial \pi_1}{\partial l_1} = -\frac{2(l_1 - l_1^0)}{b} \; ; \quad \frac{\partial^2 \pi_1}{\partial l_1^2} = -\frac{2}{b} \tag{3.9}$$

$$\frac{\partial(\beta\pi_2)}{\partial l_1} = \beta\left\{\frac{\gamma d[a + cz_2 - (b - u)y_2 + \gamma dl_1 + \gamma d^2 l_0]}{2b} + (1 - k)\alpha h y_2\right\};$$

$$\frac{\partial^2(\beta\pi_2)}{\partial l_1^2} = \frac{\beta\gamma^2 d^2}{2b} \tag{3.10}$$

where l_1^0 is the quantity of l_1 that maximizes π_1. Equations (3.9) and (3.10) show that increases in l_1 beyond l_1^0 cause π_1 to decrease and $\beta\pi_2$ to increase, both at increasing rates. Whether for some quantity of l_1 a point is reached such that $-(\partial\pi_1/\partial l_1) = \partial(\beta\pi_2)/\partial l_1$, i.e. such that $\pi = \pi_1 + \beta\pi_2$ reaches a maximum, depends upon the magnitudes of γ, d and β. Hence the expression of the second-order conditions for a profit maximum in terms of these parameters. However, increments in l_1 induce increases in $\beta\pi_2$ via the deposit relationship at a constant rate, $\beta(1 - k)\alpha h y_2$. Thus, for $\gamma d = 0$, a point must be reached as l_1 increases such that $-(\partial\pi_1/\partial l_1) = \partial(\beta\pi_2)/\partial l_1$ regardless of the value of αh provided only that $\beta(1 - k)\alpha h y_2$ is finite.

The ability of our model to explain the data in Table 1.1 is increased by the addition of the deposit relationship. Even if γ and d are small, sufficiently large values of α, h and β will cause $r - y$ to move oppositely to economic activity. For example, in the special case in which $T = 2$ and $\gamma d = 0$ so that $R_2 = 1$, it is seen from equation (3.8) that

$$\frac{\partial r_1^*}{\partial z_1} - \frac{\partial y_1}{\partial z_1} \gtrless 0 \quad \text{as} \quad (c + uf - bf) \gtrless bf\alpha h\beta(1 - k)(1 + w) \tag{3.11}$$

Unlike the case of dynamic loan demands presented in Chapter 2, knowledge of the values of the dynamic parameters of the deposit relationship (α, h, β, w) is not sufficient to determine the direction of the inequality (3.11). We must also know b, c, f, u and k, which will be estimated in Chapter 5.

3.3 THE THREE-PERIOD AND INFINITE-HORIZON MODELS

The bank's response to variations in economic activity when $T = n = 3$ may be expressed as follows:

$$\frac{\partial l_1^*}{\partial z_1} = \frac{(c + uf - bf)}{2}L_3 + \frac{bf(1 - k)\alpha h\beta\{(4 - \gamma^2 d^2\beta)[1 + w + h\beta(1 + w + w^2)] + \gamma d\beta(2 + \gamma d^2\beta)(1 + w + w^2)\}}{2[4 - 2\gamma^2 d^2\beta - (1 + \gamma)\gamma^2 d^4\beta^2]} \tag{3.12}$$

$$\frac{\partial r_1^*}{\partial z_1} - \frac{\partial y_1}{\partial z_1} = \frac{(c + uf - bf)}{2b} R_3 - \frac{f(1-k)\alpha h\beta\{(4 - \gamma^2 d^2 \beta)[1 + w + h\beta(1 + w + w^2)]}{2[4 - 2\gamma^2 d^2 \beta - (1 + \gamma)\gamma^2 d^4 \beta^2]}$$

$$\frac{+ \gamma d\beta(2 + \gamma d^2 \beta)(1 + w + w^2)\}}{}$$

(3.13)

The strength of the deposit relationship has been increased by the extension of the bank's horizon partly because of the influence of current loans on third-period deposits, which may be invested at an expected rate y_3 that has been revised upward by the amount $\partial y_3 / \partial z_1 = f(1 + w + w^2)$, and partly because of the increased interaction between the loan and deposit relationships made possible by the longer horizon. Setting $\gamma d = 0$, we see that the deposit relationship may or may not be sufficient to explain the data in Table 1.1 depending upon the direction of the following inequality:

$$\frac{\partial r_1^*}{\partial z_1} - \frac{\partial y_1}{\partial z_1} \gtrless 0 \quad \text{as} \quad (c + uf - bf) \gtrless bf\alpha h\beta(1 - k)[1 + w + h\beta(1 + w + w^2)] \quad (3.14)$$

The limits of $\partial l_1^*/\partial z_1$ and $\partial(r_1^* - y_1)/\partial z_1$ as $T = n \to \infty$ are stated in equations (A.45) and (A.46) in Appendix A.[12] Given the satisfaction of the second-order conditions for a profit maximum and $0 \leq w < 1$, the only additional assumption needed to assure finite limits is $h\beta < 1$. Letting $\gamma d = 0$ in (A.46), we see that in the infinite-horizon case

$$\frac{\partial r_1^*}{\partial z_1} - \frac{\partial y_1}{\partial z_1} \gtrless 0 \quad \text{as} \quad (c + uf - bf) \gtrless \frac{bf\alpha h\beta(1 - k)(1 + w - h\beta w)}{(1 - h\beta)(1 - h\beta w)} \quad (3.15)$$

The last term in (3.15) becomes very large as h, β and w increase in size, specifically, as h, β, $w \to 1$. This is further indication that the customer relationship as embodied in the parameters γ, d, h, β and w of the model developed in this and the preceding chapter may for large values of these parameters be sufficient to explain important aspects of the cyclical behaviour of commercial banks. But before introducing interbank competition in Chapter 4 and estimating the parameters of the model in Chapter 5 in an effort to determine whether the customer relationship has in fact exerted an important influence on bank behaviour, it may be useful to point out how the relaxation of some of our more restrictive assumptions would alter the results presented above.

3.4 SOME COMPLICATIONS

First consider a situation such as that analysed by Kane and Malkiel [1965] in which the bank maximizes expected profit under conditions of uncertainty where the principle source of uncertainty is deposit variability. Kane and Malkiel take issue with the assumption underlying many credit rationing theories that bank portfolios become more risky as the quantity of loans increases with the result that bankers refuse to accommodate the increased loan demands associated with economic expansions. 'In opposition to this view, [Kane and Malkiel] insist that there exists a class of loan applications, L^*... loans, where the very failure to grant the loan itself increases aggregate risk'. [p. 119] L^* loan requests are those from customers who (i) have access to alternative sources of credit and (ii) have maintained large, long-standing and stable deposit balances with a bank because of the past accommodation of loan requests by the bank. The refusal of L^* loan requests will both increase the variance and reduce the expected value of future profits by endangering deposit relationships.[13] Consequently, 'in booms, banks will make more loans than traditional analysis would indicate'. [p. 129] The introduction of uncertainty in the manner suggested by Kane and Malkiel would strengthen the implications of the model set forth in the present study because banks would accommodate increases in loan demands during expansions not only for the purpose of increasing future expected profits but also with a view towards reducing the variability of deposits and, therefore, profits. In common with the approach of the present paper, Kane and Malkiel use the customer relationship to explain observed increases in bank loans during periods of economic expansion. But like Hodgman and unlike this study, Kane and Malkiel do not use the loan rate as a rationing device.

Next, in contradiction to assumption (k) in Chapter 2.1, suppose that total deposits are separated into demand and time deposits. Further assume that, in addition to being influenced by past loans and the total quantities of time and demand deposits in the banking system, the quantity of time deposits in a bank is positively related to the rate of interest on time deposits and the quantity of demand deposits is negatively related to service charges on demand deposits, where both the rate on time deposits and service charges are decision variables under the control of the bank. These changes in the model would not alter the marginal conditions. The left-hand sides of (3.3) and (3.4), for example, would remain equal to y_1 and y_2, respectively, and would also equal the net marginal costs of time and demand deposits. Furthermore, if the Federal Reserve were able and willing to control both categories of deposits in response to lagged variables in the manner indicated in equation (3.6), the responses of l_1^* and $r_1^* - y_1$ to variations in economic activity would not be changed from those set forth in (3.7) and (3.8). Alternatively, if total deposits responded to current deposit demands, if those demands were positively related to current economic activity and if increases in bank reserves were rapidly invested, we might observe declines in loans as a proportion of earning assets during economic expansions even if the customer relationship were an important determinant of commercial bank behaviour. This would happen if cyclical variations in deposit demands were substantially greater than those in loan demands, the difference between deposits (less required reserves) and loans being invested in securities.

There is some evidence that the customer relationship is a small but growing factor affecting commercial bank security holdings, mainly due to increasing supplies of state and local government securities. This is because local governments sometimes prefer to keep their deposit balances with banks willing to purchase their securities.[14] If the customer relationship were as important to commercial bank security purchases as to loans and if borrowing by state and local governments were as closely attuned as loan demands to economic activity, the ability of the customer relationship to explain the data in Table 1.1 would be severely restricted; the customer relationship would act equally on the cyclical behaviour of loans and the bulk of bank security holdings and would not, therefore, have a substantial influence on either as a proportion of total earning assets.

NOTES

1. For example, see Hodgman [1961, 1963] and Kane and Malkiel [1965].
2. Hodgman [1963, pp. 16–20, 24–25]. Especially see Table 1 on page 18.
3. For example, see Staats [1969] and Bowers [1969].
4. See Sutherland [1971] for quotations from the annual reports of several banks.
5. Two of Hodgman's assumptions are stated as follows: 'To develop the significance of the customer relationship we shall begin by analysing the relationship of a commercial bank with an individual deposit customer under two simplifying assumptions: (1) that the banker is in full and certain possession of the relevant information required to assess the balance of costs and benefits associated with a particular customer account and (2) that present and future are identical, that is, static analysis suffices'. [1963, p. 98] The present study utilizes assumption (1) but discards (2).
6. However, loans are disaggregated by size in Chapter 6.
7. Hodgman states that he focuses on average relationships both for reasons of simplicity and because 'this approach has the virtue of approximating that of the practical banker who also must find simple solutions to logically complex problems'. [1961, p. 258] The model and arguments presented by Hodgman in his 1961 article are virtually identical to Chapters X–XI of his book [1963]. Papers by Gillespie, Hodgman, and Yancey [1969] and Cohen and Hodgman [1962] do not differ from Hodgman's 1961 and 1963 writings with respect to the nature of the customer relationship. Jacobs [1971] also concentrates on average relationships in his model of bank behaviour in the presence of the customer relationship.
8. Charnes and Littlechild [1970], however, have presented an interesting intertemporal non-linear programming model of commercial bank asset choice that produces the result that loans to depositors are preferred to loans to non-depositors. This result follows from the assumption of fixed interest rates and externally imposed limitations on the amounts that can be lent to different classes of customers. This paper extends an earlier work by Chambers and Charnes [1961] by introducing 'feed back relationships between loans and deposits which may be termed "customer relationships".' [p. i]
9. This represents a further departure from Hodgman's analysis in which considerable importance is attached to the costs and revenues associated with deposits and services performed for depositors.
10. This result would be accentuated if deposits entered the objective function as in Monti [1971].
11. This assumes a type of Federal Reserve behaviour similar to that in Wood [1967].
12. The statements in Appendix A should be simplified by setting $b_0 = \gamma_0 = 0$ in order to obtain results corresponding to the discussion in this chapter.
13. Garvy [1959] has also argued that stability of deposit relationships exerts an important influence on the granting of loan requests.
14. For some evidence that the customer relationship applies to municipal securities, see Murphy [1967].

CHAPTER 4

Interbank Competition

4.1 INTRODUCTION AND ASSUMPTIONS

We have so far ignored the effects of actions of other banks on the behaviour of an individual bank. Such abstraction is permissible if the bank is a monopolist or when we wish to analyse the reactions of a bank to events affecting that bank but which do not disturb its competitors. However, we are interested in the responses of banks to swings in economic activity, which affect most banks simultaneously. Furthermore, it is not likely, except perhaps in small towns in unit banking areas, that banks are free of competitive restraints. Consequently, a useful extension of the model developed in Chapters 2 and 3 will be to admit competition.[1] Perfect competition among banks in the loan market will not be considered. Given our assumption of certainty, the perfectly-elastic loan demand facing banks that perfect competition implies would exclude portfolio diversification. Neither will we consider any of the many interesting forms of oligopolistic competition. While either perfect competition or oliogopoly might be applicable to some types of loans and certain classes of banks, the simplest and most straight-forward way in which competition can be introduced into the model is in a form similar to Chamberlin's [1956] monopolistic competition. That is, although banks face negatively sloped loan demands, each bank is sufficiently small relative to the markets in which it deals that its actions have no discernible impact upon its competitors. But the behaviour of other banks in the aggregate influences the market restraints (loan demand and deposit supply) confronting the individual bank. Each bank is in competition with other banks collectively but not with any single bank or small group of banks. The implications of these assumptions for the decision process of a bank are as follows: (i) Given current and expected values of economic activity (z_t) and security yields (y_t) ($t = 1, 2, ..., T$), each bank can treat the behaviour of other banks as given and proceed to maximize profit in the manner described in the preceding chapters. It need not be concerned with the reactions of other banks since its actions will not affect those banks. (ii) However, when z_t or y_t are disturbed a bank must in deciding upon its own response take into account the expected responses of other banks to variations in z_t and y_t.

The above assumptions are incorporated in the following equations. Let the loan demand confronting a bank be written as follows, where r_t^0 is the average loan rate of other banks and l_t^0 is the sum of loans extended by other banks in the tth period:[2]

$$l_t = a - br_t + b_0 r_t^0 + cz_t + uy_t + \gamma \sum_{i=1}^{n} d^i l_{t-i} - \gamma_0 \sum_{i=1}^{n} d^i l_{t-i}^0 \qquad (4.1)$$

The newly introduced coefficients, b_0 and γ_0, are assumed to be non-negative. It is further assumed for reasons of simplicity that the geometrically declining weights d^i attached to the past loans of other banks are identical to the weights for past loans of the individual bank. This implies that (i) the impact of past loans of a bank relative to those of other banks on the current loan demand faced by the bank depends entirely on the size of γ relative to γ_0 and (ii) the rapidity with which the importance of past loans on current loan demand declines as the lag, i, increases is the same for l_{t-i} and l_{t-i}^0.

It is seen from (4.1) that banks compete through both loan rates and the customer relationship. A bank loses current borrowers by charging a high loan rate, r_t, relative to the average loan rate of other banks, r_t^0. This loss of current customers to other banks causes future loan demands faced by the bank to be lower than would have otherwise been the case because of the customer relationship effect as expressed in the last two terms of (4.1). The intensity of competition, i.e. the response of loan demands to differences between banks in current rates charged and past loans extended, is measured by the sizes of b, b_0, γ, γ_0, and d. The larger are these parameters the greater will be the effects on current and future loan demands confronted by a bank when that bank pursues an interest rate policy different from other banks. By letting b and b_0 approach infinity we cause the bank's position to approach that of a perfect competitor in a loan market in which loan demands are infinitely responsive to current interest rates and past loans have no influence. On the other hand, the bank is a monopolist of the type discussed in Chapters 2 and 3 if $b_0 = \gamma_0 = 0$ and b is finite and positive.

Competition for deposits via the deposit relationship also exists. The supply of deposits to the individual bank depends upon the past loans of that bank and of other banks and upon total deposits in the banking system:

$$q_t = a_1 + \alpha \sum_{i=1}^{n} h^i l_{t-i} - \alpha_0 \sum_{i=1}^{n} h^i l_{t-i}^0 + s(q_t + q_t^0) \qquad (4.2)$$

where α, α_0, $s > 0$. Increases in loans by other banks attract prospective depositors as well as borrowers away from the individual bank. Similarly to equation (4.1), the weights for the past loans of other banks are identical to those for the past loans of the individual bank.

Before incorporating (4.1) and (4.2) into the decision process of the individual bank, let us introduce the bank's demand for free reserves. This aspect of the portfolio decision is considered for the sake of completeness only and in such a way as not to complicate our analysis of the choice among earning assets. Let the bank's demand for free reserves be written as follows:

$$e_t = a_3 - \delta y_t \tag{4.3}$$

where e_t denotes the bank's holdings of free reserves as a proportion of earning assets plus free reserves in the tth period and $a_3, \delta > 0$. The bank desires to be liquid but there is a cost to liquidity in terms of foregone profit. Given that the bank extends loans up to the point at which the marginal revenue from loans equals the infinitely-elastic marginal revenue from securities, the opportunity cost of holding excess reserves is the rate of return on securities. The Federal Reserve's discount rate is assumed fixed.

With the addition of free reserves the bank's balance sheet becomes

$$l_t + g_t + e_t = (1 - k)q_t + \kappa \tag{4.4}$$

Equations (4.1)–(4.4) have been deflated by a new scale factor, $F_1 = L_1 + G_1 + E_1$, where L_t, G_t and E_t are dollar values of the individual bank's holdings of loans, securities and free reserves, respectively, in the tth period. The definition of F_1 has been changed from that in Chapter 3 by the addition of current free reserves. We know from (3.6) and (4.2) that q_1 is predetermined. Hence, from (4.4) and given fixed k and κ, F_1 is also predetermined. But E_1 and therefore $L_1 + G_1$ are subject to the bank's control. The responses of l_1 to variations in z_1 that will be derived below are proportional not to earning assets as in

Table 4.1. Bank loans as proportions of earning assets and of earning assets plus free reserves

	Month	L	G	E	$\dfrac{L}{L+G}$	$\dfrac{L}{L+G+E}$
(P)	11–48	41·4	71·7	0·66	0·366	0·364
(T)	10–49	41·4	77·0	0·82	0·350	0·347
(P)	7–53	65·3	75·8	0·37	0·463	0·462
(T)	8–54	66·6	81·7	0·73	0·449	0·447
(P)	7–57	91·1	73·7	−0·38	0·553	0·554
(T)	4–58	92·1	80·3	0·49	0·534	0·533
(P)	5–60	111·0	75·8	−0·03	0·594	0·594
(T)	2–61	114·8	82·1	0·52	0·583	0·582
(P)	11–66	207·2	101·4	−0·43	0·671	0·672
(T)	5–67	213·2	110·6	0·24	0·658	0·658
(P)	11–69	270·1	124·5	−0·99	0·684	0·686
(T)	11–70	284·3	138·3	−0·31	0·673	0·673
	4–73	400·2	177·1	−1·57	0·693	0·695

L = Loans of all commercial banks in billions of dollars.
G = Security holdings of all commercial banks in billions of dollars.
E = Member bank free reserves in billions of dollars.

See Appendix B for sources and descriptions of data.

Chapters 2 and 3 but to earning assets plus free reserves. This approach has been adopted because it is convenient to deal with current loans as a proportion of a predetermined variable. A proportion in which the denominator as well as the numerator varied in response to z_1 would complicate the arithmetic considerably.

While the primary objective of this study is the explanation of movements in bank loans as a proportion of total earning assets over the course of the business cycle, the treatment of loans as a proportion of F_1 rather than of earning assets has little effect on our results. This is seen in Table 4.1 in which loans as proportions of both $L_1 + G_1$ and F_1 are shown for postwar peaks and troughs.[3] The change in loans as a proportion of F_1 over the cycle is slightly more marked than the change in loans as a proportion of $L_1 + G_1$ since E_1 moves inversely to economic activity and interest rates.

4.2 THE TWO-PERIOD AND INFINITE-HORIZON MODELS

Under the monopolistically competitive conditions described in the preceding section the individual bank will maximize the sum of discounted profits (2.5) with respect to its decision variables r_t, l_t, g_t, q_t, e_t subject to the market loan and deposit restraints (4.1) and (4.2), the liquidity restraint (4.3), the balance-sheet restraint (4.4) and the Federal Reserve's behavioural equation (3.6) conditional upon current and expected levels of economic activity, z_t, security yields, y_t, and the current and expected decisions of other banks, r_t^0 and l_t^0 $(t = 1, 2, ..., T)$. This procedure yields profit-maximizing values of the decision variables, r_t^*, l_t^*, g_t^*, q_t^*, e_t^*. Now, as in Chapters 2 and 3, let us examine the effects of variations in economic activity and security yields on $r_1^* - y_1$ and l_1^*.[4] As before, the bank will revise its expectations of future z_t and y_t in the manner specified by equations (2.11) and (2.12). Furthermore, since the bank knows that cyclical expansions and contractions influence not only its own behaviour but also the decisions of other banks, its response will depend upon its expectations regarding the current and future reactions of other banks to observed changes in economic activity and security yields. I will utilize a very simple assumption with regard to an individual bank's conception of the behaviour of other banks by supposing that our bank expects other banks to respond to changes in economic activity and security yields in precisely the same way that it does.[5] This means that, where r_t^* is the loan rate planned by our bank for the tth period and r_t^0 is the average loan rate that our bank expects other banks to charge in the tth period,

$$\frac{\partial r_t^0}{\partial z_1} = \frac{\partial r_t^*}{\partial z_1}; \frac{\partial r_t^0}{\partial y_1} = \frac{\partial r_t^*}{\partial y_1} \quad (t = 1, 2, ..., T) \tag{4.5}$$

Furthermore, if there are $N + 1$ banks in the system, variations in l_t^0 are expected to be N times those in l_t^*:

$$\frac{\partial l_t^0}{\partial z_1} = N\frac{\partial l_t^*}{\partial z_1}; \frac{\partial l_t^0}{\partial y_1} = N\frac{\partial l_t^*}{\partial y_1} \quad (t = 1, 2, ..., T) \qquad (4.6)$$

Although the assumption of identical responses is a decided simplification, it will be seen in Chapter 6 that the loan rates and loans of different types of banks are positively correlated over time.

It will be assumed that $b - b_0$, $\gamma - N\gamma_0$, $\alpha - N\alpha_0 \geq 0$. That is, changes in loan rates charged and loans extended by a bank are at least as important as identical changes in rates and loans of all other banks in determining the loans and deposits of that bank. If the inequality holds, identical reductions in the loan rates charged by all banks will induce a current increase in aggregate loans demanded from the banking system and will also lead to increases in future loan demands via the loan-customer relationship. Reductions in loan rates attract business to commercial banks through increased borrowing by the non-bank public and/or the attraction of customers away from other lenders. Although a value of $\alpha > N\alpha_0$ implies that identical increases in loans extended by all banks will promote increased future demands for bank deposits, aggregate deposits (and therefore deposits in each bank in the case of identical banks) will not be affected because they are assumed to be controlled by the Federal Reserve in response to lagged variations in economic activity.

Now let us examine the implications of these assumptions for the response of a bank to changes in z_1. First consider the two-period case:

$$\frac{\partial l_1^*}{\partial z_1} = \frac{\begin{aligned}b[c + uf - (b - b_0)f][2b - b_0 + \gamma d\beta(b - b_0)(1 + w)] \\ + bf\alpha h\beta(b - b_0)(2b - b_0)(1 - k)(1 + w)\end{aligned}}{(2b - b_0)^2 - b(b - b_0)(\gamma - \gamma_0')\beta\gamma d^2} \qquad (4.7)$$

$$\frac{\partial r_1^*}{\partial z_1} - \frac{\partial y_1}{\partial z_1} = \frac{\begin{aligned}[c + uf - (b - b_0)f][2b - b_0 - b\beta\gamma(\gamma - \gamma_0')d^2 - b\beta\gamma d(1 + w)] \\ - bf\alpha h\beta(2b - b_0)(1 - k)(1 + w)\end{aligned}}{(2b - b_0)^2 - b(b - b_0)(\gamma - \gamma_0')\beta\gamma d^2} \qquad (4.8)$$

where $\gamma_0' = N\gamma_0$. Equations (4.7) and (4.8) reduce to (3.7) and (3.8), respectively, when $b_0 = \gamma_0 = 0$.[6] The denominator of (4.7) and (4.8) is positive if the second-order conditions are satisfied and $(b - b_0)$, $(\gamma - \gamma_0') \geq 0$.[7]

Let us compare the responses of the bank to fluctuations in economic activity under competitive and non-competitive conditions. The argument will be easier to follow if we make the simplifying assumption that $b_0/b = \gamma_0'/\gamma = \eta$, where we know from the discussion following equation (4.6) that $0 \leq \eta \leq 1$. Although not necessary to the results presented below, the equality of b_0/b and γ_0'/γ seems a reasonable assumption, at least for extreme values of b_0 and γ_0'. For example, under monopolistic conditions, in which the bank's customers do not have access to other banks, b_0 and γ_0' will be zero so that b_0/b and $\gamma_0'/\gamma = 0$. In competitive situations, on the other hand, where customers are quick to change banks in response to differentials between banks either in current loan rates or in the accommodation of past loan requests, b_0 and γ_0'

will approach b and γ, respectively, so that b_0/b and γ_0'/γ will approach unity. This will be true especially in those cases in which borrowers maintain accounts with several banks. Under this assumption, equations (4.7) and (4.8) may be written as follows:

$$\frac{\partial l_1^*}{\partial z_1} = \frac{\begin{aligned}&[c + uf - bf(1 - \eta)]\,[2 - \eta + \beta\gamma d(1 - \eta)(1 + w)]\\&\quad + bf\alpha h\beta(1 - \eta)(2 - \eta)(1 - k)(1 + w)\end{aligned}}{(2 - \eta)^2 - (1 - \eta)^2\beta\gamma^2 d^2} \tag{4.7a}$$

$$\frac{\partial r_1^*}{\partial z_1} - \frac{\partial y_1}{\partial z_1} = \frac{\begin{aligned}&[c + uf - bf(1 - \eta)]\,[2 - \eta - \beta\gamma^2 d^2(1 - \eta) - \beta\gamma d(1 + w)]\\&\quad - bf\alpha h\beta(2 - \eta)(1 - k)(1 + w)\end{aligned}}{b[(2 - \eta)^2 - (1 - \eta)^2\beta\gamma^2 d^2]} \tag{4.8a}$$

Disregarding the terms in αh for the present, both $\partial l_1^*/\partial z_1$ and $\partial(r_1^* - y_1)/\partial z_1$ are greater in the presence of competition ($\eta > 0$) than in the non-competitive case ($\eta = 0$) when γ, d, β and w are small. The reasons for this are as follows: As z_1 rises other banks find it profitable to increase their loans and loan rates due to the upward shift in loan demand. As a consequence, the introduction of competition causes the loan demand facing an individual bank to be higher than when $\eta = 0$ due to the effect of $b_0 r_1^0 = \eta b r_1^0$ in the loan demand equation (4.1). This is readily seen in the special case in which $d = h = 0$ and η is either zero or unity:[8]

$$\frac{\partial l_1^*}{\partial z_1} = \begin{cases} (c + uf) & , \quad \eta = 1 \\[2mm] \dfrac{(c + uf - bf)}{2} & , \quad \eta = 0 \end{cases} \quad (d = h = 0) \tag{4.7b}$$

$$\frac{\partial r_1^*}{\partial z_1} - \frac{\partial y_1}{\partial z_1} = \begin{cases} \dfrac{(c + uf)}{b} & , \quad \eta = 1 \\[2mm] \dfrac{(c + uf - bf)}{2b} & , \quad \eta = 0 \end{cases} \quad (d = h = 0) \tag{4.8b}$$

This result is reversed as the customer relationship becomes more important, i.e. as γ, d, β and w become larger. For given γ, β and w, when d is large other banks will restrain increases in their loan rates in order to achieve greater increases in their loans. Consequently, the loan demand facing an individual bank shifts upward in response to rises in z by smaller amounts under competition the larger is d. That is, increases in d reduce the amounts by which $\partial l_1^*/\partial z_1$ and $\partial(r_1^* - y_1)/\partial z_1$ under competition exceed these derivatives in the absence of competition. In fact, there are values of d such that $\partial l_1^*/\partial z_1$ and $\partial(r_1^* - y_1)/\partial z_1$ take the same values under competitive and non-competitive conditions. For example, still assuming $\alpha h = 0$, we see from (4.8a) that in the special case in which $\beta = \gamma = 1$ and $w = 0$, $\partial(r_1^* - y_1)/\partial z_1 = 0$ when $d = 1$ regardless of the value taken by η. Generally, however, the value of d that renders $\partial(r_1^* - y_1)/\partial z_1 = 0$ is dependent upon η. For example, when β, γ and w approach unity, $\partial(r_1^* - y_1)/\partial z_1 \gtrless 0$ as $d \lesseqgtr 0{\cdot}65$ and $d \lesseqgtr 0{\cdot}50$ for $\eta = 0{\cdot}50$ and $\eta = 1$, respectively.

These results may be compared with the non-competitive case ($\eta = 0$) discussed in Chapter 2.2 in which the critical value of d under these conditions was 0·73. The comparison of the effects of the deposit relationship, αh, on a bank's response to variations in economic activity under competitive and non-competitive conditions is similar to that for d.

The responses of loans and loan rates to variations in economic activity for horizons of any length ($n = T = 1, 2, ...$) are shown in (A.43) and (A.44) in Appendix A and the limits of $\partial l_1^*/\partial z_1$ and $\partial(r_1^* - y_1)/\partial z_1$ as $n = T \to \infty$ are given in (A.45) and (A.46). In the special case in which $n = T \to \infty$, $\alpha h = 0$ and $\gamma = \beta = w \to 1$, the customer relationship is sufficient to cause $\partial(r_1^* - y_1)/\partial z_1$ to be negative for $d > 0·30$ and $d > 0·29$ when $\eta = 0·5$ and $\eta = 1$, respectively. This compares with the non-competitive case discussed in Chapter 2.3 in which d was required to exceed 0·31 under these conditions. The second-order conditions require that $d < 0·50$ when $\gamma = \beta = 1$ and $n = T \to \infty$.

The strength of the deposit relationship under competitive conditions in the two-period and infinite-horizon cases is indicated by the terms in αh in equations (4.7)–(4.8) and (A.45)–(A.46), respectively. The importance of the loan-customer relationship is incorporated in L_T^0 and R_T^0 ($T = 1, 2, ...$), where our results may be expressed as follows when $\alpha h = 0$ and L_T^0 contains the terms not in αh in (4.7) and (A.45) and R_T^0 contains the terms not in αh in (4.8) and (A.46) when $T = 2$ and $T \to \infty$, respectively:

$$\frac{\partial l_1^*}{\partial z_1} = \frac{b[c + uf - (b - b_0)f]}{(2b - b_0)} L_T^0 \tag{4.9}$$
$$(T = 1, 2, ...)$$

$$\frac{\partial r_1^*}{\partial z_1} - \frac{\partial y_1}{\partial z_1} = \frac{[c + uf - (b - b_0)f]}{(2b - b_0)} R_T^0 \tag{4.10}$$

Table 4.2 lists values of R_T^0 for selected pairs of β and w in the two-period and infinite-horizon cases when $\gamma = 1$ and $\eta = 0·50$. A comparison of this table with Table 2.2 shows the impact of competition on the significance of the loan–customer relationship. However, these tables are not sufficient for a comparison of the effects of competition on $\partial(r_1^* - y_1)/\partial z_1$, which must take account of the positive influence of b_0 on the first term on the right-hand side of (4.10). Values of L_T^0 may be derived from the relation $(L_T^0 - 1) = (1 - \eta)$. $(1 - R_T^0)$. Increases in η reduce the size of the deviation of L_T^0 from unity relative to the absolute value of $1 - R_T^0$ because, as may be seen in equation (4.1), the greater is η the less are loan demands affected by equal changes in b and $b_0 = \eta b$.[9]

Table 4.3 lists approximate minimum values of d for which R_T^0 ($T = 2, \infty$) and, therefore, $\partial(r_1^* - y_1)/\partial z_1 \le 0$ for $\alpha h = 0$, $\gamma = 1$ and selected β and w. A comparison of Tables 2.3 and 4.3 illustrate the implication of the model that there is a wide range of combinations of β and w such that competition does not substantially affect the value of d for which $\partial(r_1^* - y_1)/\partial z_1 = 0$. However, as indicated by the dashes at the top of the last column in Table 4.3, unlike the

Table 4.2. Impact of the loan–customer relationship on $\partial(r_1^* - y_1)/\partial z_1$ under competition for selected β, w, d ($\gamma = 1$; $\eta = 0.5$)

	$\beta = 0.5$; $w = 0$		$\beta = 0.5$; $w = 0.5$		$\beta = 0.5$; $w = 0.9$	
d	R_2	R_∞	R_2	R_∞	R_2	R_∞
0	1·0000	1·0000	1·0000	1·0000	1·0000	1·0000
0·1	0·9655	0·9631	0·9489	0·9445	0·9355	0·9288
0·2	0·9287	0·9175	0·8953	0·8758	0·8686	0·8379
0·3	0·8894	0·8605	0·8392	0·7890	0·7990	0·7191
0·4	0·8475	0·7869	0·7803	0·6758	0·7265	0·5585
0·5	0·8028	0·6877	0·7183	0·5217	0·6507	0·3305
0·6	0·7551	0·5445	0·6531	0·2964	0·5714	−0·0192
0·7	0·7042	0·3088	0·5842	−0·0792	0·4883	−0·6357
0·8	0·6498	—	0·5115	—	0·4009	—
0·9	0·5916	—	0·4346	—	0·3089	—
1·0	0·5294	—	0·3529	—	0·2118	—

	$\beta = 0.9$; $w = 0$		$\beta = 0.9$; $w = 0.5$		$\beta = 0.9$; $w = 0.9$	
d	R_2	R_∞	R_2	R_∞	R_2	R_∞
0	1·0000	1·0000	1·0000	1·0000	1·0000	1·0000
0·1	0·9379	0·9294	0·9079	0·8930	0·8839	0·8603
0·2	0·8715	0·8299	0·8112	0·7381	0·7631	0·6443
0·3	0·8002	0·6806	0·7094	0·4984	0·6367	0·2816
0·4	0·7236	0·4314	0·6016	0·0841	0·5041	−0·4135
0·5	0·6410	−0·0808	0·4872	−0·8026	0·3641	−2·1277
0·6	0·5519	—	0·3651	—	0·2158	—
0·7	0·4553	—	0·2345	—	0·0578	—
0·8	0·3504	—	0·0940	—	−0·1111	—
0·9	0·2361	—	−0·0577	—	−0·2927	—
1·0	0·1111	—	−0·2222	—	−0·4889	—

	$\beta = 0.98$; $w = 0$		$\beta = 0.98$; $w = 0.5$		$\beta = 0.98$; $w = 0.9$	
d	R_2	R_∞	R_2	R_∞	R_2	R_∞
0	1·0000	1·0000	1·0000	1·0000	1·0000	1·0000
0·1	0·9324	0·9222	0·8997	0·8818	0·8736	0·8451
0·2	0·8600	0·8092	0·7944	0·7048	0·7419	0·5955
0·3	0·7823	0·6323	0·6833	0·4176	0·6041	0·1506
0·4	0·6986	0·3153	0·5656	−0·1181	0·4592	−0·7877
0·5	0·6082	−0·4415	0·4403	−1·4594	0·3060	−3·5975
0·6	0·5104	—	0·3064	—	0·1432	—
0·7	0·4042	—	0·1626	—	−0·0306	—
0·8	0·2884	—	0·0075	—	−0·2173	—
0·9	0·1617	—	−0·1608	—	−0·4187	—
1·0	0·0224	—	−0·3441	—	−0·6374	—

	$\beta = 1$; $w = 0$		$\beta = 1$; $w = 0.5$		$\beta = 1$; $w = 0.9$	
d	R_2	R_∞	R_2	R_∞	R_2	R_∞
0	1·0000	1·0000	1·0000	1·0000	1·0000	1·0000
0·1	0·9310	0·9204	0·8977	0·8789	0·8710	0·8412
0·2	0·8571	0·8038	0·7902	0·6962	0·7366	0·5826
0·3	0·7778	0·6193	0·6768	0·3958	0·5960	0·1145
0·4	0·6923	0·2824	0·5566	−0·1761	0·4480	−0·8986
0·5	0·6000	—	0·4286	—	0·2914	—
0·6	0·5000	—	0·2917	—	0·1250	—
0·7	0·3913	—	0·1445	—	−0·0529	—
0·8	0·2727	—	−0·0144	—	−0·2440	—
0·9	0·1429	—	−0·1868	—	−0·4505	—
1·0	0·0	—	−0·3750	—	−0·6750	—

Table 4.3. Values of d for selected β and w
($\gamma = 1$; $\eta = 0\cdot5$) above which $\partial(r_1{}^* - y_1)/\partial z_1 < 0$

β	w	$T = 2$	$T \to \infty$
0·5	0	1·65	—
0·5	0·1	1·59	—
0·5	0·5	1·38	0·69
0·5	0·8	1·24	0·62
0·5	0·9	1·21	0·60
0·9	0	1·09	0·49
0·9	0·1	1·04	0·48
0·9	0·5	0·87	0·42
0·9	0·8	0·77	0·37
0·9	0·9	0·74	0·35
0·98	0	1·02	0·46
0·98	0·1	0·97	0·45
0·98	0·5	0·81	0·39
0·98	0·8	0·72	0·34
0·98	0·9	0·69	0·33
1·00	0	1·00	0·45
1·00	0·1	0·96	0·44
1·00	0·5	0·80	0·38
1·00	0·8	0·70	0·34
1.00	0·9	0·68	0·32

case for $\eta = 0$ there are some combinations of γ, β and w such that there is no d that both satisfies the second-order conditions and causes $\partial(r_1^* - y_1)/\partial z_1$ to be negative.

NOTES

1. See Alhadeff [1954], Galbraith [1963], Guttentag and Herman [1967], Hodgman [1963] and Jacobs [1971] for discussions of interbank competition.
2. In the special case in which $n = 1$, equation (4.1) is a discrete linear version of the dynamic demands considered by Phelps and Winter [1970]. They let the change in a firm's proportion of total customers be equal to its current proportion of customers times a function of its price and a weighted average of the prices charged by other firms, the weights being current proportions of customers served by each firm.
3. Ideally, since L and G pertain to all commercial banks and E is a member bank concept, E should be adjusted upward to account for the excess reserves of non-member banks. This adjustment has not been made, however, because of the lack of data.
4. Responses of the other current decision variables to variations in z_1, where $\partial y_1/\partial z_1 = f$, may be derived from $\partial l_1^*/\partial z_1$ and the constraints. From (3.6) and (4.2), q_1 is predetermined and therefore independent of z_1. From (2.18) and (4.3), $\partial e_1^*/\partial z_1 = -\delta f$. Since $l_1 + g_1 + e_1 = 1$, $\partial g_1^*/\partial z_1 = \delta f - \partial l_1^*/\partial z_1$.
5. If the behaviour of the banking system affects economic activity and security yields

and if those effects are not offset by the fiscal and monetary authorities, current and planned variations in $l_t^* = l_t^0$ and $r_t^* = r_t^0$ ought to influence current and expected values of z_t and y_t. That is, z_t and y_t should be endogenous variables. However, we will continue to assume for the sake of simplicity in the present discussion that z_t and y_t are exogenous but will treat them as endogenous in the macroeconomic analysis in Chapter 7.

6. Note that α_0, which enters the deposit equation (4.2), does not appear in (4.7) or (4.8). The parameters of the loan demand equation (4.1) that pertain to the actions of other banks enter (4.7) and (4.8) because current and future loan demands faced by a bank are affected through b_0 and γ_0 by the actions of other banks. The influence of α_0, on the other hand, is concentrated upon future deposits and, therefore, security purchases of the bank. Assuming no corner solutions, loans and loan rates of the bank are independent of variations in deposits caused by the lending policies of other banks. Thus, while the bank's profit stream and planned future responses of g_t^* and q_t^* ($t = 2, 3, ..., T$) to variations in economic activity depend upon α_0, the responses of the other current and planned decision variables are independent of α_0.

7. It has been assumed that banks are aware of their identical behaviour. However, if we assume that (i) the time required for banks to adjust to changes in economic activity can be divided into sub-periods and (ii) banks are not aware of their identical behaviour but rather maximize profits subject to the new levels of economic activity and security yields and the loan rates and loan quantities extended by other banks in previous sub-periods, the result will be a dynamic adjustment process in which a positive value of the denominator of (4.7) and (4.8) is a necessary condition for stability.

8. The responses of both current and planned loans to variations in current and expected economic activity are constant and independent of b when $\eta = 1$ because identical changes in loan rates by all banks leave loans unchanged when $b - b_0 = b(1 - \eta) = 0$.

9. In fact, $L_T^0 = 1$ when $\eta = 1$ for the reasons given in the preceding footnote.

CHAPTER 5

Aggregation and Estimation

5.1 INTRODUCTION

This chapter is concerned with estimating the parameters of the model presented in Chapters 2–4. The objective is to determine whether time series regression estimates of these parameters are consistent with the view that the customer relationship exerts an important influence on commercial bank behaviour. These estimates will be based on the aggregate loan and deposit demands of the non-bank public using quarterly observations from the period 1948–70. The aggregation and estimation procedures are described and the results are reported in Sections 5.2 and 5.3, the performance of the estimated equations in predicting observations outside the sample period is examined in Section 5.4 and the implications of the estimates for bank behaviour are discussed in Section 5.5.

5.2 AGGREGATION

Since the model in Chapters 2–4 pertains to the behaviour of a single bank it would be desirable in estimating that model to use interest rate and balance sheet data from individual banks. But time series data of the kind required are not available for individual banks. However, in a highly-integrated system such as the American economy, variations in economic activity, loan demands, Federal Reserve credit and interest rates are rapidly diffused throughout the various sectors. This is particularly true of the commercial banking sector. Trend, cyclical and seasonal movements in loan rates and the size and compositions of the balance sheets of commercial banks widely separated in location, size and regulatory restraints tend to proceed at roughly similar rates and to have contemporaneous turning points. For example, as will be shown in Chapter 6, cyclical movements in loans as proportions of earning assets of New York City, Chicago, Other Reserve City, Country and Non-member

50

banks are similar to those of commercial banks in total. It will also be seen in Chapter 6 that, as with the average rate on all business loans, average rates on loans of all sizes surveyed by the Federal Reserve Board tend to rise during expansions and fall during contractions and are less volatile than security yields.[1] These considerations suggest that the analysis of aggregate bank data, although no doubt involving the loss of some information, ought to increase our knowledge of the behaviour of individual banks as well as the banking system as a whole.

Let the demand for loans from the jth bank in the tth period be

$$L_{jt} = A_j - B_j r_{jt} + B_{0j} r_{jt}^0 + C_j z_t + U_j y_t + \gamma_j \sum_{i=1}^{n} d_j^i L_{j,t-i} - \gamma_{0j} \sum_{i=1}^{n} d_j^i L_{j,t-i}^0 + \xi_{jt}$$

$$(j = 1, 2, ..., N + 1) \qquad (5.1)$$

where r_{jt} is the loan rate charged by the jth bank, r_{jt}^0 is an average of loan rates charged by other banks, z_t is a measure of aggregate economic activity, y_t is the expected one-period rate of return on securities and $L_{j,t-i}$ and $L_{j,t-i}^0$ are the total dollar values of loans extended by the jth bank and by all other banks, respectively, in the $(t-i)$th period. Equation (5.1) is identical to (4.1) except that (5.1) is denominated in dollars instead of proportions of the bank's earning assets and the bank index j and a stochastic disturbance ξ_{jt} with a mean of zero have been added. Given the assumptions set forth in Chapters 2–4 the presence of ξ_{jt} would not have altered the results presented in those chapters. That is, the maximization of π subject to the non-stochastic loan demand and deposit supply constraints (4.1) and (4.2) gives the same choice of decision variables as maximization of the expected value of π subject to the stochastic constraints resulting from the introduction of additive disturbances with zero means into (4.1) and (4.2).[2]

If we assume identical banks, which implies that $r_{jt} = r_{jt}^0 = r_t$ and $L_{j,t-i}^0 = NL_{j,t-i}$ for all j and t,[3] summing (5.1) over j gives the following aggregate demand for bank loans:

$$L_t = A - (B - B_0) r_t + C z_t + U y_t + \varepsilon \sum_{i=1}^{n} d^i L_{t-i} + \xi_t \qquad (5.2)$$

where $\gamma_j = \gamma$, $\gamma_{0j} = \gamma_0$, $\varepsilon = \gamma - N \gamma_0$, $d_j = d$, $A = \Sigma A_j$, $B = \Sigma B_j$, $B_0 = \Sigma B_{0j}$, $C = \Sigma C_j$, $U = \Sigma U_j$, $\xi_t = \Sigma \xi_{jt}$, $L_t = \Sigma L_{jt}$ $(j = 1, ..., N + 1)$ and, as indicated in Chapters 2–4, it is expected that $B - B_0$, C, U, ε, $d \geq 0$.

The aggregate demand for bank deposits will now be derived. Although it was assumed in Chapters 3 and 4 that aggregate bank deposits are predetermined due to the nature of the Federal Reserve's behaviour as specified in equation (3.6), the public's demand for deposits is nevertheless dependent upon current endogenous variables.[4] The public's desired holdings of deposits in the jth bank in the tth period may be written as follows:

$$Q_{jt} = A_j' - B_j' r_t - U_j' y_t + C_j' z_t + \alpha_j \sum_{i=1}^{n} h_j^i L_{j,t-i} - \alpha_{0j} \sum_{i=1}^{n} h_j^i L_{j,t-i}^0 + \zeta_{jt} \qquad (5.3)$$

where upper-case symbols denote dollar values and ζ_{jt} is a stochastic disturbance term. The loan rate that enters the demand for deposits in the jth bank is the average rate on all bank loans, which influences aggregate deposit demand. The share of total deposits in the jth bank is determined by its past loans relative to the past loans of other banks and by such factors as numbers of branch offices and relative incomes of bank marketing areas, which are assumed constant and are reflected in the parameters A'_j, B'_j, C'_j and U'_j. It is expected that the demand for bank deposits is positively related to economic activity and negatively related to rates of return on other assets so that B'_j, U'_j, $C'_j > 0$.

Again assuming identical banks and summing over j, the aggregate demand for bank deposits is

$$Q_t = A' - B'r_t - U'y_t + C'z_t + \psi \sum_{i=1}^{n} h^i L_{t-i} + \zeta_t \tag{5.4}$$

where $\alpha_j = \alpha$, $\alpha_{0j} = \alpha_0$, $\psi = \alpha - N\alpha_0$, $h_j = h$, $A' = \Sigma A'_j$, $B' = \Sigma B'_j$, $C' = \Sigma C'_j$, $U' = \Sigma U'_j$, $\zeta_t = \Sigma \zeta_{jt}$, $Q_t = \Sigma Q_{jt}$ $(j = 1, \ldots, N + 1)$.

5.3 ESTIMATION

Equations (5.2) and (5.4) may be transformed as follows, where $0 \le d, h < 1$ and $n \to \infty$;

$$L_t = (1 - d)A - (B - B_0)r_t + d(B - B_0)r_{t-1} + Cz_t - dCz_{t-1} + Uy_t - dUy_{t-1} \\ + d(1 + \varepsilon)L_{t-1} + (\xi_t - d\xi_{t-1}) \tag{5.5}$$

$$Q_t = (1 - h)A' - B'r_t + hB'r_{t-1} - U'y_t + hU'y_{t-1} + C'z_t - hC'z_{t-1} \\ + h\psi L_{t-1} + hQ_{t-1} + (\zeta_t - h\zeta_{t-1}) \tag{5.6}$$

We must deal with several problems before estimating the parameters in these equations. First note that d and h are overidentified in the coefficients of the variables. There are eight coefficients in six parameters $(A, B - B_0, C, U, \varepsilon, d)$ in (5.5) and nine coefficients in six parameters $(A', B', U', C', h, \psi)$ in (5.6). The application of unrestricted least-squares to (5.5) and (5.6) would yield three estimates of d and four estimates of h which will not in practice be the same. Second, r_t, z_t and y_t are highly autocorrelated so that estimates of the coefficients of r_t, r_{t-1}, z_t, z_{t-1}, y_t and y_{t-1} are likely to have very large errors. Third, the disturbances ξ_t and ζ_t are also probably autocorrelated when quarterly observations are used, a problem that may be accentuated by the differencing procedure that leads to the stochastic terms $(\xi_t - d\xi_{t-1})$ and $(\zeta_t - h\zeta_{t-1})$ in (5.5) and (5.6). One approach to these problems is to maximize the likelihood functions of (5.5) and (5.6) with respect to all of the parameters in those equations, including d and h, as well as the parameters of the autoregressive schemes linking current and past values of ξ_t and ζ_t. But this procedure is computationally difficult because the derivatives of the likelihood function are non-linear in the parameters to be estimated. An alternative method of estimating equations such as (5.5) and (5.6) when ξ_t and ζ_t are assumed to follow the first-order autoregressive schemes specified in (5.7) has been suggested by Dhrymes [1971, pp. 140–54].

$$\xi_t = \rho_1 \xi_{t-1} + \mu_{1t}$$
$$\zeta_t = \rho_2 \zeta_{t-1} + \mu_{2t} \tag{5.7}$$

where μ_1 and μ_2 are normally and independently distributed with zero means and variances σ_1^2 and σ_2^2. Dhrymes' approach involves, for example, the re-arrangement of (5.5) to obtain (5.8), the selection of a variety of values of d and ρ_1 in the admissible range, the calculation of $(r_t - dr_{t-1})$, $(y_t - dy_{t-1})$ and $(z_t - dz_{t-1})$ for each d and the maximization of the likelihood function with respect to the other parameters of (5.8) for each combination of d and ρ_1. This yields the Aitken estimators of A, $B - B_0$, C, U, ε and σ_1^2 as functions of d and ρ_1. The maximum likelihood estimators of d, ρ_1, A, $B - B_0$, U and ε are given by that pair d, ρ_1 that minimizes $\hat{\sigma}_1^2$.[5] A similar procedure may be applied to (5.9), which is obtained from (5.6). Dhrymes shows that these estimators are consistent.[6]

$$(L_t - dL_{t-1}) = (1 - d)A - (B - B_0)(r_t - dr_{t-1}) + C(z_t - dz_{t-1}) + U(y_t - dy_{t-1})$$
$$+ \varepsilon dL_{t-1} + (\xi_t - d\xi_{t-1}) \tag{5.8}$$

$$(Q_t - hQ_{t-1}) = (1 - h)A' - B'(r_t - hr_{t-1}) - U'(y_t - hy_{t-1}) + C'(z_t - hz_{t-1})$$
$$+ \psi hL_{t-1} + (\zeta_t - h\zeta_{t-1}) \tag{5.9}$$

This approach is cumbersome and expensive, however, because of the large number of pairs d, ρ_1 that normally must be considered — 190 pairs, for example, if we let $\rho_1 = -0.9, -0.8, ..., 0.9$ and $d = 0, 0.1, ..., 0.9$. The results reported below are based on a compromise between Dhrymes' iterative procedure and the direct maximization of the likelihood function with respect to all of the parameters of the model. We use the Autoregressive Maximum Likelihood (ARML) programme developed by Hendry and Trivedi which computes estimates of the parameters of linear equations when the disturbance terms are characterised by linear autoregressive schemes.[7] The estimators yielded by this procedure asymptotically approach maximum likelihood estimators and a Monte Carlo study by Hendry and Trivedi [1972] indicated that the small sample bias of ARML estimators is less than that of ordinary least squares estimators. The ARML programme also calculates estimates of higher-order autoregressive schemes, which may be especially useful when dealing with quarterly observations where fourth-order autocorrelation is likely to occur. This programme is not designed to deal with the problem of the overidentification of d and h, however, so that we must apply the ARML procedure to (5.8) and (5.9) for selected d and h, choosing as maximum likelihood estimators those values of d and h for which the sums of squared residuals are minimized.

Our theory implies nothing about the period of observation except that it should be sufficiently long to permit banks to adjust to new information yet short enough to enable us to capture the dynamic properties of the customer relationship. Dictated largely by the availability of data, quarterly observations are not obviously inconsistent with these criteria.

We must now decide upon empirical counterparts to the interest rates, r_t and y_t, used in the theoretical model. The use of quarterly data and the assumption that banks maximize expected profits imply a convenient empirical specification of y_t. If we are to be consistent with the assumptions of the model and the chosen period of observation, we must require banks to select their security portfolios such that expected quarterly returns net of taxes and transactions costs are equal for all securities. But the quarterly return on one of the securities held by banks is known—that on three-month Treasury bills. Given our assumptions, therefore, the expected quarterly return on security portfolios is equal to the three-month Treasury bill rate, henceforth denoted by $\bar{y}_t$.[8]

Loan rates used in the empirical work are based on the Federal Reserve's 'Quarterly Survey of Interest Rates on Business Loans'. However, contract rates, even if accurately reported, are not those relevant to our model, which requires expected returns. In the absence of time series on loan defaults I have estimated the expected return on bank loans as follows, where it is assumed that expected returns on business loans vary proportionally to those on other loans. If we assume that corporate Aaa bonds are free from default but that this is not true of Baa bonds, the differential between Moody's yield series' on Corporate Aaa and Baa bonds will reflect the market's evaluation of the expected rate of default on the latter. Letting R_A and R_B denote yields on corporate Aaa and Baa bonds, respectively, it may be observed that the ratio R_B/R_A varies inversely to economic activity. This suggests that in the eyes of investors the risk of default on medium-grade securities declines as output, employment and general economic prospects improve. By way of illustration, values of R_B, R_A and R_B/R_A at NBER turning points are listed in Table 5.1. The difference $R_B - R_A$, which is very close to $\bar{R}$ in the table, is also inversely related to economic activity, although not quite as closely as R_B/R_A.

The price of an Aaa bond is

$$P_A = \sum_{i=1}^{m} c(1 + R_A)^{-i} + V(1 + R_A)^{-m} \tag{5.10}$$

where c = coupon, V = principal and m = term to maturity. On the assumption that the risk of default on Baa bonds increases with the maturity of payment, suppose the expected payment in the ith future period on a Baa bond to be a proportion $(1 + \bar{R})^{-i}$ of the contracted payment. Then the price of a Baa bond that is identical to an Aaa bond except for risk of default is

$$P_B = \sum_{i=1}^{m} c[(1 + \bar{R})(1 + R_A)]^{-i} + V[(1 + \bar{R})(1 + R_A)]^{-m} = \sum_{i=1}^{m} c(1 + R_B)^{-i} + V(1 + R_B)^{-m} \tag{5.11}$$

Table 5.1. Published rates and expected one-period rates of return

	Month	R_B	R_A	R_B/R_A	$\bar{R}$	$\bar{r}$	$\bar{y}$	$\bar{r}-\bar{y}$	$r-y$
(P)	11–48	3·53	2·84	1·24	0·69	2·28	1·14	1·14	0·65
(T)	10–49	3·36	2·61	1·29	0·75	2·26	1·05	1·21	0·95
(P)	7–53	3·86	3·28	1·18	0·58	3·44	2·04	1·40	0·72
(T)	8–54	3·49	2·87	1·22	0·62	3·27	0·92	2·35	1·80
(P)	7–57	4·73	3·99	1·19	0·73	4·17	3·16	1·01	0·22
(T)	4–58	4·67	3·60	1·30	1·06	3·84	1·13	2·71	1·78
(P)	5–60	5·28	4·46	1·18	0·81	4·94	3·29	1·65	0·67
(T)	2–61	5·07	4·27	1·19	0·79	4·58	2·42	2·16	1·24
(P)	11–66	6·13	5·35	1·15	0·77	5·92	5·31	0·61	0·27
(T)	5–67	5·96	5·24	1·14	0·71	5·54	3·60	1·94	0·84
(P)	11–69	8·25	7·35	1·12	0·88	8·33	7·24	1·09	0·08
(T)	11–70	9·38	8·05	1·17	1·30	7·25	5·28	1·97	1·29
	4–73	8·09	7·26	1·11	0·82	6·84	6·26	0·58	0·14

R_B = Moody's corporate *Baa* bond rate.
R_A = Moody's corporate *Aaa* bond rate.
r = Average rate of interest on short-term business loans.
y = Weighted average of yields on securities.
$\bar{y}$ = Market yield on three-month Treasury bills.
$\bar{R} = \dfrac{4(R_B - R_A)}{4 + 0{\cdot}01R_A}$ = a measure of loan risk.
$\bar{r} = \dfrac{4(r - 0{\cdot}5\bar{R})}{4 + 0{\cdot}01(0{\cdot}5\bar{R})}$ = expected rate of return on short-term business loans.

All rates are per cents per annum. All series except r and $\bar{r}$ are monthly averages of daily figures. r is interpolated from the Federal Reserve's *Quarterly Survey of Interest Rates on Short-Term Business Loans of Banks* and $\bar{r}$ is calculated from r and $\bar{R}$. See Appendix B for sources and descriptions of the data.

We do not observe $\bar{R}$ directly but it may be calculated from observations on R_A and R_B using (5.10) and (5.11):

$$\bar{R} = \frac{R_B - R_A}{1 + R_A} \tag{5.12}$$

If we arbitrarily assume bank loans to be evenly divided between risky and riskless loans, where the risky loans bear the same level of risk as *Baa* bonds, the expected rate of return on one-period loans is[9]

$$\bar{r} = \frac{L(1 + r)(1 + 0{\cdot}5\bar{R})^{-1} - L}{L} = \frac{r - 0{\cdot}5\bar{R}}{1 + 0{\cdot}5\bar{R}} \tag{5.13}$$

where r is the average contract rate on business loans as reported in the Federal Reserve's *Quarterly Survey*.

The definition of $\bar{r}$ in (5.13) assumes R_A, R_B and r to be quarterly rates of return. If we follow convention by using annual rates the expected rate of return on one-period loans may be written as follows, where all rates are expressed in annual terms:[10]

56

$$\bar{r} = \frac{4(r - 0 \cdot 5\bar{R})}{4 + 0 \cdot 5\bar{R}} \text{ where } \bar{R} = \frac{4(R_B - \bar{R}_A)}{4 + \bar{R}_A} \tag{5.14}$$

Values of $\bar{r} - \bar{y}$ at cyclical turning points are shown in Table 5.1 above. These may be compared with the values of $r - y$ listed in Table 1.1 and repeated in Table 5.1. The only qualitative disagreement between movements in these two series occurred during the 1949–53 expansion when $r - y$ declined while $\bar{r} - \bar{y}$ rose.

Quarterly averages of $\bar{R}$, $\bar{r}$, $\bar{y}$, $\bar{r} - \bar{y}$ and $l = L/F$ from II/1948 to I/1973 are depicted in Chart 5.1; L is total commercial bank loans and F is total earning

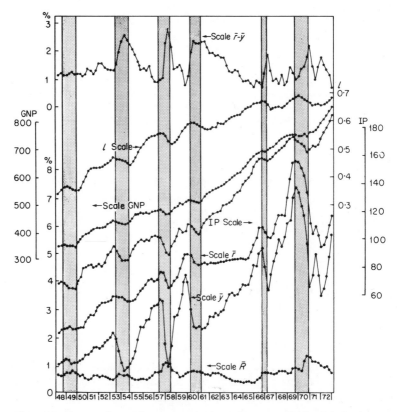

Chart 5.1. Economic activity, interest rates and commercial bank behaviour: II/1948–I/1973

assets plus free reserves of banks. Also shown are alternative specifications of our index of economic activity, z: Gross National Product in constant (1958) dollars, GNP, and quarterly averages of the Federal Reserve Board's Index of Industrial Production, IP (1957–59 = 100). The data in Chart 5.1 are discussed at length in Appendix B and are listed in Table B.1. Interpreting Chart 5.1

within the framework of the model developed in Chapters 2–4, these data suggest a strong customer relationship. That is, the data appear to be consistent with values of γ, d, α, h, β and w sufficiently large to cause $\partial(\bar{r}_1 - \bar{y}_1)/\partial z_1 < 0$.

The Autoregressive Maximum Likelihood (ARML) estimates of equations (5.8) and (5.9) for d, $h = 0, 0{\cdot}1, 0{\cdot}2, ..., 0{\cdot}9$ are listed in Tables 5.2 and 5.3 where first-order autoregressive schemes are assumed to hold. The data upon which these estimates were based may be summarized as follows. (Sources, detailed descriptions and lists of these data are contained in Appendix B).

Quarterly data were used for the period II/1948–IV/1970, the sample size being dictated by the availability of data. It was decided to end the sample period with 1970 in order to leave at least two years upon which to test the ability of the estimated equations to predict observations outside the sample period.

Except for interest rates, which contain little or no seasonal variation, the data are seasonally adjusted.

L is an estimated quarterly average of total commercial bank loans based on straight-line interpolation of end-of-month figures—in billions of dollars deflated by the GNP price deflator ($1958 = 100$).

GNP (z) is in billions of constant (1958) dollars at annual rates.

Interest rates are measured in percentages at annual rates. $\bar{y}$ is a quarterly average of daily figures on the three-month Treasury bill rate. $\bar{r}$ depends on R_A, R_B and r as shown in equation (5.14). R_A and R_B are quarterly averages

Table 5.2.   Loan demand

d	Constant	$\bar{r}_t - d\bar{r}_{t-1}$	$\bar{y}_t - d\bar{y}_{t-1}$	$z_t - dz_{t-1}$	dL_{t-1}	ρ	s^2
			Dependent variable $= L_t - dL_{t-1}$				
0	− 98·27	3·14	− 2·00	0·404		0·712	3·40
	(24·53)	(2·61)	(2·85)	(32·58)		(9·43)	
0·1	− 16·77	− 1·53	0·16	0·093	7·39	0·490	0·84
	(3·36)	(2·73)	(0·43)	(4·30)	(15·13)	(4·60)	
0·2	− 15·16	− 1·66	0·19	0·095	3·23	0·472	0·87
	(3·26)	(2·74)	(0·48)	(4·23)	(14·43)	(4·46)	
0·3	− 13·29	− 1·81	0·22	0·097	1·91	0·458	0·90
	(3·11)	(2·74)	(0·55)	(4·11)	(13·75)	(4·35)	
0·4	− 11·22	− 1·97	0·27	0·097	1·24	0·445	0·94
	(2·91)	(2·71)	(0·62)	(3·94)	(13·14)	(4·27)	
0·5	− 9·13	− 2·06	0·29	0·097	0·83	0·437	0·99
	(2·70)	(2·57)	(0·66)	(3·75)	(12·59)	(4·24)	
0·6	− 6·81	− 2·09	0·32	0·093	0·56	0·440	1·05
	(2·38)	(2·36)	(0·69)	(3·44)	(12·19)	(4·35)	
0·7	− 4·42	− 1·92	0·32	0·084	0·37	0·452	1·12
	(1·93)	(1·99)	(0·69)	(2·99)	(11·96)	(4·57)	
0·8	− 1·91	− 1·49	0·24	0·064	0·23	0·488	1·17
	(1·15)	(1·45)	(0·53)	(2·21)	(12·05)	(5·12)	
0·9	0·38	− 1·48	0·19	0·030	0·12	0·695	1·16
	(0·27)	(1·47)	(0·48)	(1·05)	(9·74)	(7·89)	

of Moody's daily series on corporate *Aaa* and *Baa* bonds. r is an estimate of the quarterly average of business loan rates derived by straight-line interpolation of data reported for the first fifteen days of one month in each quarter.

Q is a quarterly average of monthly data on total commercial bank time and demand deposits net of interbank deposits in billions of dollars deflated by the GNP price deflator ($1958 = 100$).

The estimated residual error variances adjusted for degrees of freedom are listed in the last columns of Tables 5.2 and 5.3. Referring to Table 5.2, we see that the sum of squared residuals is minimized for $d = 0.1$. When $d = 0.1$ all of the estimated slope coefficients have the expected signs and all are significant at the five per cent level except $\hat{U}$, the estimated coefficient of $y_t - dy_{t-1}$. Values of Student's t are given in parentheses below the estimates. The estimated first-order autocorrelation coefficient is significant for all d.

Estimates of the deposit demand equation for selected values of h are shown in Table 5.3, which shows that the sum of squared residuals is minimized for $h = 0.8$. As for the loan demand equation, the maximum likelihood estimates of the coefficients of the deposit demand equation have the expected signs and, except for the coefficient of $y_t - hy_{t-1}$, are significantly different from zero at the five per cent level. The estimated first-order autocorrelation coefficient is not significant for large h. The sum of squared residuals for h in the vicinity of 0.8 is not as clearly a global minimum as was the case for d in the vicinity of 0.1. In fact, a reasonable interpretation of the pattern of values of s^2 in Table 5.3 might be that the true variance σ^2 is a monotonically decreasing function of h,

Table 5.3.   Deposit demand

h	Constant	$\bar{r}_t - h\bar{r}_{t-1}$	$\bar{y}_t - h\bar{y}_{t-1}$	$z_t - hz_{t-1}$	hL_{t-1}	ρ	s^2
			Dependent variable $= Q_t - hQ_{t-1}$				
0	−10.00	−4.75	−2.56	0.470		0.834	8.16
	(1.00)	(2.26)	(2.33)	(18.48)		(13.57)	
0.1	38.89	−7.97	−0.99	0.263	4.95	0.843	7.15
	(2.34)	(3.44)	(0.88)	(3.97)	(3.25)	(12.55)	
0.2	37.00	−7.58	−0.88	0.249	2.27	0.801	7.12
	(2.50)	(3.25)	(0.77)	(3.65)	(3.27)	(11.01)	
0.3	35.19	−7.47	−0.67	0.233	1.39	0.743	7.12
	(2.70)	(3.17)	(0.58)	(3.33)	(3.35)	(9.35)	
0.4	32.40	−7.40	−0.51	0.218	0.94	0.668	7.12
	(2.87)	(3.16)	(0.44)	(3.06)	(3.45)	(7.65)	
0.5	27.90	−7.40	−0.44	0.211	0.64	0.568	7.12
	(2.97)	(3.19)	(0.37)	(2.95)	(3.51)	(5.88)	
0.6	23.06	−7.85	−0.29	0.207	0.44	0.442	6.99
	(3.11)	(3.43)	(0.25)	(2.95)	(3.68)	(4.18)	
0.7	17.25	−8.16	−0.25	0.209	0.29	0.299	6.82
	(3.17)	(3.61)	(0.21)	(3.10)	(3.86)	(2.64)	
0.8	11.73	−8.73	−0.07	0.208	0.18	0.167	6.57
	(3.28)	(3.90)	(0.06)	(3.23)	(4.21)	(1.42)	
0.9	5.91	−8.57	−0.06	0.201	0.09	0.099	6.59
	(3.00)	(3.91)	(0.05)	(3.17)	(4.44)	(0.83)	

the increase in s^2 between $h = 0.8$ and $h = 0.9$ being well within the range of statistical error. To test this interpretation the deposit demand equation was also estimated for $h = 1.0$. The resulting s^2 was much greater than that corresponding to $h = 0.9$. This suggests that σ^2 is in fact minimized for h approximately equal to 0.8 since s^2 falls as h rises to 0.8 and then increases for $h = 0.9$ and 1.0.[11]

ARML estimates were also computed under the assumption of the joint occurrence of first-order through fourth-order autocorrelation without any significant differences from the estimates obtained under the assumption of only first-order autocorrelation. Equations (5.7)–(5.9) suggest the possibility of moving-average as well as autoregressive elements in the errors and, accordingly, the loan demand and deposit demand equations were estimated following a mixed autoregressive–moving–average maximum likelihood procedure.[12] Except for the ρ_i, the estimates computed using this method were not significantly different from those obtained using the ARML programme.

These estimation procedures were also applied to the loan demand function using seasonally unadjusted data and seasonal dummies. The estimate of d remained unchanged at 0.1 and the estimated interest rate coefficients were not significantly different from those reported in Table 5.2. Estimates of the coefficients of $z_t - 0.1z_{t-1}$ and $0.1L_{t-1}$ increased substantially, however, to approximately 0.18 and 9.1, respectively.

These estimates lend support to the many economists and bankers who have argued that the customer relationship exerts an important influence on commercial bank behaviour. However, as with all empirical studies, we must be careful not to infer too much from our results. All that we can confidently say is that these results are consistent with the customer relationship hypothesis. Empirical results seldom if ever have unambiguous theoretical interpretations in the sense of being consistent with only one hypothesis. This problem is especially acute in the case of distributed-lag models. It is well-known that distributed-lag models with quite different theoretical rationales are often empirically indistinguishable.[13] For example, the demand equations estimated here are sufficiently similar to the forms implied by adaptive expectations and partial adjustment theories that we cannot have very much confidence in the ability of regressions to discriminate between those theories and the customer relationship. But these problems do not necessarily detract from the usefulness of the estimates presented above, which are not intended to be conclusive or to stand alone as a test of the importance of the customer relationship. Rather, these results should be considered in conjunction with the evidence cited in Chapters 2 and 3, especially Hodgman's surveys. That evidence in combination with the results presented in this chapter forms the basis of a persuasive argument that the customer relationship is an empirically significant phenomenon. Additional evidence in support of this position will be offered in Chapter 6.

5.4 PREDICTION

The estimated loan demand equation for $d = 0.1$ in Table 5.2 explains 99.97 per cent of the variance of L_t during the sample period 1948–70. An example of

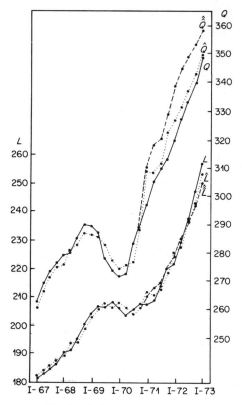

Chart 5.2. Predictive performance of the estimated loan and deposit demand equations

the closeness of this fit is shown for 1967–70 in Chart 5.2, where actual and estimated L_t are indicated by solid and dotted lines, respectively.[14] This equation also predicts L_t very well outside the sample period from the first quarter of 1971 through the first quarter of 1973, the last period for which data were available when this study was completed. When actual values of L_{t-1} are used in predicting L_t the estimated equation explains 98.78 per cent of the variance of L_t during 1971–73; this set of predictions, $\hat{L}_t$, is represented by a continuation of the dotted line. If predicted values of L_{t-1} are used, 91·03 per cent of the variance of L_t is explained: this set of predictions, $\hat{L}_t$, is indicated by a dashed line.

The estimated deposit demand equation for $h = 0.8$ in Table 5.3 performs almost as well as the estimated loan demand equation. This equation explains 99·69 per cent of the variance of Q_t during the sample period and predicts 95·71 and 96·73 per cent of the variance of Q_t during 1971–73 depending upon whether actual or estimated Q_{t-1} is used; the predictions are shown by dotted and dashed lines, respectively, in Chart 5.2.

5.5 THEORETICAL IMPLICATIONS OF THE ESTIMATES

Although the estimates reported in Section 5.3 indicate that the customer relationship is empirically significant we have yet to answer the question of whether or not these estimates are consistent with a customer relationship sufficiently strong to account for the opposite movements in $r - y$ and l shown in Table 1.1. We may go some way towards an answer to this question by examining the conditions under which our estimates are consistent with the results $\partial(r_1 - y_1)/\partial z_1 < 0$, $\partial l_1/\partial z_1 > 0$ as discussed in connection with equations (4.7)–(4.8) in Chapter 4 and (A.45)–(A.46) in Appendix A. As in Chapter 4, assume that $b_0/b = N\gamma_0/\gamma = \eta$ and let the same parameter apply to deposit demands so that $N\alpha_0/\alpha = \eta$. In the unscaled regression equation (5.8), the upper-case coefficients $B - B_0$, C and U correspond to their lower-case counterparts in Chapter 4.[15]

In both the two-period and infinite-horizon cases, bank responses to variations in economic activity (GNP) depend upon C, $B - B_0 = B(1 - \eta)$, U, d, h, $\gamma - N\gamma_0 = \gamma(1 - \eta) = \varepsilon$, $\alpha - N\alpha_0 = \alpha(1 - \eta) = \psi$, k, f, β, w. From Tables 5.2 and 5.3, estimates of the first seven of these parameters are approximately 0·093, 1·53, 0·1, 0·1, 0·8, 7·39, 0·18. The average reserve requirement ratio on all bank deposits during 1948–70 was approximately 0·11, which was used as an estimate of k. An estimate of f was obtained from a regression of the three-month Treasury bill rate on GNP, the data and sample period being the same as for the results in Tables 5.2 and 5.3. This provided an estimate of $\partial \bar{y}/\partial z = \hat{f} = 0.012$.[16] We have assumed throughout this study that $[c + uf - (b - b_0)f] = [C + Uf - (B - B_0)f]/F > 0$.[17] This assumption is supported by our estimates, which give a value of $[C + Uf - (B - B_0)f] = 0.077$.

The implications of these estimates for bank behaviour are conditional upon the values assumed with respect to η, β and w, for which our empirical analysis has not provided independent evidence. The expectations equation (2.11) requires $0 \le w < 1$ while the discount factor may assume any value in the range $0 \le \beta \le 1$, although it is probably not far from unity. Given the maximum admissible $\beta = 1$ and our estimates of d and ε, the range of admissible η is dictated by the second-order conditions which, when $T \to \infty$, include the statement $(1 + \gamma)d\beta^{1/2} = [1 + \varepsilon/(1 - \eta)]d\beta^{1/2} = [1 + 7.39/(1 - \eta)](0.1)(1) < 1$ or $\eta < 0.179$.[18]

The curves in Figure 5.1 are loci of combinations of β and w for the estimates listed above and selected $\eta = 0, 0.085, 0.170$ such that $\partial(r_1 - y_1)/\partial z_1 = 0$ for $T = 2$ and $T \to \infty$.[19] Figure 5.1(a) shows these loci for $d = 0.1$, $h = 0$, i.e. in the absence of the deposit relationship. Figure 5.1(b) shows these loci for $d = 0.1$, $h = 0.8$. The solid and dashed curves correspond to $T = 2$ and $T \to \infty$, respectively. Combinations of β and w above the curves imply $\partial(r_1 - y_1)/\partial z_1 < 0$. There are three curves for each value of T, one for each of the three assumed values of η. The greater is η the smaller are the values of β and w necessary to cause $\partial(r_1 - y_1)/\partial z_1 \le 0$. This is because, given ε and ψ, high values of η imply large γ and α and therefore a strong customer relationship.[20] Curves for $d = 0$,

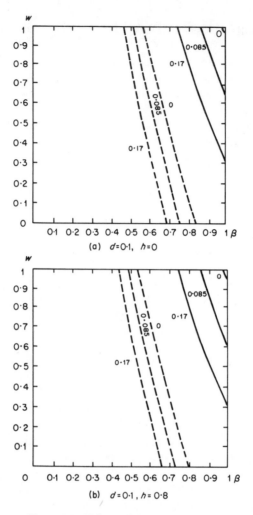

Figure 5.1. Values of β and w consistent with $\partial\,(r_1^* - y_1)/\partial z_1 = 0$ given the estimates in Tables 5.2 and 5.3

$h = 0.8$ are not shown because no combinations of w, $\beta \leq 1$ are consistent with $\partial(r_1 - y_1)/\partial z_1 \leq 0$. Thus, our estimates suggest that the loan–customer relationship discussed in Chapter 2 exerts a greater impact on bank behaviour than the deposit relationship introduced in Chapter 3.

Considering the case in which $T \to \infty$, Figure 5.1(*b*) shows that, given the estimates in Tables 5.2 and 5.3 and letting w and η assume any values in the ranges $0 \leq w < 1$ and $0 \leq \eta \leq 0.17$, we have $\partial(r_1 - y_1)/\partial z_1 \leq 0$ for all values of $\beta \geq 0.794$. It is seen in Figure 5.1(*a*) that, under these same conditions except that the deposit relationship is excluded ($h = 0$), $\partial(r_1 - y_1)/\partial z_1 \leq 0$ for $\beta \geq 0.841$.

It is unlikely that the true value of β is less than 0·97 and it certainly exceeds 0·79.[21] Therefore, even for small w, our estimates are consistent with a customer relationship that is capable of explaining those aspects of bank behaviour discussed in Chapter 1.

NOTES

1. Compare Tables 6.1 and 6.2 with Table 1.1.
2. See Theil [1961, pp. 414–24] for discussion of certainty equivalence. This certainty equivalence property of the model is dependent upon our assumptions and would not hold, for example, if the stochastic terms were multiplicative instead of additive or if predictions of rates of return were stochastic.
3. See the discussion of equations (4.5) and (4.6).
4. This means that r_t, y_t and z_t must adjust so as to be consistent with Federal Reserve behaviour, which is determined by z_{t-1}.
5. More precisely, Dhrymes recommends the minimization of $\hat{\sigma}_1^2/(1 - \hat{\rho}_1^2)^{1/T}$ where T is the number of observations. But the minimization of this quantity rather than $\hat{\sigma}_1^2$ does not influence the choice of estimators presented below due to our large sample size.
6. See Johnston [1972, pp. 315–16] for a discussion of a similar procedure suggested by Zellner and Geisel [1968]. An earlier iterative maximum likelihood approach to the problem of overidentification of the parameters of distributed-lag models in the absence of autocorrelation was suggested by Nerlove [1960] and discussed by Wallis [1969].
7. See Hendry [1971], Hendry and Trivedi [1972] and Wallis [1972]. I first used Nerlove's procedure but Durbin's [1970] method of testing for autocorrelation in the presence of lagged dependent variables indicated substantial autocorrelation in the disturbances. See Wood [1973] for an earlier version of portions of this study.
8. Since capital gains and losses are not relevant to Treasury bills we do not have to worry about differential tax treatments of earnings on loans and bills.
9. In Chapter 6, where we consider large and small loans separately, $\bar{R}$ instead of $0·5\bar{R}$ is used as the estimate of the risk of default on small loans while large loans are assumed to be riskless.
10. The difference between the definitions of $\bar{R}$ and $\bar{r}$ in (5.13) and Table 5.1 are due to the expression of interest rates as percentages in the table.
11. Although useful for purposes of comparison such as that discussed above, a value of h equal to unity is not consistent with the model in this study because the transformation of equation (5.4) into (5.6) requires that the absolute value of h be less than unity. A similar comparison was carried out for the loan demand equation, for which the s^2 when $d = 1·0$ was substantially greater than that corresponding to $d = 0·9$.
12. As in the case of the ARML procedure, the mixed autoregressive moving-average maximum likelihood programme is based on an iterative technique developed by Powell [1965] designed for minimizing sums of squares of non-linear functions.
13. This problem has been discussed in many places, including Griliches [1967] and Wallis [1969].
14. Actual and estimated values of L_t and Q_t are not shown for the entire sample period because this would have required such a small scale that, due to the close fit, the actual and estimated values would have been virtually indistinguishable.
15. By 'unscaled' I mean not divided by bank earning assets plus free reserves, F_r. The use of estimated coefficients based on unscaled regressions does not affect the qualitative nature of the results in Chapters 2–4. Equations in $\partial(r_1 - y_1)/\partial z_1$ in the unscaled parameters B, B_0, C and U are identical to those in b, b_0, c and u because both the numerators and denominators of these equations are proportional to linear combi-

nations of these parameters. When upper-case parameters are used, equations in $\partial l_1/\partial z_1$ become $\partial L_1/\partial z_1 = F_1(\partial l_1/\partial z_1)$.

16. That is, the three-month Treasury bill rate has tended to change by slightly more than one basis point for each billion dollar change in GNP. The $\bar{R}^2$ for the regression was 0·87 and the t-statistic for $\hat{f}$ was 23·8.

17. See the discussion relating to Figure 2.2.

18. Smaller values of β and T permit the consideration of $\eta > 0\cdot179$. However, in order to be able to treat the full ranges of β and w in Figure 5.1, only values of $\eta < 0\cdot179$ are considered.

19. $\partial l_1/\partial z_1 > 0$ for all values of the parameters considered.

20. $\gamma = \varepsilon(1 - \eta) = 7\cdot39,\ 8\cdot08,\ 8\cdot90$ and $\alpha = \psi/(1 - \eta) = 0\cdot18,\ 0\cdot20,\ 0\cdot22$ for $\eta = 0,\ 0\cdot085,\ 0\cdot170$, respectively.

21. Member bank after-tax income as a percentage of total capital accounts has averaged 8·7 per cent on an annual basis since 1948, varying between a low of 7·2 per cent in 1948 and a high of 10·4 per cent in 1970. (For example, see the *Federal Reserve Bulletin*, June 1971, pp. 445–51). Using the generous figure of 12 per cent per annum as the appropriate rate of discount on bank profits and converting this to a quarterly basis to be consistent with the estimates upon which Figure 5.1 above is based, we arrive at a value of β equal to (approximately) 0·97.

CHAPTER 6

Alternative Theories of Bank Behaviour: Credit Rationing and the Customer Relationship

6.1 INTRODUCTION

This chapter has two objectives: First, to disaggregate the model developed in the preceding chapters in order to examine the implications of the customer relationship for the behaviour of banks of different size. Second, to compare the empirical validity of this disaggregated model of the customer relationship with that of credit rationing theories. Credit rationing and credit availability theories of commercial bank behaviour became popular in the 1950s, particularly in defence of the effectiveness of monetary policy despite the apparent lack of response of investment to variations in interest rates. Most contributors to this literature sought to explain why rational lenders might both restrict loans and resist increases in loan rates during periods of rising interest rates and loan demands. At least one study went so far as to apply a model of credit availability to an explanation of why banks might shift out of loans into securities during periods of rising interest rates.[1] But, as seen in Table 1.1 and Chart 5.1, (i) although only modest rises in loan rates occur during economic expansions, (ii) banks tend to move vigorously from securities into loans during such periods. Early credit rationing theories were consistent with (i) but inconsistent with (ii). The theory of bank behaviour developed in Chapters 2–4 above, based on the customer relationship, was seen in Chapter 5 to be consistent with both (i) and (ii).

None of the early work on credit rationing was based on a complete framework of commercial bank profit maximization subject to constraints imposed by loan demands and market interest rates. As a result, the determination of loan rates lay outside the scope of those theories and loan rates were assumed to be given exogenously. Furthermore, because of the absence of explicit loan demands, the implications of those theories for the composition of bank portfolios were extremely tenuous. Recently, however, Jaffee and Modigliani [1969] have built upon the earlier work in credit rationing by supplying the missing loan demands and thus making possible the explanation of loan rates and bank portfolios within the framework of a theory of credit rationing.

The J–M model requires the disaggregation of borrowers according to size. Therefore, in order to be able to compare the theory advanced in Chapters 2–4 with J–M's credit rationing theory, as well as to obtain some results that are interesting in their own right, a disaggregated model of the customer relationship is presented in Section 6.2. J–M's model is summarized in Section 6.3 and an attempt is made in Section 6.4 to compare the usefulness of the two models as explanations of observed bank behaviour.

6.2 DISAGGREGATION OF THE CUSTOMER RELATIONSHIP

All borrowers were assumed to be identical in Chapters 2–5.[2] Let us relax this condition by making the less restrictive assumption that a particular bank is confronted by J homogeneous classes of borrowers whose demands for loans from that bank may be written as follows:

$$l_{jt} = a_j - b_j r_{jt} + c_j z_t + u_j y_t + \gamma_j \sum_{i=1}^{n_j} d_j^i l_{j,t-i} \quad (j = 1, ..., J; t = 1, ..., T) \quad (6.1)$$

These demands assume that the bank is in a position to practice price discrimination, i.e. that borrowers may be separated into distinct classes, with each class being charged a rate r_j that may be different from the rates paid by other classes.

The bank wishes to maximize the sum of discounted profits

$$\pi = \sum_{t=1}^{T} \beta^{t-1}(y_t g_t + \sum_{j=1}^{J} r_{jt} l_{jt}) \quad (6.2)$$

subject to (6.1) and the balance sheet constraint

$$\sum_{j=1}^{J} l_{jt} + g_t = 1. \quad (t = 1, ..., T) \quad (6.3)$$

where deposits are assumed to be fixed. The deposit relationship and interbank competition will be referred to in the following discussion, but for reasons of simplicity these concepts do not enter the formal analysis. It will be remembered from Chapters 3 and 4 that the deposit relationship accentuates the interest rate and portfolio effects of the loan relationship while the introduction of interbank competition may either accentuate or moderate those effects.

In the two-period case the marginal conditions may be written as follows:

$$r_{j1} + \frac{l_{j1}}{\frac{\partial l_{j1}}{\partial r_{j1}}} - \frac{\beta l_{j2}}{\frac{\partial l_{j2}}{\partial l_{j2}}} \frac{\partial l_{j2}}{\partial l_{j1}} = y_1 \quad (6.4)$$

$$(j = 1, ..., J)$$

$$r_{j2} + \frac{l_{j2}}{\dfrac{\partial l_{j2}}{\partial r_{j2}}} = y_2 \tag{6.5}$$

Equations (6.4) and (6.5) are, except for the index j, identical to the marginal conditions (2.6) and (2.7) obtained under the assumption of a single homogeneous class of borrowers. This reflects the fact that the loan and loan rate decisions of the bank are separable as between customers. Thus, we can solve for the bank's decision with respect to each of the J classes individually in precisely the way that we did when it was assumed that there was only one class of customers, this separability characteristic of the model depending crucially upon the assumptions of fixed marginal revenues from securities, rate discrimination between customers and no corner solutions. The bank extends loans to each class of customers up to the point at which the marginal revenue obtained from each class is equal to the rate of return on securities. This approach has much in common with Shull's [1963] treatment of the bank as a multi-product price discriminating firm, which in turn is based on Clemens. [1950]

The objective of the remainder of this section is to apply this model to an analysis of the determination of loan rates charged and loans granted to different classes of borrowers. Ideally for this purpose, we need time series of loans extended to borrowers classified, for example, by size or credit rating. This would enable us to estimate the parameters of some of the J demand equations given in (6.1). If, in addition, banks could be classified according to the kinds of customers with which they principally do business, we might be able to develop the implications of those parameter estimates for the portfolios of different classes of banks. Although such data do not exist in ideal form, time series on loans and loan rates by size of loan are available. If loan size and size of borrower are highly correlated and banks may be classified according to the average size of borrowers with which they do business, then data classified by size of loan may be useful in evaluating the importance of the customer relationship for borrowers of different size and their banks. In fact, there exists a substantial amount of evidence from survey data to support these assumptions.[3]

Time series on average short-term business loan rates by size of loan are available in the *Federal Reserve Bulletin* in the 'Quarterly Survey of Interest Rates on Business Loans'. Estimated monthly averages of these rates in cyclical peak and trough months are listed in the top-left portion of Table 6.1 along with the prime rate (r_6) and an average yield on securities (y). The differences $r_j - y$ ($j = 1, \ldots, 6$) are shown in the top-right portion of the table. The lower half of the table lists changes in r_j, y and $r_j - y$ between peaks and troughs; average changes in these data during expansions and contractions are denoted by ΔE and ΔC, respectively.[4] Note that, as with the average of all short-term business loan rates in Table 1.1, the difference between each of the loan rates and y shown in Table 6.1 is inversely related to economic activity. We see

Table 6.1. Average loan rates by size of loan (thousands of dollars)

Levels — small loans

	Month	r_1 (1–10)	r_2 (10–100)	r_3 (100–200)	r_4 (200+)	r_6 (Prime rate)	y	r_1-y	r_2-y	r_3-y	r_4-y	r_6-y
(P)	11–48	4·51	3·58	2·96	2·33	2·00	1·98	2·53	1·60	0·98	0·35	0·02
(T)	10–49	4·58	3·63	2·98	2·33	2·00	1·69	2·89	1·94	1·29	0·64	0·31
(P)	7–53	4·99	4·39	3·92	3·53	3·25	3·01	1·98	1·38	0·91	0·52	0·24
(T)	8–54	4·99	4·33	3·84	3·33	3·00	1·78	3·21	2·55	2·06	1·55	1·22
(P)	7–57	5·50	5·09	4·78	4·42	4·00	4·32	1·18	0·77	0·46	0·10	−0·32
(T)	4–58	5·51	5·01	4·60	4·15	3·83	2·60	2·91	2·41	2·00	1·55	1·23
(P)	5–60	6·00	5·76	5·52	5·22	5·00	4·68	1·32	1·08	0·84	0·54	0·32
(T)	2–61	5·89	5·54	5·20	4·81	4·50	3·74	2·15	1·80	1·46	1·07	0·76
(P)	11–66	6·77	6·69	6·51	6·19	6·00	6·04	0·73	0·65	0·47	0·15	−0·04

Levels — large loans

	Month	r_1 (1–10)	r_2 (10–100)	r_3 (100–500)	r_4 (500–1000)	r_5 (1000+)	r_6 (Prime rate)	y	r_1-y	r_2-y	r_3-y	r_4-y	r_5-y	r_6-y
(T)	5–67	6·69	6·53	6·15	5·85	5·71	5·50	5·06	1·63	1·47	1·09	0·79	0·65	0·44
(P)	11–69	9·14	9·25	8·99	8·80	8·64	8·50	8·70	0·44	0·55	0·29	0·10	−0·06	−0·20
(P)	11–70	8·91	8·74	8·22	7·93	7·60	7·28	6·62	2·29	2·12	1·60	1·31	0·98	0·66
(T)	4–73	8·10	7·92	7·52	7·14	7·01	6·61	7·12	0·98	0·80	0·40	0·02	−0·11	−0·51

Differences — small loans

	Month	Δr_1 (1–10)	Δr_2 (10–100)	Δr_3 (100–500)	Δr_4 (500–1000)	Δr_6	Δy	$\Delta(r_1-y)$	$\Delta(r_2-y)$	$\Delta(r_3-y)$	$\Delta(r_4-y)$	$\Delta(r_6-y)$
(T)	10–49	0·07	0·05	0·02	0·00	0·00	−0·29	0·36	0·34	0·31	0·29	0·29
(P)	7–53	0·41	0·76	0·94	1·20	1·25	1·32	−0·91	−0·56	−0·38	−0·12	−0·07
(T)	8–54	0·00	−0·06	−0·08	−0·20	−0·25	−1·23	1·23	1·17	1·15	1·03	0·98
(P)	7–57	0·51	0·76	0·94	1·09	1·00	2·54	−2·03	−1·78	−1·60	−1·45	−1·54
(T)	4–58	0·01	−0·08	−0·18	−0·27	−0·17	−1·72	1·73	1·64	1·54	1·45	1·55
(T)	5–60	0·49	0·75	0·92	1·07	1·17	2·08	−1·59	−1·33	−1·16	−1·01	−0·91
(P)	2–61	−0·11	−0·22	−0·32	−0·41	−0·50	−0·94	0·83	0·72	0·62	0·53	0·44
(P)	11–66	0·88	1·15	1·31	1·38	1·50	2·30	−1·42	−1·15	−0·99	−0·92	−0·80

Differences — large loans

	Month	Δr_1	Δr_2	Δr_3	Δr_4	Δr_5	Δr_6	Δy	$\Delta(r_1-y)$	$\Delta(r_2-y)$	$\Delta(r_3-y)$	$\Delta(r_4-y)$	$\Delta(r_5-y)$	$\Delta(r_6-y)$
(P)	11–69	2·45	2·72	2·84	2·95	2·93	3·00	3·64	−1·19	−0·92	−0·80	−0·69	−0·71	−0·64
(P)	11–70	−0·23	−0·51	−0·77	−0·87	−1·04	−1·22	−2·08	1·85	1·57	1·31	1·21	1·04	0·86
(T)	4–73	−0·81	−0·82	−0·70	−0·79	−0·59	−0·67	0·50	−1·31	−1·32	−1·20	−1·29	−1·09	−1·17
ΔE		0·95	1·23	1·39	1·54		1·58	2·38	−1·43	−1·15	−0·99	−0·79	−0·84	−0·79
ΔC		−0·06	−0·16	−0·27	−0·37		−0·43	−1·25	1·20	1·09	0·99		0·88	0·82

See Appendix B for sources and descriptions of data.

Table 6.2. Loans and investments of commercial banks by Federal Reserve class (billions of dollars)

Month	Non-member			Country			Other reserve cities			Chicago			New York City		
	L	G	L/(L+G)	L	G	L/(L+G)	L	G	L/(L+G)	L	G	L/(L+G)	L	G	L/(L+G)
(P) 11–48	6·4	12·3	0·342	11·9	25·0	0·322	14·2	21·1	0·402	1·8	2·9	0·383	7·8	10·9	0·417
(T) 10–49	6·6	12·1	0·353	12·3	25·5	0·325	13·8	23·9	0·366	1·5	3·7	0·288	7·4	12·1	0·379
(P) 7–53	9·5	12·9	0·424	19·1	26·8	0·416	22·2	23·1	0·490	2·6	3·2	0·448	11·9	9·2	0·564
(T) 8–54	10·1	13·3	0·432	20·5	27·6	0·426	22·3	25·7	0·465	2·5	3·6	0·410	11·5	11·4	0·502
(P) 7–57	12·7	14·0	0·476	27·7	27·6	0·501	32·1	21·6	0·598	3·9	2·4	0·619	16·4	7·0	0·701
(T) 4–58	13·0	14·8	0·468	28·3	28·9	0·495	32·0	24·4	0·567	3·5	3·0	0·538	16·4	9·1	0·643
(P) 5–60	16·7	15·6	0·517	35·6	29·6	0·546	39·1	20·5	0·656	4·2	2·3	0·646	17·9	7·3	0·710
(T) 2–61	17·3	16·2	0·516	36·5	31·2	0·539	39·5	23·2	0·630	4·4	2·6	0·629	17·8	9·5	0·652
(P) 11–66	34·3	23·3	0·595	67·2	40·3	0·625	68·6	25·5	0·729	8·2	3·1	0·726	34·5	10·0	0·775
(T) 5–67	36·2	24·4	0·598	70·4	41·7	0·628	68·9	29·5	0·700	8·5	3·6	0·702	35·7	11·1	0·763
(P) 11–69	50·4	30·7	0·621	88·4	48·7	0·645	85·9	30·5	0·738	10·1	3·6	0·737	45·1	11·7	0·794
(T) 11–70	56·2	34·3	0·621	94·2	52·3	0·643	89·8	35·2	0·718	10·6	4·1	0·721	44·9	13·6	0·768
(P) 4–73	85·6	47·3	0·644	128·4	69·3	0·649	129·0	42·6	0·752	17·8	4·6	0·795	61·7	13·6	0·819

Δ[L/(L+G)]

Month	Non-member	Country	Other reserve cities	Chicago	New York City
(T) 10–49	0·011	0·003	−0·036	−0·095	−0·038
(P) 7–53	0·071	0·091	0·124	0·160	0·185
(T) 8–54	−0·008	−0·010	−0·025	−0·038	−0·062
(P) 7–57	0·044	0·075	0·133	0·209	0·199
(T) 4–58	−0·008	−0·006	−0·031	−0·081	−0·058
(P) 5–60	0·049	0·051	0·089	0·108	0·067
(T) 2–61	−0·001	−0·007	−0·026	−0·017	−0·058
(P) 10–66	0·079	0·086	0·099	0·097	0·123
(T) 3–67	0·003	0·003	−0·029	−0·024	−0·012
(P) 11–69	0·023	0·017	0·038	0·035	0·031
(T) 11–70	0·000	−0·002	−0·020	−0·016	−0·026
(P) 4–73	0·023	0·006	0·034	0·074	0·051
ΔE	−0·053	0·064	0·097	0·122	0·121
ΔC	−0·002	0·000	−0·028	−0·045	−0·042

Average end-of-year bank assets
(millions of dollars)

	1947	1960	1970
New York City	756	2651	7663
Chicago	490	922	2222
Other reserve Cities	141	385	1080
Country	7	14	33
Non-member	3	6	14

See **Appendix B** for sources and descriptions of data.

further that, because rates on large loans are cyclically more volatile than those on small loans, the differences between rates on large loans and y are cyclically less volatile than the differences between rates on small loans and y.

It is possible to achieve a reasonably good understanding of the cyclical behaviour of banks of various sizes from the monthly series on 'Principal Assets and Liabilities and Number, by Class of Bank' published in the *Federal Reserve Bulletin*. As indicated in the lower-right portion of Table 6.2, there are marked differences in the average sizes of commercial banks in different Federal Reserve classes. The top half of that table lists loans (L), securities (G) and $[L/(L + G)] = l$ by class of bank at cyclical peaks and troughs. Changes in these l during expansions and contractions are given in the lower-left of the table; ΔE and ΔC denote average changes in l during expansions and contractions. As in the case of all commercial banks shown in Table 1.1, l has tended to increase during expansions and to decline during contractions for each Federal Reserve Class.[5] But the volatility of l has been much greater for large than for small banks.[6]

Further evidence of these differences between movements in rates on large and small loans and in the portfolios of large and small banks is presented in Chart 6.1. This chart shows quarterly averages of the average rate on small short-term business loans, adjusted for risk ($\bar{r}_s$), the average rate on large short-term business loans, assumed to be risk-free (r_L), differentials between these loan rates and the Treasury bill rate, ($\bar{r}_s - \bar{y}$) and ($r_L - \bar{y}$), and loans as proportions of the earning assets of Non-member and New York City banks, (l_s) and (l_L). The chart shows l_L to be more volatile than l_s, r_L to be more volatile than r_s and, therefore, $r_L - \bar{y}$ to be less volatile than $\bar{r}_s - \bar{y}$. Sources and descriptions of these data are contained in Appendix B.

Given the survey evidence cited above, which indicates that both loan size and size of bank tend to be strongly positively correlated with the size of borrower, the data in Tables 6.1 and 6.2 and Chart 6.1 suggest that loans and loan rates are cyclically more volatile and $r - y$ is less volatile for large than for small borrowers. I now wish to determine whether our theory of the customer relationship is consistent with these empirical regularities under the following assumptions: The loan demands of large borrowers are more responsive than those of small borrowers to loan rates and other rates; and loans demanded from and deposits supplied to a specific bank in future periods are more responsive to current loans extended for large than for small borrowers. These assumptions are, I think, realistic, at least when contrasting the behaviour of very large and very small borrowers. National firms, which borrow from and maintain deposits in banks in several cities, are likely to be quite responsive in their dealings with a particular bank to the rate charged by that bank relative to money market rates and rates charged by other banks. The failure of Chase Manhattan to lend to General Motors at a rate competitive with other banks is likely to induce General Motors to transfer its loan and deposit accounts to banks from which it can borrow at favourable rates. The profitability of large accounts and the ability of large firms to obtain funds from a variety of sources

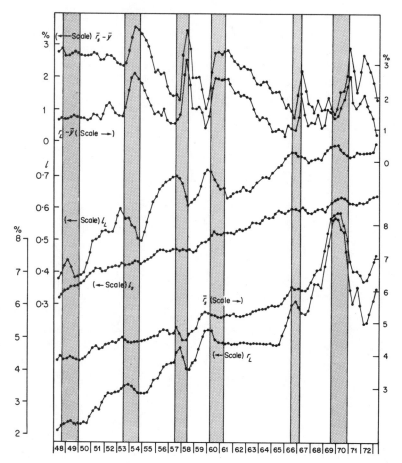

Chart 6.1. The behaviour of large and small banks, II/1948–I/1973

force banks into vigorous competition for the business of those firms and leads to a substantial uniformity of rates charged to large customers, even by banks in widely separated locations.

On the other hand, if the Citizens' Bank of Podunk either refuses accommodation or offers to lend to Joe's Bakery only at a high rate, the effect on either Joe's current demand for loans or his future dealings with that bank may be affected only slightly because Joe's alternative sources of credit are limited. These are examples of the tendencies of demand and supply elasticities to be positively related to the availability of convenient alternative supplies and demands.

Now let us derive the implications of our model for cyclical movements in loan rates charged and loans extended by large banks relative to small banks. Consider two banks and two classes of borrowers. Specifically, a homogeneous group of large firms borrows from the large bank, both bank and firms denoted by $j = 1$, while a homogeneous group of small firms borrows from the small bank, both denoted by $j = 2$. Then the influence of a change in the level of economic activity on loans of the jth bank as a proportion of its earning assets and on the difference between the loan rate charged by the jth bank and the yield on securities may be written as follows:

$$L_j = \frac{\partial l_{j1}}{\partial z_1} = \frac{(c + u_j f - b_j f)}{2} L_{jT} = \Lambda_j L_{jT} \tag{6.6}$$

$$(j = 1, 2)$$

$$R_j = \frac{\partial r_{j1}}{\partial z_1} - \frac{\partial y_1}{\partial z_1} = \frac{(c + u_j f - b_j f)}{2b_j} R_{jT} = \rho_j R_{jT} \tag{6.7}$$

where $(c + u_j f - b_j f)/2 = \Lambda_j = b_j \rho_j$. The principal difference between the two classes of borrowers is that the large firms have access to a greater variety of sources of finance. Consequently, the responsiveness of the loan demands of large firms to both interest rates and past loan accommodation is greater than that of small firms; i.e. $b_1 > b_2$, $u_1 > u_2$.[7] It is assumed that variations in economic activity have identical impacts on the loan demands of large and small firms relative to the sizes of their banks: i.e. c is independent of j. L_{jT} and R_{jT} are defined for a single class of borrowers (so that j is suppressed) in (2.28) and (2.29) and examples for $T = 2,3$ are given in (2.19), (2.21), (2.25), (2.26). Under the assumption that the loan demands of large firms are more responsive than those of small firms to past loan accommodation and the additional assumptions that the discount factors (β) and expectations (w) of large and small firms are identical,[8] $L_{1T} > L_{2T}$ and $R_{1T} < R_{2T}$.

Consider a specific case in which $b_1/b_2 = u_1/u_2 > 1$. We continue to assume values of c, b_j and u_j such that Λ_j, $\rho_j > 0$ and also assume that own-partial derivatives exceed cross-partials; i.e. $(b_j - u_j) > 0$ ($j = 1, 2$). Given these assumptions and in the absence of the customer relationship ($L_{jT} = R_{jT} = 1$; $j = 1, 2$), we have

$$R_2 = \rho_2 > \rho_1 = R_1 > 0 \tag{6.8}$$

$$L_2 = \Lambda_2 > \Lambda_1 = L_1 > 0 \tag{6.9}$$

Expression (6.8) indicates that both r_1 and r_2 will rise more than y during economic expansions. However, because of the greater responsiveness of the loan demands of large firms to interest rates, including the differential between rates on loans and securities, r_1 rises less relative to y than does r_2. Associated with this result is the smaller increase in l_1 than in l_2, which is shown in (6.9). Thus, in the absence of the customer relationship, our model is inconsistent with the data in Tables 6.1 and 6.2 and Chart 6.1, which show that $L_1 > L_2$ and $R_2 < R_1 < 0$.

It will now be shown that the inequalities in (6.8) and (6.9) may be reversed when the customer relationship is introduced in conjunction with the assumption that the customer relationship is more important for large firms than for small firms; i.e. $L_{1T} > L_{2T}$, $R_{1T} < R_{2T}$. In terms of (6.6) and (6.7) and our assumptions regarding the relative values of L_{jT}, R_{jT}, b_j and u_j, the data imply the following:

$$L_1 = \Lambda_1 L_{1T} > \Lambda_2 L_{2T} = L_2 ; \frac{L_{1T}}{L_{2T}} > \frac{\Lambda_2}{\Lambda_1} > 1 \qquad (6.10)$$

$$R_2 = \rho_2 R_{2T} < \rho_1 R_{1T} = R_1 < 0 ; \frac{\rho_2}{\rho_1} > \frac{R_{1T}}{R_{2T}} > 1 \qquad (6.11)$$

where R_{1T}, $R_{2T} < 0$. That is, within the framework of our model, the cyclical behaviour of commercial bank portfolios suggests that the customer relationship is sufficiently strong even for small banks to restrain increases in loan rates relative to security yields during economic expansions. While both r_1 and r_2 rise less than y, r_1 rises more than r_2 because of the greater responsiveness of loan demands of large firms to variations in y. However, this upward influence on r_1 relative to r_2 is moderated by the greater efforts of banks to increase loans to large firms in order to create or strengthen customer relationships. As shown in (6.10) and (6.11), our model is consistent with the data if the customer relationship is sufficiently greater for large than for small firms so as to induce greater increases in loans to large firms during cyclical upswings yet not large enough to reverse the forces that cause r_1 to rise relative to r_2.[9]

Although there is a wide range of plausible values of the parameters of our model that are consistent with the data—i.e. satisfy (6.10) and (6.11)—this does not constitute 'proof' of the validity of our theory. For there are other theories which, it is claimed, are also consistent with variations in commercial bank portfolios. One of these is the theory of credit rationing as it has been extended by Jaffee and Modigliani, who have built upon the work of Freimer and Gordon and others. This theory is summarized and its empirical implications are developed and compared with the data in Section 6.3.

6.3   CREDIT RATIONING

6.3.1   Freimer and Gordon

Perhaps the best known demonstration of the rationality of credit rationing within a profit maximizing framework is that of Freimer and Gordon [1965]. They considered a bank presented with loan requests by firms desiring finance for investment projects. The proceeds from the ith borrower's project, equal to the end-of-period value of the firm, is a continuous random variable x with density function $f_i(x)$. Assume for simplicity that the size of the project is fixed so that $f_i(x)$ is independent of the size of loan.[10] The firm has alternative, though more costly, sources of finance with which it complements bank credit. The borrower contracts to pay the bank an amount $R_i L_i$, where L_i is the size of the loan, r_i is the rate of interest on the loan and $R_i = 1 + r_i$. The actual payment to the bank, which is limited to the proceeds from the investment, is

$$Z = \text{minimum} \left[x, R_i L_i \right] \qquad (6.12)$$

with density function $f_i(x)$. Sure minimum outcomes, k_i, and maximum possible outcomes, K_i, for projects are assumed so that

$$f_i(x) = 0 \text{ for } x < k_i \text{ and } x > K_i. \tag{6.13}$$

The bank's expected profit, P_i, from a loan is the excess of the expected payment by the firm over the opportunity cost of making the loan, IL_i, where $I = 1 + j$ and j is the certain rate of return on alternative bank investments, say Treasury bills.

$$P_i = P_i(R_iL_i) = \bar{Z} - IL_i = R_iL_i \int_{R_iL_i}^{K_i} f_i(x)dx + \int_{k_i}^{R_iL_i} x f_i(x)dx - IL_i \tag{6.14}$$

The first term in (6.14) is the contracted repayment weighted by the probability that the proceeds from the investment will be sufficient to repay the loan in full. The second term is the expected repayment if the proceeds from the investment fall short of the contracted repayment, in which case the bank receives the entire outcome x. The last term is the bank's opportunity cost, where I is independent of L_i.

Now let us derive the bank's loan-offer curve to the ith customer, which is the locus of loan sizes that maximize the bank's expected profit from that customer for given loan rates. Maximizing (6.14) with respect to L_i for given R_i yields the following first-order condition:[11]

$$1 - \int_{R_iL_i}^{K_i} f_i(x)dx = \int_{k_i}^{R_iL_i} f_i(x)dx = F_i(R_iL_i) = \frac{R_i - I}{R_i} = \frac{r_i - j}{1 + r_i} \tag{6.15}$$

where $F_i(A)$ is the probability that $x < A$. The bank maximizes expected profit by granting a loan of a size such that the probability of default, $F_i(R_iL_i)$, is equal to the excess of the loan rate over the opportunity cost discounted by $1 + r_i$.

Solving (6.15) for L_i gives the offer curve in terms of R_i, defined as $\hat{L}_i = \hat{L}_i(R_i)$. F–G consider a uniform distribution on the interval k_i to K_i, for which the offer curve is

$$\hat{L}_i = \frac{k_i}{R_i} + \frac{(K_i - k_i)(R_i - I)}{R_i^2} \quad \text{for } R_i \geq I \tag{6.16}$$

Jaffee and Modigliani show that the offer curve has the following properties, which are illustrated in Figure 6.1 and may be checked using (6.16) for the special case of a uniform distribution: (i) $\hat{L}_i = 0$ when $r_i < j$; i.e. the bank extends no loan to the ith customer when r_i is less than the certain rate of return on Treasury bills. (ii) If $r_i = j$, then $0 < \hat{L}_i < k_i/I$; i.e. the bank is indifferent between a loan to the ith customer and investments in Treasury bills when $r_i = j$ as long as the loan and interest are certain to be repaid. This is the meaning of the vertical (perfectly elastic) portion of the offer curve lying below k_i/I in Figure 6.1. (iii) The bank will not extend a loan beyond an amount such that the contracted repayment exceeds the maximum possible proceeds of the

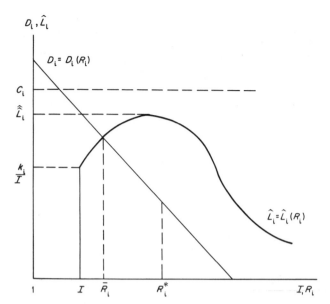

Figure 6.1. Loan demand and loan offer curves

borrower's investment; i.e. $(1 + r_i)\hat{L}_i \leq K_i$. (iv) The limit of $\hat{L}_i$ as $r_i \rightarrow \infty$ is zero; this follows from (iii) and implies that as r_i increases beyond some point the optimal loan does not increase and eventually declines. (v) It also follows from the second-order condition for a maximum that for given R_i 'expected profits decrease monotonically as the loan size varies from the optimal size $[\hat{L}_i(R_i)]$ in either direction'. [J–M, p. 854] That is, it pays the bank to grant a loan as close in size to the offer curve as possible.

The above analysis was based on the assumption that the 'banker sets an interest rate… and extends whatever credit a borrower wants at this rate up to a limit determined by the borrower's financial circumstances', the limit being the $\hat{L}_i$ that corresponds to the rate that has been set. [F–G, p. 397] Depending upon the cost of the project, the probability distribution of outcomes from the project and the rate of return on alternative bank investments, it is quite possible that the customer will be unable to borrow the full cost of his project regardless of the interest rate he is willing to pay.[12] This is what F–G mean by 'weak credit rationing'. [pp. 398, 402][13]

6.3.2 Jaffee and Modigliani: Theory

Differing from F–G, J–M define credit rationing as an excess demand for loans at the ruling loan rate. A complete theory of credit rationing so defined requires an explicit statement of the demand for loans by the ith customer, which J–M specify as negatively related to the loan rate. Such a loan demand curve, $D_i = D_i(R_i)$, is depicted in Figure 6.1. If the bank charges an interest factor less than $\bar{R}_i = (1 + \bar{r}_i)$, rationing will occur since 'the bank's optimum loan offer is less than the amount demanded by the customer.' [p. 855][14] The introduction of a demand curve for loans also enables us to determine the optimum loan rate as well as the optimum loan size. The existence of a finite optimum loan rate depends upon the presence of a downward sloping demand curve because 'expected profits increase along the offer curve for successively higher interest rate factors'.[15] This implies 'that the bank will obtain maximum potential profits when allowed to charge an infinite interest rate. Of course, this only serves to emphasize that the offer curve is defined independently of the demand for loans and thus many points on the offer locus may not prove feasible for the lender'. [J–M, p. 854] J–M go on to discuss the conditions under which credit rationing may exist given loan demand and loan offer curves such as those shown in Figure 6.1. They demonstrate that credit rationing will not occur when the bank is a discriminating monopolist but that rationing may occur under either equilibrium or disequilibrium conditions when the bank is constrained to charge different classes of borrowers the same rate of interest.

The bank as a discriminating monopolist. It will now be shown that credit rationing is not profitable when the bank is free to charge a different rate to each customer. The interest factor R_i^* that maximizes profit from the ith customer will not be less than $\bar{R}_i$ because all points on the offer curve to the left of $\bar{R}_i$ are feasible (lie below the demand curve) and expected profits increase along the offer curve for successively higher R_i. Furthermore, since for given R_i the bank finds it profitable to grant a loan as close in size to the offer curve, $\hat{L}_i$, as possible, and since the demand curve places a ceiling on the feasible loan size when $R_i > \bar{R}_i$, the bank will maximize profit by charging a rate $R_i^* \geq \bar{R}_i$ and lending the amount demanded at that rate, $D_i(R_i^*)$.

The bank must charge all customers a uniform rate of interest. Consider the case in which the bank faces only two customers, where initially we rule out credit rationing by requiring the bank to satisfy the loan demands of both customers at the chosen uniform rate. The bank's expected profit is

$$P = P_1(RD_1) + P_2(RD_2) \qquad (6.17)$$

where D_i is the size of loan demanded by the ith customer when $R = R_i$ ($i = 1, 2$).

Maximizing (6.17) with respect to R gives the optimal common interest factor, R^*. It will now be shown that R^* lies between the optimal interest rate factors that would be charged by a discriminating monopolist, R_1^* and R_2^*. For a discriminating monopolist, expected profit from each customer is a concave function of R in the neighbourhood of R_1^* and R_2^*, respectively, as shown in Figure 6.2. Letting $R_1^* < R_2^*$, if the bank chooses a uniform rate less than R_1^*, say R', it would find that expected profits from both customers would be increased by charging a higher rate. If the uniform rate is $R'' > R_2^*$, profits from both customers would be increased by charging a lower rate. Thus, the uniform rate that mazimises profits lies between R_1^* and R_2^*. The optimum uniform

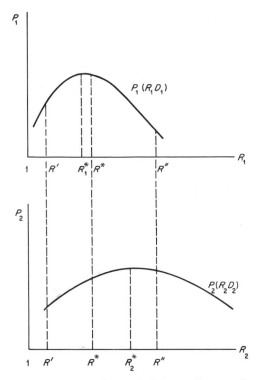

Figure 6.2. Profit maximizing uniform and discriminatory rates with no credit rationing

rate is that rate lying between R_1^* and R_2^* such that $\partial P_1/\partial R_1 = -\partial P_2/\partial R_2$: A reduction in R^* below this point induces a decline in P_2 in excess of the increase in P_1, while a higher R^* leads to a reduction in P_1 greater than the rise in P_2.

Now admit the possibility of credit rationing by dropping the requirement that the loan demands of both customers must be satisfied at the common rate. Remember that credit rationing will not occur under rate discrimination, for which $R_i^* \geq \bar{R}_i$. When a uniform rate is charged such that $R_2^* > R^* > R_1^*$, customer 1 will not be rationed because $R^* > R_1^* \geq \bar{R}_1$ and the bank maximizes profit by granting loans so as to get as close to the offer curve as possible, which means operating on customer 1's demand curve. For customer 2, on the other hand, $R_2^* > R^* \gtreqless \bar{R}_2$. That is, we may have $R^* < \bar{R}_2$, which implies that customer 2 may be rationed.

If credit rationing is in fact profitable, the optimum uniform rate may differ from R^*, which is the optimum rate in the absence of credit rationing. But J–M show that the above propositions remain valid when R^* is replaced by the more general optimum, $\hat{R}$; i.e. $R^* \leq \bar{R}_2$ implies $\hat{R} \leq \bar{R}_2$.

Equilibrium credit rationing. J–M generalize their analysis by considering n customers which the bank assigns to m classes, where within each class the bank must charge a uniform rate. They argue that 'usury ceilings, the pressure of legal restrictions and considerations of good will and social mores', as well as tacit rate fixing agreements among banks, tend to keep the number of rate classes small and to 'make it inadvisable if not impossible for the banker to charge widely different rates to different customers'. After thus justifying the use of their uniform loan rate model, J–M 'conclude that equilibrium rationing is consistent with rational economic behaviour', where '*equilibrium rationing* is defined as credit rationing which occurs when the loan rate is set at its long-run equilibrium level', $\hat{R}$. [pp. 851, 861]

J–M consider the comparative static properties of equilibrium rationing, in particular the impact of a change in I. Assume a bank with two groups of customers to whom it is constrained to charge a common rate: risk free customers, who will not be rationed as long as $R > I$, and risky customers, who may be rationed.[16] A rise in I from I' to I'' causes the offer curve of loans to the

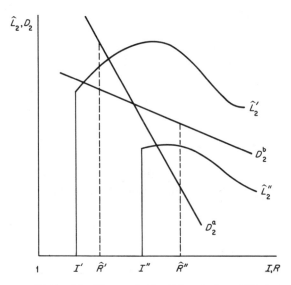

Figure 6.3. Changes in I and changes in equilibrium rationing

risky customers to shift downward and to the right from $\hat{L}'_2$ to $\hat{L}''_2$ as shown in Figure 6.3. The increase in I also induces an increase in the optimal common rate factor from $\hat{R}'$ to $\hat{R}''$. The rise in I is consistent with an increase, a decrease or no change in rationing, depending upon the demand curve of the risky customers. If that demand curve is D^a_2, those customers move from a rationed to a non-rationed status as I increases from I' to I''; the opposite is true if the demand curve is D^b_2. It is equally possible to draw demand curves such that rationing status is unchanged. Therefore, '*no systematic relationship exists between the extent of equilibrium rationing and the absolute level of interest rates*'. [p. 862; J–M's emphasis]

Downward sloping demand curves imply declines in loans to both risky and risk free customers as $\hat{R}$ increases if those demands do not shift upward. If the rise in I induces increased loan demands, loans to each type of customer may rise, fall or remain unchanged. In neither case is there an unambiguous relationship between variations in I and the allocation of loans between risky and risk free customers.

Now suppose equilibrium is disturbed by increases in the loan demands of both risky and riskless customers. This induces a rise in the common loan rate and may lead to either an increase or a decrease in rationing. Let the offer curve of loans to risky customers be $\hat{L}'_2$ in Figure 6.3. An upward shift in loan demand from D^b_2 and the associated increase in $\hat{R}$ may lead either to rationing or to a continued absence of rationing. If the demand curve is D^a_2, an increase in demand accompanied by a rise in $\hat{R}$ may lead either to a non-rationing status or to the continued existence of rationing depending upon the magnitude of the shift in demand relative to the increase in $\hat{R}$ and the shape of the offer curve. The change in the volume of loans depends upon the same factors.

It is reasonable to suppose that periods of economic expansion are associated with increases in both I and loan demands, while opposite movements occur during recessions. However, since J–M's model is consistent with either increases or decreases in equilibrium rationing and either increases or decreases in risky relative to risk free loans in response to variations in each of the factors influencing the supply and demand for loans, that model has no unambiguous implications for cyclical movements in either commercial bank portfolios or credit rationing in the absence of knowledge of the parameters of the loan demand and loan offer curves. J–M choose not to estimate or make assumptions about those parameters but instead devote the remainder of their analysis to the impact of changes in market forces on rationing in disequilibrium situations.

Dynamic credit rationing. J–M 'define dynamic rationing as the difference between equilibrium rationing and the volume of rationing that arises when the actual rate charged customers, R, differs from the long-run equilibrium rate, $\hat{R}$'. Dynamic rationing may be positive or negative and J–M are concerned to 'show that its magnitude will be positively associated with the spread, $\hat{R} - R$', where because of 'the oligopolistic structure of the banking industry', R adjusts slowly to changes in $\hat{R}$. [J–M, pp. 862–63] They consider disturbances to equilibrium such that the equilibrium rate changes from $\hat{R}'$ to $\hat{R}''$ while the quoted rate remains unchanged at $\hat{R}'$.

Suppose, for example, that an equilibrium position is disturbed by a rise in I from I' to I'', which shifts the offer curve of loans to risky customers from $\hat{L}'_2$ to $\hat{L}''_2$ as shown in Figure 6.4. Since, by assumption, the quoted rate remains at $\hat{R}'$ and all demand curves are unchanged, '*there must be an aggregate increase in rationing*'. [p. 863; J–M's emphasis] If the loan demand of risky customers is D^b_2, rationing will increase from CE and AE and loans to those customers

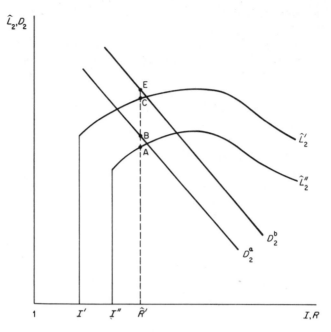

Figure 6.4. Dynamic credit rationing

will fall by AC. If the demand curve is D_2^a, rationing will increase from zero to AB and risky loans will fall by AB. On the other hand, if the demand curve had been substantially below D_2^a, neither rationing nor risky loans would be affected by the rise in I. In the aggregate, if any borrowers had been rationed or near the point of being rationed prior to the disturbance, an increase in I will cause an increase in rationing and a decrease in risky loans, both absolutely and relative to riskless loans, which have not been affected.

These results are modified somewhat when account is taken of the upward influence of I on loan demands. Those customers who were rationed previously will now be rationed even more severely as loan demand increases in conjunction with the downward shift in the offer curve; and the decline in loans to these customers will be the same as if D were independent of I. The increase in D increases the chances that customers who were not rationed previously will now be rationed but loans to these customers may increase. Furthermore, loans will increase to those risky customers not rationed either before or after the increase in I. Thus, while rationing is again likely to increase we do not know whether total loans to risky customers will rise or fall. However, if loan demands of riskless customers are more responsive to I than are the demands of risky customers, riskless loans will rise relative to risky loans.

Now suppose equilibrium is disturbed by increases in all loan demands, the shift in demand by risky customers being from D_2^a to D_2^b in Figure 6.4. If the offer curve and the quoted rate are $\hat{L}_2'$ and $\hat{R}'$, respectively, rationing will increase from zero to CE and risky loans will rise by BC. If the offer curve is $\hat{L}_2''$, rationing will increase from AB to AE and risky loans will be unchanged at A. Those customers who were rationed previously will suffer an increase in rationing and will experience no increase in loans. But loans will increase to those risky customers not rationed prior to the upward shift in loan demands. Overall, both rationing and risky loans are likely to increase. But, because loans to riskless customers have also increased, risky loans may either rise or fall relative to riskless loans.

Briefly considering a final type of disturbance, if loan demands and market rates of interest are unchanged but the system is shocked by an upward revision in the outcomes expected by banks from risky projects, the offer curve of loans to risky customers will shift upwards. As a result, rationing will decrease and loans to risky customers will increase, while riskless loans will be unchanged.

Unlike equilibrium rationing, the responses of dynamic rationing to changes in market forces, taken one at a time, are unambiguous. It is not clear, however, whether rationing becomes more or less severe during periods of either economic expansion or recession, when these market forces tend to move together. For example, (a) rising loan demand tends to be associated with (b) a rise in I and (c) 'an increase in the anticipated profitability of the investment projects, the latter producing a decrease in risk as measured by $F(x)$'. [J–M, p. 864] Suppose equilibrium is disturbed by simultaneous increases in loan demand and I and a decrease in $F(x)$. The effects of (a) and (b) will be to increase rationing while (c) acts to reduce rationing. The net effect on rationing is ambiguous, as are the net effects on the volume of risky loans and risky loans as a proportion of total loans.

6.3.3 Jaffee and Modigliani: A Measure and Test of Credit Rationing

Some of this ambiguity may be eliminated if we are willing, as are J–M, to make assumptions regarding the relative magnitudes of shifts in loan demand and offer curves. J–M 'anticipate an increase in rationing because the demand curve is likely to shift further than the offer curve, reflecting an increase in the optimism of firms relative to that of banks. ... We should then expect that as the gap between $\hat{R}$ and R widens and dynamic rationing becomes more severe, loans to the riskless customers will tend to represent a growing share of the total loan portfolio'. Given these assumptions, because of the lack of data enabling them to measure the volume of credit rationing directly, J–M adopt an 'operational proxy', H, which 'is simply the percentage of total loans which are granted to risk free customers, and hence is positively related to the degree of rationing'. [J–M, pp. 864–65]

$$H = \frac{L_1}{L_1 + L_2} \tag{6.18}$$

where L_1 and L_2 are loans granted to risk free prime customers and rationed customers, respectively.

It should be noted that the assumption that 'the optimism of firms relative to that of banks' increases during economic expansions must apply only to risky firms. Otherwise, those firms that were formerly risk free would become risky and subject to rationing. But this means that increases in the loan demands of risky customers exceed those of risk-free borrowers. As a consequence, if many risky firms were well below the rationing point prior to the expansion, it is quite conceivable that an increase in rationing may be associated with a fall in H. Thus, a stronger assumption is needed if H is to be positively associated with rationing; viz. that loan demands of small (risky) firms shift further than their offer curves or the demands of large (risk-free) firms without substantially exceeding the shift in the demands of large firms, which nevertheless remain free of risk.

In the absence of information about which loans are risk free and which are risky, J–M approximate H by the percentage of loans granted at the prime rate or which were large in size. Specifically, they use the first principal component of the four series listed in Table 6.3. The table shows that H rises during

Table 6.3.   Jaffee and Modigliani's credit rationing proxy at cyclical peaks and troughs

	Quarter	H
(P)	III–53	− 1·14
(T)	III–54	− 1·48
(P)	III–57	1·09
(T)	II–58	− 0·96
(P)	II–60	− 0·01
(T)	I–61	− 0·07
(P)	IV–66	1·87
(T)	II–67	0·39
(P)	IV–69	2·23

H is the principal component of the following four series with the computed factor loadings of each series shown in parentheses:
1. Proportion of total loans granted at the prime rate (0·980).
2. Proportion of total loans over $200,000 in size (0·969).
3. Proportion of loans over $200,000 granted at the prime rate (0·921).
4. Proportion of total loans $1,000 to $10,000 in size (− 0·959).

Source data: Jaffee [1971, pp. 87, 100–103].

expansions and falls during contractions.[17] This is what one would expect on the basis of Table 6.2, since H is a measure of large loans as a proportion of total loans.

If we accept J–M's explicit and implicit assumptions underlying a positive relationship between H and the incidence of credit rationing and further assume that variations in I and loan demands dominate the effects of changes in risk on the equilibrium loan rate, r^*, then H (rationing) will be positively related to the spread between r^* and the sticky rate actually prevailing, r:

$$H = a_0 + a_1(r^* - r) + \varepsilon. \tag{6.19}$$

J–M hypothesise that r^* is a function of the Treasury bill rate, j, and various measures of the liquidity yields or costs of Treasury bills and loans. They do not include explanatory variables intended to account for fluctuations in either loan demands or loan offer curves. Substituting their explanatory equation for r^* into (6.19) and regressing H on the result using quarterly observations for the period 1952–65, they obtain a good fit and, as expected, significantly negative and positive coefficients of r and j, respectively. J–M interpret these results as confirming the implications of their model. In particular, the positive coefficient of j indicates that j tends 'to increase rationing given the commercial loan rate'. Furthermore, the negative coefficient of r 'supports one of the most distinctive implications of our model, to wit, that a rise in the commercial loan rate given the optimal level of this rate as measured by the remaining variables in the equation, tends to reduce rationing as it reduces the demand and increases the supply'. [p. 870]

6.4 SUMMARY AND COMPARISONS

The theory of bank behaviour set forth in Chapters 2–5 and 6.2 was motivated by a desire to explain why banks move out of securities into loans at the same time that loan rates are increasing substantially less than security yields. That theory is consistent not only with the observed behaviour of banks in the aggregate but also with differences in behaviour between large and small banks if (i) future loan demands and deposit supplies of both large and small borrowers are responsive to current loan accommodation but the responsiveness of large borrowers is greater than that of small borrowers, (ii) loan demands of large borrowers are more sensitive than those of small borrowers to variations in both loan rates and money market rates, (iii) the sizes of loans, borrowers and banks are positively correlated, (iv) cyclical shifts in the loan demands of small borrowers are not substantially greater than those of large borrowers and (v) loan rates adjust rapidly to changes in market conditions.

J–M's theory of dynamic rationing, on the other hand, was shown to be consistent with the data if (i) large borrowers are less risky than small borrowers, (ii) interest rate elasticities of demand are greater for large than for small borrowers (see footnote 16), (iii) fluctuations in the loan demands of risky customers must exceed those in the offer curve of loans to those customers without substantially exceeding fluctuations in the loan demands of large customers who, nevertheless, remain risk free in the eyes of bankers and (iv) because of the oligopolistic structure of banking markets and other restrictions imposed by legal rate ceilings and 'considerations of good will and social mores', loan rates do not vary substantially either over time or among different classes of customers.

Given that sizes of loans, borrowers and banks are positively related, a choice between the two theories depends upon (i) the nature of the loan demands of large and small borrowers, (ii) the speed of response of loan rates to changes in market conditions and the variability of those rates among different kinds of customers and (iii) the size and cyclical variability of default risk on small loans. With respect to (i), what we need in order to choose between these theories are estimates of loan demands classified by size of borrower. Jaffee estimated loan demands by asset size of firms using quarterly balance sheet data from the Federal Trade Commission—Securities and Exchange Commission 'Quarterly Financial Report for Manufacturing Corporations' for the period III/1952 to IV/1969. Among other results, he found that the size and significance of interest rate coefficients increase with the size of firms but that the coefficient of his credit rationing proxy had the wrong sign and was not statistically significant. [pp. 139–44] Not too much importance should be attached to these results, however, since the FTC–SEC data are defective in several respects and Jaffee included no measure of variations in the expected proceeds from investments or any other variables designed to account for responses of either loan demands or loan offer curves to variations in economic activity. As indicated in note 9, estimates of the parameters of the customer relationship model based on data similar to those presented in Tables 6.1 and 6.2 above were also statistically insignificant. Useful estimates of loan demands for different classes of banks and borrowers await better data than those now available and, probably, more completely specified models than those that Jaffee and I have estimated.

Whether or not one regards loan rates as adjusting slowly or rapidly to market conditions and as having a narrow or wide spread between different types of borrowers depends upon one's ideas of how fast is 'fast' and how wide is 'wide'. Although the business loan rate is classified by the National Bureau of Economic Research as a lagging indicator, that lag has typically been short during the postwar period. [Moore, 1961, p. 107] The average lag has been slightly less than one quarter and has tended to be shorter in recent years. And, as may be seen above in Table 6.1, although loan rates have not fluctuated as widely as money market rates, they have been far from constant. This is especially true of rates on large loans. 'Sluggish' and 'sticky' would seem to be too strong to apply to movements in loan rates. As may also be seen in Table 6.1, the spread of rates between large and small loans may be regarded as substantial, the average difference between the prime rate and the average rate on loans of the smallest size, for example, being 155 basis points on the dates listed in the table. This compares with an average difference of 82 basis points between yields on Moody's Baa and Aaa securities on these dates. Although a credit rationing theory of some kind may potentially be of some assistance in our efforts to understand bank behaviour, it would appear that any model that requires loan rates to be invariant over time or between customers is not very helpful.

Finally, the available evidence on loan defaults suggests that default risk has been very small, perhaps negligible, during the postwar period. For example, Alhadeff [1954, p. 117] reported the estimates of a California branch loan officer that losses on small loans had not averaged more than 0·0015 per cent of those loans for several years. A survey by Smith [1964] of instalment accounts of consumer credit organizations, based on 1952–58 data (which included two recessions), indicated that only 1.15 per cent of these loans, which are often regarded as high risk loans, were 'bad accounts'. Data supplied by 994 banks in twelve Federal Reserve districts and reported in *Functional Cost Analysis*, 1971 indicated that five-year averages of losses on 'commercial, agricultural and other loans' were 0.240, 0.254 and 0.304 per cent of those loans extended by small, medium-size and large banks, respectively.[18] While these data are not conclusive, they do not lend much support to those who argue that the large differences between rates on small loans and money market rates are due to the riskiness of the former.

Freimer and Gordon's analysis suggests that if bankers' estimates of loan risk are unbiased, then loan losses during the five years ending in 1971 should have been $(r - y)/(1 + r) = 1.66$ per cent of loans, where r is the average rate on all business loans and y is the average rate on three-month Treasury bills during 1967–71.[19] This is five or six times the losses actually experienced.[20] The loss rate implied by Jaffee and Modigliani will on average be less than that implied by Freimer and Gordon because loans will be smaller than permitted by the offer curve for unrationed customers. Nevertheless, the apparently very small risk of default on loans casts considerable doubt on the usefulness of the F–G or J–M theories as important explanations of bank behaviour. Still less is there any evidence that small loans are more risky than large loans. In fact, as seen from the data in the preceding paragraph, loan losses were positively related to bank size during 1967–71. It will be remembered that loan size and bank size tend to be positively related, although it may be argued that these figures are due to greater risk aversion on the part of small banks.

A credit rationing model may be consistent with few or no losses on loans actually extended if it is assumed that banks refuse to extend loans involving any degree of risk whatever. But the F–G and J–M models assume that banks are not risk averse but will extend loans to risky customers up to the point at which the marginal contribution to expected profit equals some risk-free money market rate.

NOTES

1. See Scott [1957]. Also see Roosa [1951] and the surveys in Guttentag [1960], Jaffee [1971, pp. 16–31], Kane and Malkiel [1965] and Galbraith [1963, Ch. 2]. Hodgman [1960] was also a devotee of credit rationing theories until he took a close look at actual bank behaviour, after which he emphasised the customer relationship.

2. See assumption (c) in Chapter 2.1.

3. Hester, for example, using the 1955 survey of business loans collected by the Board of Governors of the Federal Reserve System, found a significant positive relationship between total assets of borrowers and loan size [1962, pp. 205–210]. Jacobs writes that 'surveys which studied bank loan portfolios indicate that large banks make a large fraction of their loans to large business and a small fraction to small business. The opposite is true of small banks' [1971, p. 344] Also see the discussion in Guttentag and Herman [1967, pp. 143–46].

4. There is a break between 1966 and 1967 in Table 6.1 because of changes in the 'Quarterly Survey'. The fourth and tenth columns corresponding to ΔE and ΔC are the averages of first Δr_4 and Δr_5 and second, $\Delta(r_4 - y)$ and $\Delta(r_5 - y)$. Although these and the other ΔE and ΔC are averages of data that are not strictly comparable over time because of changes in definitions and sample size, these averages nevertheless provide a good idea of differences in the volatility of rates on large and small loans.

5. As may be seen in Table 6.2, there have been some exceptions, l declining during contractions only about half the time for smaller (Country and Non-member) banks.

6. This observation is supported by data published in the Federal Reserve Bulletin on 'Assets and Liabilities of Large Weekly Reporting Commercial Banks' in and outside of New York City. Over ninety per cent of the assets of New York City banks are in 'large' banks.

7. Since b and u are proportions of bank earning assets, it is not enough merely that the interest rate coefficients of loan demands of large firms be greater than those of small firms in order that $b_1 > b_2$, $u_1 > u_2$. It is necessary that these interest rate coefficients be greater for large than for small firms as proportions of the earning assets of the banks with which they do business. The same considerations apply to comparisons of c_1 and c_2.

8. That is, β and w, which are discussed in Section 2.2, are independent of j.

9. I had hoped to obtain estimates of the parameters of loan demands facing large and small banks in order to determine whether the inequalities in (6.10) and (6.11) were consistent with such estimates. To this end, equations of the form shown in (5.8) were estimated for New York City banks (letting r be the average rate on large short-term business loans) and Non-member banks (letting r be the average rate on small short-term business loans). The data used are defined and listed in Appendix B. Since data broken down by class of bank are available only in seasonally unadjusted form, seasonally unadjusted GNP was used along with seasonal dummies. The results proved unhelpful, however, because all of the interest rate coefficients were statistically insignificant and most has 'wrong' signs. It appears that the procedure followed was too restrictive and that, if useful estimates are to be obtained, a simultaneous equations approach will probably have to be followed in which both borrowers and banks are classified in more detail and each class of borrowers is permitted access to several classes of banks. However, suitable data with which to conduct such an empirical analysis are not yet available. (See the discussion in Section 6.4 of Jaffee's use of data from the Federal Trade Commission—Securities and Exchange Commission 'Quarterly Financial Report for Manufacturing Corporations'.)

10. Jaffee shows that the principal conclusions of the analysis do not change when the size of the investment project is influenced by the size of the loan. [1971, pp. 57–62].

11. This yields a profit maximizing loan size because $\partial^2 P_i / \partial L_i^2 < 0$. The bank's linear utility function in terms of expected profit makes it unnecessary to take into account higher moments of $F_i(x)$ or covariances of outcomes between customers. The bank extends loans to each customer such that expected profit from each customer is maximized.

12. Consider the case of a uniform distribution. Setting the derivative of (6.16) with respect to R_i equal to zero and substituting the solution for R_i into (6.16) gives the maximum loan, $\hat{L}_i$, that the bank is willing to grant to the ith borrower. Let C_i be the cost of the

investment project. The expected value of the proceeds from the investment is $(k_i + K_i)/2$ so that the expected rate of return from the investment is $q_i = (k_i + K_i)/2C_i$. The firm will not be able to obtain a loan from the bank in the full amount of the project's cost regardless of the rate of interest it is willing to pay—i.e. $\hat{L}_i < C_i$ and credit rationing exists as shown in Figure 6.1—unless $q_i \geq 2(1 - z_i^2)I$, where $z_i = k_i/K_i$. But $\hat{L}_i > 0$ requires that $\hat{R}_i \geq I$, where $\hat{R}_i$ is the value of R_i corresponding to $\hat{L}_i$. This condition in turn requires that $z_i \leq 1/2$, which means that credit will always be rationed unless $q_i \geq 3I/2$.

13. 'A banker who practices weak credit rationing will vary the amount he is willing to lend a borrower with the interest rate up to a limit [that limit being $\hat{L}_i$ at interest rate $\hat{r}_i$]. Only beyond this limit will be refuse to extend credit regardless of the interest rate. A banker who sets an interest rate, lends a borrower whatever he wants up to a predetermined level at this rate and refuses to lend him more regardless of the rate will be referred to as practicing *strict credit rationing*'. [F–G's emphasis, p. 398]

14. F–G implicitly assume a perfectly inelastic loan demand equal to the cost of the investment, C_i. For such a demand curve, rationing occurs regardless of the rate that the customer is willing to pay if $C_i > \hat{L}_i$ as shown in Figure 6.1.

15. This proposition is proved by substituting the solution of (6.15) for $\hat{L}_i$ into (6.14) and differentiating with respect to R_i.

16. If the bank were free to charge discriminatory rates, it would charge a rate, say R_1^*, to its riskless customers such that marginal revenue from riskless loans equals the rate of return on Treasury bills, j. Profit from the riskless customers, P_1, is a quadratic function of R_1 in the case of a linear demand curve and may be drawn as in Figure 6.2, where for purposes of this discussion we let customers 1 and 2 be riskless and risky, respectively. The principles determining the optimal uniform rate in this case are identical to those in the case of two risky customers discussed above. The uniform rate will be closer to R_1^* than to R_2^* if, as one might expect, the slope of the demand curve of riskless customers is greater than that of risky customers. It is interesting to note that if D_1 were not more elastic than D_2 it would be easy to draw demand curves and an offer curve of loans to risky customers such that $R_1^* > R_2^*$. Thus, even within the framework of J–M's risk model, observed rate differentials are as amenable to explanation by differences in demand elasticities as to differences in risk.

17. Quarterly data are shown in Table 6.3 rather than monthly data as in earlier tables because Jaffee lists H only on a quarterly basis.

18. *Functional Cost Analysis* may be obtained from Federal Reserve Banks or the Board of Governors of the Federal Reserve system. 'Commercial, agricultural and other loans' include all loans except real estate mortgage loans, instalment loans and credit card loans. 'Small', 'medium-size' and 'large' banks are those with deposits up to $50 million, from $50 million to $200 million and over $200 million, respectively.

19. See equation (6.15) above.

20. These data suggest that the risk adjustments presented in equations (5.12)–(5.14) and used in the empirical work of Chapter 5 substantially overstate actual risk. This was done deliberately in order to stack the cards against the customer relationship hypothesis by giving risk differences a better than even chance of explaining the data. However, as seen from a comparison of Tables 1.1 and 5.1, this made no difference in the qualitative nature of the results.

CHAPTER 7

The Customer Relationship and Monetary Policy

7.1 INTRODUCTION

The main conclusion of the preceding chapters was that the customer relationship tends to accentuate the volatility of bank loans and to moderate the volatility of loan rates. We should expect these primary effects of the customer relationship to carry over into other financial markets and, if commodity demands are responsive to interest rates, into the markets for commodities and labour services. The principal objective of this chapter is to determine, within a general equilibrium framework, the qualitative nature of the responses of variables determined in these markets to variations in the strength of the customer relationship. After the presentation of a short-run static equilibrium model in Section 7.2, Section 7.3 is devoted to an analysis of the implications of the customer relationship for (i) the magnitudes of fluctuations in interest rates, the price level and output and (ii) the ability of the monetary authority to moderate those fluctuations. Finally, in Sections 7.4 and 7.5 fluctuations in interest rates, the price level and output in a regime in which bank behaviour is dominated by the customer relationship are compared with those that might occur if banks were permitted to compete for deposits by means of unrestricted variations in the rate of return on deposits.

Bankers and others have advanced several arguments opposed to legalizing interest payments on demand deposits.[1] One argument is that such a step, which would reduce the importance of the customer relationship as banks competed for deposits by means of variations in deposit rates rather than through preferential loan rates, might 'tend to increase the magnitude and frequency' of fluctuations of the entire structure of interest rates. [Hodgman, 1961, pp. 267–68]. On the other hand, Hodgman continues, the legalization of interest on demand deposits would tend to make the structure of rates more responsive to actions by the monetary authority. 'The balance of advantage for central monetary policy is difficult to assess'. [p. 268][2]

Some of Hodgman's conclusions are consistent with those that will be obtained below. But there are differences, the most important of which may be stated as follows. In the models presented in Chapters 2–4 and 6 it was seen that the stronger is the customer relationship the smaller are variations in loan rates. So far, we are in agreement with Hodgman. However, it was also seen that the reduced volatility of loan rates is associated with increased variation in the composition of bank portfolios. As interest rates rise with economic activity, for example, the customer relationship causes banks to raise loan rates less than would otherwise be the case so that the increase in loans relative to bank security holdings is accentuated. Thus, the customer relationship induces a reduction in bank demands for securities, which reinforces increases in security rates.

Whether or not these effects of the customer relationship intensify fluctuations in output and commodity prices will be seen to depend upon the relative importance of security and loan rates in the aggregate demands for commodities and money, although it is possible to be more precise in certain cases. Specifically, it is shown in Section 7.3.1 that the customer relationship tends to accentuate fluctuations in prices and output during periods of low interest rates but to moderate such fluctuations when interest rates are high.

It is further shown in Section 7.4 that the introduction of a variable deposit rate does not necessarily render loan and security rates more responsive either to monetary policy or to shifts in aggregate demand. As in the models set forth by Gramley and Chase [1965, pp. 1401–1402] and Hendershott [1969, pp. 288–91], endogenous variations in deposit rates may either intensify or reduce fluctuations in other rates depending upon the substitutionary relations existing among deposits, securities, loans and commodities.[3]

There are, however, several unambiguous consequences of the removal of restrictions on deposit rates within the framework of the model presented below. One of the most important of these consequences is an increase in the efficacy of monetary stabilization measures, specifically, a reduction in the scale of Federal Reserve open market operations required to neutralize the effects of fluctuations in aggregate demand on prices and output.

7.2   A MACROECONOMIC MODEL

7.2.1   The Model

The model consists of four sectors—the Federal Reserve, commercial banks, the non-bank public and the government—which trade in the markets for six goods—Federal Reserve liabilities, commercial bank loans and deposits, commodities, labour and securities. The variables appearing in the model may be defined as follows:

R = bank reserves = Federal Reserve liabilities = government securities held by the Federal Reserve (in dollars).

G, G^b, G^p = total government securities outstanding, government securities held by banks and those held by the non-bank public, respectively (in dollars).

L = bank loans (in dollars).

Q = bank deposits (in dollars).

K_b = real value of commercial bank capital accounts.

K_p = real assets of the non-bank public.

V = net wealth of the non-bank public (in dollars).

P = commodity price level.

Z = commodity output (real income).

y = yield on securities.

r = rate of interest on bank loans.

q = rate of interest on bank deposits.

N = employment.

W = money wage rate.

S = an exogenously determined shift variable in the commodity demand function.

The balance sheets of commercial banks and the non-bank public may be expressed as follows:

$$R + G^b + L = Q + PK_b \tag{7.1}$$

$$Q + G^p + PK_p = L + V \tag{7.2}$$

For reasons of simplicity, we abstract from currency holdings of the non-bank public so that all Federal Reserve liabilities, R, are held by banks as reserves. Banks and the Federal Reserve hold government securities, G^b and R, but not those of the non-bank public.[4] Thus, the security issues of the non-bank public, which are assumed perfectly substitutable for government securities, do not enter our model explicitly since they are netted out in the transactions of the non-bank public. The balance sheets of the Federal Reserve and government sectors are not included since we are interested only in certain exogenous aspects of those sectors, viz. the security issues, G, of the government and the holdings of those issues, R, by the Federal Reserve. Bank reserves equal Federal Reserve holdings of securities because we abstract from other sources of reserves.

The non-bank public's demands for (homogeneous) bank deposits and government securities may be written as follows, where, except for (7.13) below, demands and supplies are expressed in real terms:

$$\frac{Q}{P} = Q(y,r,q,Z) \qquad Q_z, Q_q > 0 \, ; Q_y, Q_r < 0 \tag{7.3}$$

$$\frac{G^p}{P} = G^p(y,r,q,Z) \qquad G^p_y, G^p_z > 0 \, ; G^p_r, G^p_q < 0 \tag{7.4}$$

Signs of derivatives are given at the right of the equations; e.g. $\partial(Q/P)/\partial Z = Q_z$. The non-bank public's demand for bank loans is

$$\frac{L}{P} = L(y,r,q,Z) \qquad L_y,L_q,L_z > 0 \, ; L_r < 0 \tag{7.5}$$

It will be remembered that in the microeconomic model developed in the preceding chapters loan and deposit demands were crucially dependent upon past loans. However, in the short-run equilibrium model presented here, lagged variables may be taken as fixed and will therefore be suppressed. This is tantamount to assuming that all markets clear and the system attains a new equilibrium following a disturbance within a span of time equal to one decision period of banks. A long-run equilibrium model that allowed variations in the capital stock and the long-run adjustments in bank behaviour discussed in Chapter 2.4 would be considerably more complex and in some cases yield results substantially different from those that will be presented below.

Since all money is of the inside variety and under our assumptions government debt does not influence the public's net wealth, there are no real balance or wealth effects. The stock of capital goods should influence the non-bank public's demands, but because this stock is assumed fixed in our short-run analysis and all commodity prices are assumed to vary equiproportionally, the real value of capital goods is exogenous to the model and has been excluded from the behavioural equations.

Commercial bank demands for reserves and government securities are

$$\frac{R}{P} = R(y,\frac{Q}{P}) \qquad R_y < 0 \, ; R_q > 0 \tag{7.6}$$

$$\frac{G^b}{P} = G^b(y,Z) \qquad G_y^b > 0 \, ; G_z^b < 0 \tag{7.7}$$

These equations follow from the microeconomic analysis in Chapters 2–4. Excess reserves respond negatively to the yield on securities. Required reserves are proportional to Q. The positive and negative responses of G^b to y and Z, respectively, follow from the opposite responses of bank preferences for loans. Bank demands are expressed in real terms; it is assumed that bank owners are not subject to money illusion.

The key equation in our macroeconomic analysis follows from the principal result of our microeconomic analysis, viz. the response of the loan rate to movements in economic activity and the rate of return on securities. Many of the microeconomic results were based on the assumption that y is a stable linear function of Z. That assumption was useful because it enabled us to focus on variations in r relative to y. But such an approach is valid only if the macroeconomic system always responds to disturbances in such a way that movements in y and Z are highly correlated. This is acceptable in microeconomic analysis but we will see below that the relationship between movements in y and Z in a general equilibrium framework depends upon the way in which the system is disturbed. Therefore, the analysis in this chapter will take account of the independent effects of y and Z on r.

$$r = r(y,Z) \qquad r_y > 0 ; r_z < 0 \qquad (7.8)$$

The empirical results in Chapter 5 indicated that $\partial r/\partial y > 0$, $\partial r/\partial Z < 0$.

In order to be able to compare the influence of the customer relationship on our macro-variables with that of a regime in which banks compete for deposits by means of the deposit rate rather than through loans, the following deposit-rate equation is introduced:[5]

$$q = q(y) \qquad q_y > 0 \qquad (7.9)$$

If banks are allowed to vary the deposit rate freely they will be more or less energetic in their efforts to attract deposits via the deposit rate as the rate of return on securities is high or low; i.e. $q_y > 0$.

All government securities must be held so that

$$G = G^b + G^p + R \qquad (7.10)$$

This completes the financial side of the model—the markets for deposits, securities, loans and Federal Reserve liabilities. Now let us complete the model by introducing the real sector—the markets for labour and commodities. The production function, which in combination with the labour market determines the supply of commodities, is written as follows:

$$Z = Z(N) \qquad Z_n > 0 ; Z_{nn} < 0 \qquad (7.11)$$

The marginal product of labour, Z_n, is assumed positive but decreasing in the vicinity of equilibrium. The capital stock is assumed fixed and is omitted from the production function.

Assume perfect competition among firms in both the labour and commodity markets so that firms hire labour up to the point at which the marginal product of labour equals the real wage. The demand for labour is thus

$$N = N^d\left(\frac{W}{P}\right) \qquad \frac{dN^d}{d(W/P)} = \frac{1}{Z_{nn}} \qquad (7.12)$$

The supply of labour depends upon both the money wage and the commodity price level but does not necessarily depend uniquely upon the real wage; i.e. we allow for the possibility of money illusion in the supply of labour, which may be written as follows:

$$N = N^s(W,P) \qquad N_w^s > 0 ; N_p^s < 0 \qquad (7.13)$$

where it is assumed that

$$W N_w^s + P N_p^s \geq 0. \qquad (7.13.1)$$

If the equality in (7.13.1) holds, we are in the classical world; equiproportional changes in W and P induce no change in the real wage or, hence, in the quantity of labour supplied. If the inequality in (7.13.1) holds, we approach the Keynesian system; workers are more responsive to W than to P so that, for example, equiproportional increases in W and P induce an increase in the quantity of labour supplied.

Let the demand for commodities be denoted by X so that the commodity market is in equilibrium when

$$X(y,r,q,Z,S) = Z \qquad X_y, X_r, X_q < 0; \quad X_z, X_s > 0 \qquad (7.14)$$

The model consists of fourteen equations in eleven jointly-determined variables—$Q, G^p, G^b, L, P, y, r, q, Z, N, W$. But because ours is a closed system not all of these equations are independent. If by Walras' Law we drop one of the markets, say the securities market, from explicit consideration we are left with nine equations—(7.3), (7.5), (7.6), (7.8), (7.9), (7.11)—(7.14) in nine unknowns—$Q, L, P, y, r, q, Z, N, W$.

7.2.2 The Workings of the Model: The General Case

Now let us examine the impacts of shifts in the aggregate demand for commodities and Federal Reserve credit on the equilibrium values of selected variables. The derivative dq/dS, for example, indicates the impact of a change in the exogenous variable S on the equilibrium value of q when R and other exogenous variables are held constant.

$$\frac{dq}{dS} = X_s q_y [B + AR_Q(Q_r r_z + Q_z)] > 0 \qquad (7.15)$$

$$\frac{dr}{dS} = X_s \left[Br_y + A\{r_y R_Q(Q_r r_z + Q_z) - r_z[R_y + R_Q(Q_y + Q_r r_y + Q_q q_y)]\} \right] \gtreqless 0 \qquad (7.16)$$

$$\frac{dy}{dS} = X_s [B + AR_Q(Q_r r_z + Q_z)] > 0 \qquad (7.17)$$

$$\frac{dP}{dS} = \frac{-X_s P^2 B}{R} [R_y + R_Q(Q_y + Q_r r_y + Q_q q_y)] > 0 \qquad (7.18)$$

$$\frac{dZ}{dS} = -X_s A[R_y + R_Q(Q_y + Q_r r_y + Q_q q_y)] > 0 \qquad (7.19)$$

$$\frac{dq}{dR} = \frac{-A}{P}(1 - X_z - X_r r_z) < 0 \qquad (7.20)$$

$$\frac{dr}{dR} = \frac{-A}{P}[r_y(1 - X_z - X_r r_z) + r_z(X_y + X_r r_y + X_q q_y)] < 0 \qquad (7.21)$$

$$\frac{dy}{dR} = \frac{-A}{P}(1 - X_z - X_r r_z) < 0 \qquad (7.22)$$

$$\frac{dP}{dR} = \frac{-BP}{R}(X_y + X_r r_y + X_q q_y) > 0 \qquad (7.23)$$

$$\frac{dZ}{dR} = \frac{-A}{P}(X_y + X_r r_y + X_q q_y) > 0 \qquad (7.24)$$

where $A = Z_n(WN_w^s + PN_p^s)/\Delta \geq 0$; $B = R(1 - PZ_{nn}N_w^s)/P\Delta > 0$;

$$\Delta = \frac{-R}{P}(1 - PZ_{nn}N_w^s)(X_y + X_r r_y + X_q q_y)$$

$$- Z_n(WN_w^s + PN_p^s)\{R_Q(X_y + X_r r_y + X_q q_y)(Q_r r_z + Q_z) + (1 - X_z - X_r r_z) \cdot$$

$$[R_y + R_Q(Q_y + Q_r r_y + Q_q q_y)]\}$$

The signs of these derivatives are the same as in most post-Keynesian models and are conditional upon assumptions (7.25)–(7.27).[6] Given our assumptions with respect to the signs of the derivatives of (7.1)–(7.14) and the additional assumption

$$[R_y + R_Q(Q_y + Q_r r_y + Q_q q_y)] < 0, \tag{7.25}$$

then a sufficient condition for $\Delta > 0$ is

$$\frac{(1 - X_z - X_r r_z)}{(X_y + X_r r_y + X_q q_y)} < \frac{-R_Q(Q_r r_z + Q_z)}{[R_y + R_Q(Q_y + Q_r r_y + Q_q q_y)]} \tag{7.26}$$

The inequality in (7.25) holds if a change in the rate of return on securities induces an opposite movement in the demand for bank reserves. There are direct and indirect effects of changes in y on bank demands for R. The direct effect, R_y, is simply the inverse impact of y on the demand for excess reserves. The indirect effects are the responses of deposit demands and therefore required reserves to variations in y and the associated variations in r and q. The direct effect and all of the indirect effects except $R_Q Q_q q_y$ are negative. It is assumed that the sum of these direct and indirect effects is negative, i.e. that securities and bank reserves are substitutes.[7]

Inequality (7.26) is the analogue in our model of the familiar stability condition that the slope of the IS curve be less than that of the LL curve. [Hicks, 1937] The difference between (7.26) and the requirement for stability in Hicks' model are due to the presence of bank reserves and loan and deposit rates in our model. If r and q are fixed and banks hold no excess reserves, (7.26) reduces to the stability condition derived by Modigliani [1944] in his analysis of Hicks' model.[8]

It is shown in Appendix C that stability requires $\Delta > 0$ if excess demands induce increases in prices proportional to the magnitudes of the excess demands. Unlike Hicks' model, (7.26) is not a necessary condition for stability. This is because of the contribution of the labour market, ignored by Hicks, to the stability of the system analysed here. Nevertheless, we will assume that (7.25) and (7.26) are satisfied, which is sufficient for $\Delta > 0$ and the indicated signs of (7.15), (7.17), (7.18), (7.19), (7.23) and (7.24). The signs indicated for (7.20)–(7.22) also depend upon (7.27), which is stated below.

Starting from a position of equilibrium, an upward shift in the demand for commodities influences the system in the following ways.[9] The initial effect is an excess demand for commodities, which induces an increase in the price level. The rise in commodity prices leads to an increased demand for transactions balances and, therefore, an excess demand for money which induces an increase in interest rates. These money market effects are only partially offset by a reduction in commercial bank demands for reserves in response to the higher yield on securities. Interest rates and prices continue to rise until the commodity and money markets are equilibrated for the same price level and structure of interest rates. The rise in the price level disturbs the equilibrium in the labour market by reducing the real wage, thereby causing an excess demand for labour and an increase in the money wage rate. If money illusion is absent from the supply of labour, the new labour market equilibrium is described by the same real wage, employment and output that existed prior to the disturbance. On the other hand, if money illusion exists such that workers are more responsive to wage rates than to commodity prices, equiproportional rises in wages and prices induce increases in employment and output. In the absence of the customer relationship, all interest rates will be higher in the new equilibrium. However, as seen in (7.16), because $r_z < 0$ when the customer relationship is strong, dr/dS may be either positive or negative.

Referring to (7.23) and (7.24), we see that injections of reserves into the system by the Federal Reserve induce increases in the price level and output. For example, an open market purchase reduces interest rates and, hence, induces an increase in the demand for commodities. This leads to increases in the price level, employment and output in the manner described above in connection with a shift in the demand for commodities. These increases in Z and P induce an increase in the demand for money such that the initial downward movement in y is reversed. The level of y in the new equilibrium relative to that which existed prior to the Federal Reserve's action depends on the responses of the saving and investment schedules to the increase in output. I will make the usual assumption that the induced increment in the demand for commodities is less than the increase in output. This means that the analogue in our model of the Hicksian IS schedule is downward sloping; i.e.

$$(1 - X_z - X_r r_z) > 0 \qquad (7.27)$$

Inequality (7.27) implies that the sum of the direct, X_z, and indirect, $X_r r_z$, components of the marginal propensity to spend is less than unity. Given our earlier assumptions, this is a necessary and sufficient condition for inverse responses of y, q and r to changes in Federal Reserve credit.

7.2.3 The Workings of the Model: The Classical Case

A better understanding of the model can be achieved by a consideration of its workings under limiting classical and Keynesian assumptions. First consider the classical case, which exists when the equality in (7.13.1) is assumed to hold, i.e. when there is no money illusion in the supply of labour. In the classical world, equations (7.15)–(7.19) reduce to the following:

$$\frac{dq}{dS} = \frac{-X_s q_y}{(X_y + X_r r_y + X_q q_y)} > 0 \qquad (7.28)$$

$$\frac{dr}{dS} = \frac{-X_s r_y}{(X_y + X_r r_y + X_q q_y)} > 0 \qquad (7.29)$$

$$\frac{dy}{dS} = \frac{-X_s}{(X_y + X_r r_y + X_q q_y)} > 0 \qquad (7.30)$$

$$\frac{dP}{dS} = \frac{X_s P^2 [R_y + R_Q(Q_y + Q_r r_y + Q_q q_y)]}{R(X_y + X_r r_y + X_q q_y)} > 0 \qquad (7.31)$$

$$\frac{dZ}{dS} = 0 \qquad (7.32)$$

The upward shift in the demand for commodities induces increases in the securities rate and the price level. However, with no money illusion in the labour market, that market reaches a new equilibrium in which the wage rate and the price of commodities increase equiproportionally with no change in employment or output. With an unchanged Z there are no further effects on y, the upward movement in which is due entirely to the upward shift in the demand for commodities. The loan and deposit rates also increase since they respond positively to y.

In the classical world, (7.20)–(7.24) become

$$\frac{dP}{dR} = \frac{P}{R}, \frac{dq}{dR}, \frac{dr}{dR}, \frac{dy}{dR}, \frac{dZ}{dR} = 0 \qquad (7.33)$$

We obtain the classical result that liabilities of the central bank are neutral. Changes in R induce equiproportional changes in the price level, the wage rate, bank deposits and all other nominal values while relative prices, interest rates, output and other real quantites are unchanged.

It should be noted that, although R is neutral in the classical case due to the absence of money illusion in the private sectors of the economy, the pricing process is not dichotomized. This is due to the introduction of loan and deposit rates.[10] For example, a shift in bank behaviour regarding the determination of r will alter the combination of r, q, y and Z that equilibrates the commodity market. Such a shift will in general induce changes in the equilibrium values of r, q and y (though the equilibrium real wage, employment and output will be unaffected). Another way of indicating that the pricing process is not dichotomized in our model even in the absence of money illusion and wealth effects is to point out that the four equations in the real sector, (7.11)–(7.14), include six unknowns – Z, N, W/P, y, r, q. Hence, the financial sector is required for the determination of the real variables.

7.2.4 The Workings of the Model: The Keynesian Case

The limiting Keynesian case is defined by assuming that (i) commodity demands are independent of interest rates, i.e. $X_y = X_r = X_q = 0$, and (ii) there is money illusion in the supply of labour, i.e. the inequality in (7.13.1) holds.

Under these assumptions (7.15)–(7.19) may be written as shown in Section 7.2.2, but Δ, which enters A and B, reduces to

$$\Delta = - Z_n(WN_w^s + PN_p^s)(1 - X_z)[R_y + R_Q(Q_y + Q_r r_y + Q_q q_y)]$$

The familiar multiplier effect on output is obtained, $dZ/dS = X_s/(1 - X_z)$, because (7.14) reduces to the Keynesian 45-degree model when commodity demands are independent of interest rates.

However, interest rates respond to variations in output even though the reverse is not true. This is because increases in prices and output induce an increased transactions demand for money. The result is an increase in the rate of return on securities which is now completely determined according to the Keynesian liquidity preference theory of interest. The effects of a shift in the demand for commodities on the loan and deposit rates are determined by the factors discussed in connection with (7.15) and (7.16), i.e. by changes in y and Z acting through r_y, r_z and q_y.

The effects of open market operations when commodity demands are independent of interest rates are as follows:

$$\frac{dq}{dR} = \frac{q_y}{P[R_y + R_q(Q_y + Q_r r_y + Q_q q_y)]} < 0 \tag{7.34}$$

$$\frac{dr}{dR} = \frac{r_y}{P[R_y + R_Q(Q_y + Q_r r_y + Q_q q_y)]} < 0 \tag{7.35}$$

$$\frac{dy}{dR} = \frac{1}{P[R_y + R_Q(Q_y + Q_r r_y + Q_q q_y)]} < 0 \tag{7.36}$$

$$\frac{dP}{dR}, \frac{\partial Z}{\partial R} = 0 \tag{7.37}$$

The influence of R on y is determined solely by the slope of the demand for deposits as a function of y (taking into account the responses of r and q to y), i.e. by our model's analogue of the liquidity preference function. However, since the demand for commodities is independent of interest rates, these money market effects of open market operations are not transmitted to the real sector. Since Z is unchanged, changes in r and q are functions solely of y.

7.3 THE CUSTOMER RELATIONSHIP

7.3.1 Shifts in Commodity Demand

We are now in a position to examine the macroeconomic implications of variations in the strength of the customer relationship. As indicated in Chapters 2–4, a strong customer relationship (i.e. large values of d, h, β, γ, α) implies a small r_z but has conflicting effects on r_y.[11] The empirical results in Chapter 5 suggest that alterations in the values of d, h, β, γ and α, if these parameters change equiproportionally, leave r_y virtually unchanged. Thus, we may examine the effects of the customer relationship on the responses of interest rates, prices and output to shifts in commodity demand if we know how these responses are affected by changes in r_z, i.e. by partially differentiating (7.16)–(7.19) with respect to r_z. The deposit rate is held constant while the effects of variations in r_z are analysed. The effects of a variable q are examined in Section 7.4.

The partial derivatives of (7.16)–(7.17) with respect to r_z take the following signs:[12]

$$\frac{\partial(dr/dS)}{\partial r_z} > 0 ; \frac{\partial(dy/dS)}{\partial r_z} < 0 \qquad (7.38)$$

The first inequality in (7.38) indicates that an increase in the strength of the customer relationship—reduction in r_z—means a reduction in the response of loan rates to increases in economic activity. Increases in loan rates are moderated or decreases in r are accentuated in order to attract a greater quantity of loans, which through the customer relationship will induce increased future loan and deposit demands. A smaller variation in r is associated with an increased variation in y. For example, the action by banks in maintaining loan rates at relatively low levels during an economic expansion, which accentuates the increase in their loan portfolio, implies a reduced demand by banks for securities. This induces higher security yields than would otherwise prevail. In summary, the strength of the customer relationship is positively and negatively related to the magnitudes of fluctuations in y and r, respectively.

The impacts of the customer relationship on fluctuations in the price level and output are obtained by differentiating (7.18) and (7.19) with respect to r_z. This yields the following qualitative results:[13]

$$\frac{\partial(dP/dS)}{\partial r_z}, \frac{\partial(dZ/dS)}{\partial r_z} \underset{<}{\overset{>}{\gtreqless}} 0 \text{ as } C \underset{>}{\overset{<}{\lesseqgtr}} 0, \qquad (7.39)$$

where

$$C = X_r[R_y + R_Q(Q_y + Q_r r_y + Q_q q_y)] - R_Q Q_r(X_y + X_r r_y + X_q q_y) \qquad (7.40)$$

and

$$C \underset{>}{\overset{<}{\lesseqgtr}} 0 \text{ as } \frac{X_r}{(X_y + X_q q_y)} \underset{>}{\overset{<}{\lesseqgtr}} \frac{R_Q Q_r}{[R_y + R_Q(Q_y + Q_q q_y)]} \qquad (7.41)$$

or, when deposit rates are fixed,

$$C \underset{>}{\overset{<}{\lesseqgtr}} 0 \text{ as } \frac{X_r}{X_y} \underset{>}{\overset{<}{\lesseqgtr}} \frac{R_Q Q_r}{R_y + R_Q Q_y} \qquad (7.42)$$

These results may be interpreted as follows. An upward shift in the demand for commodities implies, at existing prices and interest rates, an excess demand for commodities. This excess demand induces a rise in the price level and, given money illusion in the supply of labour, increases in employment and output. If the demand for commodities is independent of interest rates, we obtain the full Keynesian multiplier impact on output. However, interest rate movements will usually moderate movements in prices and output. Under these conditions, the impact of the customer relationship on the responses of P and Z to S depends upon the relative importance of r and y in the demands for commodities and money. As indicated in (7.38), a reduction in r_z accentuates the increase in y and moderates the increase in r during an economic expansion. Consequently, given the terms on the right-hand side of the second inequality in (7.42), an increase in the strength of the customer relationship is more likely to accentuate the responses of P and Z to S the more important is r relative to y in the commodity demand function, i.e. the larger is X_r/X_y.

Variations in the demand for the monetary base, as well as in the demand for commodities, cause changes in prices and output. In simpler Hicksian–Keynesian models from which banking systems are absent, the monetary base is equivalent to the money supply. In the present model, with an endogenous banking system but no currency, the monetary base is held entirely by commercial banks as reserves. Suppose that at an existing array of interest rates, price level and output the demand for reserves exceeds the quantity of reserves available. Banks attempt to shift out of other assets (loans and securities) into reserves, bidding loan and security rates up until they are just satisfied to hold the existing supply of reserves. If the commodity market was in equilibrium prior to this disturbance in the money market, these increases in interest rates induce an excess supply of commodities which in turn causes decreases in the price level, employment and output.

The customer relationship influences the demand for the monetary base through its impact on interest rates. The stronger is the customer relationship so that the smaller is the rise in r and the larger is the rise in y due to an increase in S, the less will be the increase in the demand for reserves the more important is y relative to r in the demand for reserves. The yield on securities influences the demand for reserves (i) through the non-bank public's demand for deposits and, hence, the demand by banks for required reserves and (ii) by directly affecting the choice between excess reserves and securities. The sum of these two effects of y on the demand for reserves is $R_Q Q_y + R_y$. Only the first of these two effects is relevant to the loan rate. Therefore, a strengthening of the customer relationship is more likely to strengthen (weaken) the responses of P and Z to S the greater (smaller) is $|R_y + R_Q Q_y|$ relative to $|R_Q Q_r|$, i.e. the smaller (greater) is the ratio on the right-hand side of the second inequality in (7.42). If it is assumed that bank demands for reserves and the public's demand for money are relatively unresponsive to changes in security yields when security yields are high but are very responsive to changes in security yields when those yields are low, these conditions suggest that a strengthening of the customer relationship is more likely to strengthen the responses of P and Z to S the lower is the structure of interest rates.[14]

We can most easily understand the conditions stated in (7.39) by means of an analysis of the impact of a shift in the demand for commodities within the familiar framework of a model with no banking system, an exogenously determined money stock and only one rate of interest. The commodity and

100

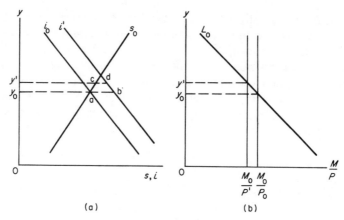

Figure 7.1. Interest rate responses and the effects of a shift in the demand for commodities

money markets in such a model are depicted in Figures 7.1(a) and 7.1(b), respectively. The demand for commodities is separated into saving, s, and investment, i, in real terms per unit of time as functions of the rate on securities, y, for a given level of output, Z_0. The saving and investment schedules are initially s_0 and i_0. The demand for money in real terms, L, is also shown as a function of y for given $Z = Z_0$. The exogenously determined stock of money is M_0. The initial equilibrium values of the security rate and the price level are y_0 and P_0, respectively.

Now assume an autonomous increase in the demand for commodities as reflected in a rightward shift in the investment function to i'. This causes an excess demand for commodities in the amount ab. The resulting increase in the commodity price level, $P' - P_0$, implies a decreased supply of real money balances and, as a consequence, an excess demand for money. While the money market must in the long run accommodate itself to the commodity market because of the effects of price level changes on the supply of real balances, the rate of interest is determined in the short run in the money market. Consequently, the rate of interest corresponding to the fixed money stock, M_0, and the new price level, P', is y'. The excess commodity demand corresponding to the higher interest rate is cd.

The price rises resulting from the excess demands ab and cd induce increases in employment and output. These increases in Z induce further shifts in the demands for commodities and money until a rate of interest is attained such that both the commodity and money markets are equilibrated. The amounts by which the levels of P and Z in the new equilibrium exceed P_0 and Z_0 depend upon the magnitudes of the excess demands and, hence, the price rises caused by increases (autonomous and induced) in the demand for commodities. These excess demands depend upon the slopes of the saving, investment and money demand functions. For example, the greater is the absolute value of the slope of the money demand function $|L_y|$, the smaller will be the initial increase in in y and, hence, the greater will be the excess demand for commodities, $i - s = X - Z$ after the increase in P to P'. For a given increase in y, the reduction in the excess demand for commodities is less the smaller is the absolute value of the difference between the slopes of the investment and savings functions, $|i_y - s_y| = |X_y|$. These considerations, taken together, imply that an autonomous shift in the demand for commodities induces greater changes in P and Z the greater is the ratio L_y/X_y. If a banking system is introduced into a regime in which the monetary base is held only by banks as reserves, then the derivative of the demand for the monetary base with respect to the securities rate is $R_y + R_Q Q_y$ and the relevant ratio is $(R_y + R_Q Q_y)/X_y$.

When bank loans are added, the responses of money and commodity demands to the loan rate also influence the impact of shifts in commodity demand on the price level and output. These effects are analogous to those of the security rate. Specifically, a shift in the demand for commodities induces greater variation in P and Z the greater is $R_Q Q_r/X_r$. Structural changes affecting the volatility of r relative to that of y may imply either greater or smaller cyclical fluctuations in P and Z depending upon the relative sizes of $R_Q Q_r/X_r$ and $(R_y + R_Q Q_y)/X_y$. In particular, an increase in the strength of the customer relationship, which intensifies the response of y and reduces the response of r to an autonomous shift in the demand for commodities, results in greater (smaller) fluctuations in P and Z if $(R_y + R_Q Q_y)/X_y$ exceeds (is less than) $R_Q Q_r/X_r$. This statement is equivalent to (7.39).

Now let us examine the effects of the customer relationship on the responses of interest rates, the price level and output to variations in commodity demand under the limiting classical and Keynesian cases discussed in Sections 7.2.3 and 7.2.4. In the classical world, since aggregate output is invariant in the presence of shifts in the demand for commodities, the derivatives in (7.38) and (7.39) are zero—variations in the strength of the response of r to Z are irrelevant because Z does not change. In the Keynesian case, the qualitative effects of the customer relationship on interest rates are unchanged from those shown in (7.38).[15] However, since interest rates no longer influence the demand for commodities, the effects of the customer relationship on interest rate fluctuations are not transmitted to the price level and output—the derivatives in (7.39) are zero.

7.3.2 Federal Reserve Credit

The effects of changes in the strength of the customer relationship on the response of the system to open market operations is obtained by partially differentiating (7.21)–(7.24) with respect to r_z.[16] The results of this differentiation are qualitatively as follows:

$$\frac{\partial(dr/dR)}{\partial r_z} > 0; \; \frac{\partial(dy/dR)}{\partial r_z} < 0 \qquad (7.43)$$

$$\frac{\partial(dP/dR)}{\partial r_z}, \frac{\partial(dZ/dR)}{\partial r_z} \gtreqless 0 \text{ as } C \lesseqgtr 0 \tag{7.44}$$

Remembering that dr/dR, $dy/dR < 0$ and $dZ/dR > 0$, (7.43) indicates that increases in the strength of the customer relationship accentuate the response of r and moderate the response of y to open market operations. The effects of changes in r_z on dP/dR and dZ/dR depend upon the relative slopes of the demands for commodities and money in the manner described in Section 7.3.1.

In the classical case, all of the derivatives in (7.43) and (7.44) are zero. Variations in R do not affect equilibrium values of Z so that the response of r to Z does not come into play. The derivatives in (7.44) and (7.45) are also zero in the Keynesian case. Variations in R exert no influence on r, y, P or Z in this situation regardless of the value r_z.

7.3.3 Stabilization Policy

Suppose the Federal Reserve wishes to offset the effects of shifts in aggregate demand on the price level or output. In the case of the price level, equation (7.45) must hold if the offsetting action is to be complete.

$$dP = \left(\frac{dP}{dS}\right)dS + \left(\frac{dP}{dR}\right)dR = 0 \tag{7.45}$$

Substituting (7.18) and (7.23) into (7.45) gives (7.46), which governs the Federal Reserve action necessary for an unchanged P in the presence of a change in S:

$$\left(\frac{dR}{dS}\right)_p = \left(\frac{dR}{dS}\right)_z = \frac{-X_s P[R_y + R_Q(Q_y + Q_r R_y + Q_q q_y)]}{(X_y + X_r r_y + X_q q_y)} < 0 \tag{7.46}$$

The response of R to S necessary to achieve stable output is the same as for price stability because, in the present model, changes in both R and S influence Z only through P. Since increases in aggregate demand and Federal Reserve credit both have positive effects on the price level and output, increases in S must be accompanied by open market sales if P and Z are to remain constant; thus the negative sign of (7.46).

Note that r_z does not enter (7.46) and that, therefore, the strength of the customer relationship does not influence the scale of open market operations required to neutralize the impacts of shifts in commodity demand on the price level and output. This is because variations in r_z are irrelevant under conditions in which $dP = dZ = 0$. However, it will be seen in Section 7.4.3 that the introduction of a variable deposit rate reduces the quantity of open market operations required to offset the effects of S on P and Z.

7.4 A VARIABLE DEPOSIT RATE

7.4.1 Shifts in Commodity Demand

In this section we examine the macroeconomic implications of a variable deposit rate. Partially differentiating (7.15)–(7.19) with respect to q_y, we see the effects of increased variability of q on the responses of interest rates, prices and output to shifts in the demand for commodities. These derivatives take the following signs:[17]

$$\frac{\partial(dq/dS)}{\partial q_y} > 0 \tag{7.47}$$

$$\frac{\partial(dr/dS)}{\partial q_y}, \frac{\partial(dy/dS)}{\partial q_y} \gtrless 0 \tag{7.48}$$

$$\frac{\partial(dP/dS)}{\partial q_y}, \frac{\partial(dZ/dS)}{\partial q_y} < 0 \tag{7.49}$$

It was seen from (7.15) and (7.17) that dq/dS and dy/dS are positive. Therefore, as indicated in (7.47), an increase in the responsiveness of q to y—a rise in q_y—accentuates the responsiveness of q to S. The higher q exerts direct and indirect effects on the commodity and money markets and therefore on other interest rates. The direct effect of a more pronounced increase in q is a moderation of the increase in commodity demand and, hence, smaller increases in P and Z and also smaller increases in y and r because of a reduction in borrowing to finance commodity purchases. This negative direct effect of a change in q_y on r and y is embodied in the first terms in X_q in (D.10) and (D.11).

The indirect effects on y arise from the reaction of Z on the money and commodity markets and may be analysed in terms of the slopes of the IS and LL schedules when these schedules are loci of Z and q such that the commodity and money markets are equilibrated for given y. In the money market, the smaller Z due to the higher q_y means a smaller demand for deposits and, hence, lower y and r. But the higher q induces a greater demand for money and, hence, higher y and r. Therefore, an increase in q_y is more likely to accentuate the positive response of y to S the greater is Q_q relative to $Q_r r_z + Q_z$, i.e. the smaller is $(Q_r r_z + Q_z)/Q_q$, which is the negative of the slope of LL when r is expressed as a function of Z. (Note that the slope of this LL schedule is negative because $Q_q > 0$).

The moderation of the rise in Z due to an increase in q_y means that the elimination of the excess demand for commodities falls more heavily upon increases in interest rates, which suggests an accentuation of the upward movements in y and r. This effect is greater the greater is the absolute value of the derivative of the excess demand for commodities with respect to Z, which is $X_r r_z + X_z - 1$, where r is a function of Z. But the higher q reduces the excess demand for commodities and so moderates the increases in y and r. Consequently, an increase in q_y is more likely to accentuate the rise in y the greater is $(X_r r_z + X_z - 1)/X_q$, which is the negative of the slope of IS. Combining the money and commodity markets, dy/dS is more likely to respond positively to q_y the greater is the absolute value of the slope of IS relative to that of LL, i.e. the greater is $(X_r r_z + X_z - 1)/X_q$ relative to $(Q_r r_z + Q_z)/Q_q$ or, rearranging, the greater is $X_q(Q_r r_z + Q_z) + Q_q(1 - X_z - X_r r_z)$.[18] This term, which incorporates the indirect effects of changes in q_y on dy/dS, may be seen in (D.11).

As indicated in (7.49), the impact of q_y on P and Z is unambiguous. Expressing

r as a function of y, we see from (7.14) that if increases in q and y are both accentuated, moderating the increase in demand, the responses of P and Z to S must be reduced. On the other hand, if dq/dS increases but dy/dS falls, the demand for the monetary base is increased and, again, increases in q_y act to moderate the responses of P and Z to shifts in the demand for commodities.

The last derivative in (7.49) is zero in the classical case, in which Z is independent of shifts in commodity demand. It will be remembered that an increase in q_y, which accentuates the rise in q following an increase in S, moderates the increase in the demand for commodities. This results in smaller rises in r and y than would otherwise occur. There are no further effects on interest rates in the classical case, in which interest rates are determined in the commodity market in conjunction with (7.8) and (7.9). Consequently, the derivatives in (7.48) are negative in the classical case. The upward influence of q_y on q and its downward influence on r and y induce increases in the demand for the monetary base and therefore a reduction in the response of P to the increased demand for commodities.[19]

Interest rates are determined solely in the markets for financial assets in the Keynesian case because commodity demands and therefore prices and output are independent of interest rates. Consequently, the derivatives in (7.49) are zero and, because of the increased demand for deposits due to higher dq/dS, rises in r and y are accentuated; i.e. the derivatives in (7.48) are positive in the Keynesian case.[20]

7.4.2 Federal Reserve Credit

The effects of changes in the variability of the deposit rate on the efficacy of monetary policy may be seen by partially differentiating (7.20)–(7.24) with respect to q_y. The signs of these derivatives are shown in (7.50)–(7.52).[21]

$$\frac{\partial(dq/dR)}{\partial q_y} < 0 \tag{7.50}$$

$$\frac{\partial(dr/dR)}{\partial q_y}, \frac{\partial(dy/dR)}{\partial q_y} \gtreqless 0 \tag{7.51}$$

$$\frac{\partial(dP/dR)}{\partial q_y}, \frac{\partial(dZ/dR)}{\partial q_y} > 0 \tag{7.52}$$

As shown in equation (7.20), dq/dR is negative because $q_y(dy/dR)$ is negative. An increase in the responsiveness of the deposit rate to variations in y—a more positive q_y—intensifies the negative response of q to open market operations. In the Keynesian case, in which interest rates are completely determined in the markets for financial assets, the fall in the demand for deposits due to the accentuated decline in q induces further declines in r and y. Thus the derivatives in (7.51) are negative in the Keynesian case.[22] The derivatives in (7.52) become zero because P and Z are not affected by q when commodity demands are independent of interest rates.

Going to the general case, since dy/dR is negative while dy/dS is positive, changes in q_y exert opposite influences on the responses of the system to R and S. This means that increases in q_y unambiguously accentuate the positive responses of P and Z to changes in Federal Reserve credit. The effects of changes in q_y on dr/dR and dy/dR continue to depend upon the relative responses of the demands for money and commodities to income and interest rates in the manner described in Section 7.4.1.

7.4.3 Stabilization Policy

Partial differentiation of (7.46) with respect to q_y enables us to analyse the implications of a variable deposit rate for the scale of open market operations required to offset shifts in the demand for commodities. This derivative is

$$\frac{\partial(dR/dS)_p}{\partial q_y} = \frac{\partial(dR/dS)_z}{\partial q_y} = \frac{X_s PD}{(X_y + X_r r_y + X_q q_y)^2} > 0 \qquad (7.53)$$

It was seen from Sections 7.4.1 and 7.4.2 that increases in q_y reduce the effect of S on Z and accentuate the impact of R on Z. Consequently, the introduction of a variable deposit rate reduces the negative response of R to shifts in demand that is necessary to maintain constant P and Z.

7.5 IMPLICATIONS FOR DEPOSIT RATE POLICY

Suppose restrictions on the payment of interest on deposits to be removed so that the deposit rate may respond freely to variations in the yield on securities. This policy change will, if legal restrictions had been binding, lead to an increase in q_y. Further assume that the importance of the customer relationship is reduced as banks compete for deposits by means of the deposit rate rather than loan policy. Since the strength of the customer relationship is negatively associated with r_z, this means an increase in r_z.

Table 7.1, which brings together the results presented in Sections 7.3 and 7.4, shows the directions of the effects of these changes in r_z and q_y in general and under the alternative assumptions of high and low interest rates. This table contains eight rows and three columns of boxes, which for ease of reference are identified as T_{ij} ($i = 1, \ldots, 8; j = 1, 2, 3$). The third column contains only the elements T_{33} and T_{63}. The top rows of T_{11} and T_{12}, for example, show the signs of the derivatives first of dr/dS and then of dr/dR with respect to r_z and q_y in the intermediate case (i.e. when neither of the extreme classical or Keynesian cases prevail) and when the equilibrium structure of interest rates may be at any level. These signs, some of which are ambiguous and are therefore indicated by question marks, were given in (7.38), (7.48), (7.43) and (7.51). The second and third rows of T_{11} and T_{12} indicate the signs of the same derivatives under the assumptions of high and low interest rates, respectively. The signs following the colons in each box indicate the total effects of the introduction

Table 7.1. Effects of introducing variable deposit rates

		dS r_z, q_y	dR r_z, q_y	dR/dS r_z, q_y
Intermediate	dr	+ ? : ? + ? : ? + − : ?	+ ? : ? + ? : ? + + : +	
	dy	− ? : ? − ? : ? − ? : ?	− ? : ? − ? : ? − ? : ?	
	dP,dZ	? − : ? + − : ? − − : −	? + : ? + + : + − + : ?	0 + : + 0 + : + 0 + : +
Classical	dr	0 − : − 0 − : − 0 − : −	0 0 : 0 0 0 : 0 0 0 : 0	
	dy	0 − : − 0 − : − 0 − : −	0 0 : 0 0 0 : 0 0 0 : 0	
	dP	0 − : − 0 − : − 0 − : −	0 0 : 0 0 0 : 0 0 0 : 0	0 + : + 0 + : + 0 + : +
Keynesian	dr	+ + : + + + : + + + : +	0 − : − 0 − : − 0 − : −	
	dy	− + : ? − + : ? − + : ?	0 − : − 0 − : − 0 − : −	

of a variable deposit rate regime. Examining T_{31}, for example, the total effect on dP/dS is ambiguous in general and when interest rates are high, but dP/dS is clearly reduced when interest rates are low. The fourth and seventh rows of boxes show the analogous results in the classical and Keynesian cases. The second, fifth and eighth rows of boxes contain the signs of the derivatives of dy/dS and dy/dR with respect to r_z and q_y under the nine combinations of assumptions of any level, high or low interest rates and the intermediate, classical or Keynesian cases. P and Z are considered together in the third row of boxes because S and R influence Z through P so that the relevant derivatives take identical signs. Z has been omitted from the classical case, in which aggregate output is independent of S and R. P and Z do not appear in the Keynesian case, in which these variables are independent of interest rates and therefore of changes in r_z and q_y. The third column of boxes gives the signs of the derivatives of $(dR/dS)_p$ and $(dR/dS)_z$ with respect to r_z and q_y.

Referring to the top row of T_{81}, we see that the derivatives of dy/dS with respect to r_z and q_y in the Keynesian case are negative and positive, respectively. Because, under our assumptions, the abolition of restrictions on the deposit rate leads to increases in r_z and q_y, the removal of these restrictions has conflicting impacts on dy/dS in the Keynesian case so that the net effect is not clear. Thus the question mark. The top row of T_{82} shows that $\partial(dy/dR)/\partial q_y$ is negative in the Keynesian case. The derivative of dy/dR with respect to r_z is zero because Z is independent of r in the Keynesian case. Therefore, the negative impact of R on y is accentuated by the removal of restrictions on the deposit rate. This is the meaning of the minus sign following the colon. In summary, if the Keynesian case holds the introduction of variable deposit rates causes the impact of open market operations on r and y to be accentuated. The response of r to shifts in commodity demand also becomes more pronounced but the effect on dy/dS is not clear.

In the classical case, the introduction of variable deposit rates moderates the influence of shifts in commodity demand on interest rates and the price level but leaves the impact of open market operations unaffected. (See the penultimate paragraph of Section 7.4.1 and note 22). Consequently, the scale of open market operations needed to maintain stable prices in the face of fluctuations in aggregate demand is reduced. This result, which is repeated in the intermediate case discussed below, is independent of the level of interest rates and is indicated by the column of plus signs following the colons in T_{63}.

It will be remembered from the discussions in Sections 7.3.1, 7.3.2, 7.4.1 and 7.4.2 that changes in the strength of the customer relationship and in the volatility of the deposit rate often have ambiguous effects on the responsiveness of interest rates, prices and output to open market operations and shifts in the demand for commodities. The signs of these effects for the intermediate case are shown in Table 7.1 above and were seen to depend upon the substitutionary relationships between money, commodities, loans and securities. The implications for stabilization policy are, however, more clear-cut. We saw in Section 7.3.3 that the strength of the customer relationship does not affect the scale of open market operations necessary to offset the impacts of shifts in commodity demand on the price level and output. But it was shown in Section 7.4.3 that an increase in the variability of the deposit rate reduces the scale of open market operations required to neutralize the effects of fluctuations in commodity demand on P and Z. That is, within the framework of the model presented in this chapter, the abolition of restrictions on deposit rates tends to increase the monetary authority's ability to stabilize prices and output.

NOTES

1. See Hodgman [1963, pp. 162–63] for examples.
2. It is not obvious to this writer why an increase in the volatility of interest rates should necessarily be regarded as undesirable; the structural changes discussed in this chapter should not be judged good or bad as they contribute to smaller or greater variations in interest rates.
3. I have been unable to ascertain why Hodgman's results differ from the results of the present study and from those of Gramley and Chase and Hendershott. This is due to Hodgman's failure to specify completely either his microeconomic or his macroeconomic framework. (See the discussion of Hodgman's work in Chapter 3 above). However, it should be added in fairness to Hodgman that his 'implications for national monetary policy . . . [are offered] as tentative suggestions rather than as definitive statements'. [1961, p. 267]
4. Strictly, the value of government security holdings is a function of y. The simpler forms of expression used here will not, however, affect our analysis since, applying Walras' Law, the securities market will be dropped when we solve the model. It will further be assumed that the interest burden of government securities is financed by taxes. 'Hence if the private sector discounts its future tax liabilities in the same way that it discounts future interest receipts, the existence of government securities will not generate any net wealth effect.' [Patinkin, 1965, p. 289]. Consistency with this assumption requires that V in (7.2) be net of the interest burden of government securities.
5. We might also have considered the influence of Z on the determination of q. Conflicting forces act on the sign of $\partial q/\partial Z$. On the one hand, an increase in economic activity is associated with an increase in the demand for deposits, which *ceteris paribus* induces a reduction in the rate offered for deposits by the profit-maximizing bank. On the other hand, a rise in Z causes an upward shift in the loan demand function facing the bank so that the bank might raise q in order to attract deposits for investment in the now more attractive loans. In order to simplify the analysis, it is assumed that these forces exactly cancel one another so that $\partial q/\partial Z = 0$.
6. It is assumed for purposes of this section that $A, X_r, X_y, X_q \neq 0$. In the classical and Keynesian cases discussed below we shall let $A = 0$ and $X_r = X_y = X_q = 0$, respectively.
7. See Tobin and Brainard [1963] for discussions of the importance of a similar assumption for stability and monetary control.
8. The model presented in this study, with an explicit factor market, is more akin to Modigliani's later model [1963] than to the one he analysed in 1944.
9. The manner in which S enters the model, i.e. only in the commodity demand equation (7.14), implies that shifts in the demand for commodities take place completely at the expense of the suppressed market, securities. If this were not so, S would also enter loan and/or deposit demands, in which case our results would differ from those presented here. See Patinkin [1965, pp. 244–52, 488–94] on this point.
10. See Gurley and Shaw [1960, pp. 247–64] on this point.
11. It was noted following (2.17) that the loan-customer relationship accentuates the positive response of r to y. But the deposit relationship acts to reduce the response of r to y because, for example, a rise in y, which causes expectations of future y's to be revised upwards, induces banks to seek to expand current loans in order to attract future deposits which may be invested in securities at the higher expected y's.
12. These derivatives are listed in equations (D.1)–(D.2) in Appendix D. Signs of the derivatives in (7.38)–(7.53) hold when $A, X_r, X_y, X_q \neq 0$, i.e. in circumstances other than the extreme classical or Keynesian cases. Many of these derivatives reduce to zero in the classical or Keynesian cases and some others, which are otherwise ambiguous, become unambiguous in the classical or Keynesian cases.
13. These derivatives are listed in (D.3)–(D.4).
14. This is consistent with much theoretical and empirical work and is usually explained

in terms of Keynes' hypothesis that investors' expectations of capital gains and losses on securities are based on the concept of a 'normal' level of the structure of interest rates. For example, see Laidler [1969] and Cagan [1969]. The evidence strongly supports a non-linear money demand function of the form assumed here, although the evidence regarding the demand for reserves is mixed. Because loans and deposits are not subject to capital gains and losses, the highly non-linear way in which y enters the demands for money and reserves is not likely to be quite so pronounced for r and q.

15. The derivatives (7.38) in the Keynesian case are listed in (D.1.1)–(D.2.1).
16. These derivatives are listed in (D.5)–(D.8).
17. These derivatives are listed in (D.9)–(D.13).
18. This analysis of the indirect effects of variable deposit rates on the securities rate is similar in some respects to Pye and Young's [1972] analysis of the effects of the relaxation of deposit rate ceilings on aggregate income.
19. The derivatives (7.47)–(7.49) in the classical case are listed in (D.9.1)–(D.12.1).
20. These derivatives are listed in (D.9.2)–(D.11.2).
21. These derivatives are listed in (D.14)–(D.18).
22. These derivatives are listed in (D.14.1)–(D.16.1). All of the derivatives (7.50)–(7.52) are zero in the classical case, in which changes in R have no influence on equilibrium values of y or q so that the responses of q to y do not come into play.

APPENDIX A

The General Customer Relationship Model

This appendix contains a derivation for the general (T-period) case of the model presented in Chapters 2–4. It begins with a statement of the problem in the most complicated form presented in the text—that put forward in Chapter 4 in which deposits and loan demand are dynamic, there is competition, free reserves are endogenous and the bank's horizon is T periods. The effects of changes in economic activity on loans and loan rates of the individual bank are then derived, both in general and as the bank's horizon approaches an infinite length. While this appendix may be read independently of the text, the reader must refer to Chapters 2–4 for discussions of the assumptions and rationale underlying the model.

A.1 STATEMENT OF THE PROBLEM

The bank wishes to maximize the discounted sum of current and future profits:

$$\pi = \sum_{t=1}^{T} \beta^{t-1}(r_t l_t + y_t g_t) \tag{A.1}$$

where r_t and y_t are rates of return in the tth period on bank loans and bonds, respectively. Loans and bonds are homogeneous and mutually exclusive one-period assets, where l_t and g_t indicate loans and bonds planned by the bank for its tth period portfolio as proportions of the sum of first-period earning assets and free-reserves, F_1, of the bank. Profit, π, is also expressed as a proportion F_1. The discount factor is $0 \leq \beta \leq 1$ and the bank's horizon is T periods. The bank chooses portfolios for periods $t = 1, 2, \ldots, T$ such that π is maximized subject to constraints that will be stated below.

The loan demand confronting the bank in the tth period depends upon r_t and y_t as well as the average loan rate of other banks, r_t^0, an index of economic activity, z_t, and past loans of our bank, l_{t-i}, and of other banks, l_{t-i}^0 $(i = 1, 2, \ldots, n)$:

$$l_t = a - br_t + b_0 r_t^0 + cz_t + uy_t + \gamma \sum_{i=1}^{n} d^i l_{t-i} - \gamma_0 \sum_{i=1}^{n} d^i l_{t-i}^0$$

$$(t = 1, 2, \ldots, T) \qquad \text{(A.2)}$$

All dollar values here and elsewhere are expressed as proportions of $F_1 = L_1 + G_1 + E_1$, where L_t, G_t and E_t are dollar values of loans, bonds and free reserves, respectively, in period t.

The bank's deposits, q_t, depend upon its past loans and the past loans of other banks as well as upon total deposits in the banking system, $q_t + q_t^0$:

$$q_t = a_1 + \alpha \sum_{i=1}^{n} h^i l_{t-i} - \alpha_0 \sum_{i=1}^{n} h^i l_{t-i}^0 + s(q_t + q_t^0)$$

$$(t = 1, 2, \ldots T) \qquad \text{(A.3)}$$

Now assume that the Federal Reserve fixes total deposits in the banking system in response to economic activity with a one-period lag:

$$q_t + q_t^0 = a_2 + \sigma z_{t-1} \qquad (t = 1, 2, \ldots T) \qquad \text{(A.4)}$$

The bank's balance sheet is

$$l_t + g_t + e_t = (1 - k)q_t + \kappa_t \qquad (t = 1, 2, \ldots, T) \qquad \text{(A.5)}$$

where κ_t and e_t are the bank's capital and free reserves as proportions of F_1 and k is the required reserve ratio, which is expected to continue unchanged. It is assumed that all profits are paid to the owners so that κ_t is also invariant.

The bank's demand for free reserves in period t is

$$e_t = a_3 - \delta y_t \qquad (t = 1, 2, \ldots, T) \qquad \text{(A.6)}$$

Neglecting problems of risk and uncertainty, the bank has direct control over its loan rate, r_t, bond holdings, g_t, and excess reserves, e_t $(t = 1, 2, \ldots, T)$. Through its selection of r_t the bank determines its current and future loans and future deposits subject to its own past behaviour (l_{t-i}), the past, current and expected future behaviour of other banks $(l_{t-i}^0, r_t^0, l_t^0)$ and current and expected levels of bond rates and economic activity (y_t, z_t).

At the beginning of the first period the bank decides upon those values of r_t, g_t, e_t, l_t and q_t $(t = 1, 2, \ldots, T)$ that maximize π subject to (A.2)–(A.6) and those variables that are, from the standpoint of the bank, predetermined—l_{1-i}, r_t^0, l_t^0, l_{1-i}^0, y_t and z_t $(i = 1, 2, \ldots, n; t = 1, 2, \ldots, T)$. But we are interested primarily in r_t and l_t. Substituting (A.3)–(A.6) into (A.1) and maximizing the result with respect to r_t and l_t subject to (A.2) is equivalent to maximizing the following

Lagrangian function, expressed in matrix notation, with respect to r_t, l_t and λ_t ($t = 1, 2, ..., T$):

$$
\begin{aligned}
\Phi = \ & L'BR + (1-k)(a_1 + sa_2)B_1'Y + (1-k)s\sigma Y'B_2 Z \\
& + (1-k)s\sigma Z_0'Y + (1-k)\alpha L'HBY + (1-k)\alpha L_1'H_1 BY \\
& - (1-k)\alpha_0 L_0'HBY - (1-k)\alpha_0 L_{01}'H_1 BY + (\kappa - a_3)B_1'Y \\
& + \delta Y'BY - L'BY + \Lambda'L - a\Lambda'I_1 + b\Lambda'R - b_0\Lambda'R_0 \\
& - c\Lambda'Z - u\Lambda'Y - \gamma L'D\Lambda - \gamma L_1'D_1\Lambda + \gamma_0 L_0'DA + \gamma_0 L_{01}'D_1\Lambda \quad \text{(A.7)}
\end{aligned}
$$

where, letting $n = T, L, L_1, L_0, L_{01}, I_1, R, R_0, Y, B_1, Z, Z_0$ and Λ are $T \times 1$ vectors and B, B_2, H, H_1, D and D_1 are $T \times T$ matrices. These vectors and matrices are defined as follows, where the subscripts i and j denote rows and columns, respectively ($i, j = 1, 2, ..., T$):

$$
\begin{aligned}
& L_i = l_i; \ (L_1)_i = l_{1-i}; \ (L_0)_i = l_i^0; \ (L_{01})_i = l_{1-i}^0; \\
& (I_1)_i = 1; \ R_i = r_i; \ (R_0)_i = r_i^0; \ Y_i = y_i; \ (B_1)_i = \beta^{i-1}; \\
& Z_i = z_i; \ \Lambda_i = \lambda_i;
\end{aligned}
$$

$$
(Z_0)_i = \begin{cases} z_0, & i = 1 \\ 0, & i > 1 \end{cases};
\qquad
B_{ij} = \begin{cases} \beta^{i-1}, & i = j \\ 0, & i \neq j \end{cases};
$$

$$
(B_2)_{ij} = \begin{cases} \beta^j, & i = j+1 \\ 0, & i \neq j+1 \end{cases};
\qquad
H_{ij} = \begin{cases} h^{j-i}, & i < j \\ 0, & i \geq j \end{cases};
$$

$$
(H_1)_{ij} = \begin{cases} h^{i+j-1}, & i+j \leq T+1 \\ 0, & i+j > T+1 \end{cases};
\qquad
D_{ij} = \begin{cases} d^{j-i}, & i < j \\ 0, & i \geq j \end{cases};
$$

$$
(D_1)_{ij} = \begin{cases} d^{i+j-1}, & i+j \leq T+1 \\ 0, & i+j > T+1 \end{cases};
$$

Setting the derivatives of (A.7) with respect to L, R and Λ equal to zero and solving for the profit maximizing values of L and R gives

$$
\begin{aligned}
L = \ & M^{-1}B[aI_1 + cZ + (u-b)Y + b(1-k)\alpha B^{-1}HBY \\
& + \gamma D_1' L_1 + b_0 R_0 - \gamma_0 D'L_0 - \gamma_0 D_1' L_{01}] \quad \text{(A.8)}
\end{aligned}
$$

$$
\begin{aligned}
R = \ & K'M^{-1}\{[I - (1-k)\alpha H]BY + \frac{1}{b}KBK'^{-1}(aI_1 + cZ + uY \\
& + \gamma D_1' L_1 + b_0 R_0 - \gamma_0 D'L_0 - \gamma_0 D_1' L_{01})\} \quad \text{(A.9)}
\end{aligned}
$$

where $K = I - \gamma D$; $M = KB + BK'$.

Now let us find the responses of l_1 and r_1 to variations in current economic activity, z_1. In order to do this we must be explicit about the manner in which the bank revises its expectations of future bond rates and levels of economic activity in response to observed changes in current economic activity. We assume first that the bank expects the bond rate in each period to respond in a linear fashion to variations in economic activity during that period:

$$\frac{\partial y_t}{\partial z_t} = f \qquad (t = 1, 2, ..., T) \tag{A.10}$$

Further, the bank is assumed to revise its expectations of future economic activity in response to variations in current economic activity in the following manner:

$$\frac{\partial z_t}{\partial z_1} = w_t = \sum_{i=0}^{t-1} w^i = \frac{1 - w^t}{1 - w}, \quad 0 \le w < 1 \quad (t = 1, 2, ..., T) \tag{A.11}$$

From (A.10) and (A.11),

$$\frac{\partial Y_t}{\partial z_1} = \frac{\partial Y_t}{\partial z_t} \frac{\partial z_t}{\partial z_1} = f w_t = \frac{f(1 - w^t)}{(1 - w)} \quad (t = 1, 2, ..., T) \tag{A.12}$$

Before our bank revises its portfolio strategy in response to variations in z_1 it must take into account the probable reactions of other banks. We make the simplifying assumption that our bank expects other banks to react to changes in z_1 in precisely the same way that it does. This means that

$$\frac{\partial r_t^0}{\partial z_1} = \frac{\partial r_t}{\partial z_1} \quad (t = 1, 2, ..., T) \tag{A.13}$$

and

$$\frac{\partial l_t^0}{\partial z_1} = N \frac{\partial l_t}{\partial z_1} \quad (t = 1, 2, ..., T) \tag{A.14}$$

where there are $N + 1$ banks.

Assumptions (A.11)–(A.14) may be expressed in vector form as follows:

$$\frac{\partial Z}{\partial z_1} = W; \quad \frac{\partial Y}{\partial z_1} = fW; \quad \frac{\partial R_0}{\partial z_1} = \frac{\partial R}{\partial z_1}; \quad \frac{\partial L_0}{\partial z_1} = N \frac{\partial L}{\partial z_1} \tag{A.15}$$

where

$$W_i = w_i; \quad \left(\frac{\partial R}{\partial z_1}\right)_i = \frac{\partial r_i}{\partial z_1}; \quad \left(\frac{\partial L}{\partial z_1}\right)_i = \frac{\partial l_i}{\partial z_1} \quad (i = 1, 2, ..., T)$$

Substituting (A.15) into (A.8) and (A.9) and differentiating with respect to z_1 gives

$$\frac{\partial L}{\partial z_1} = M^{-1} B \left\{ [c + (u - b)f]W + bf\alpha(1 - k)B^{-1} HBW + b_0 \frac{\partial R}{\partial z_1} \right.$$
$$\left. - N\gamma_0 D' \frac{\partial L}{\partial z_1} \right\} \tag{A.16}$$

$$\frac{\partial R}{\partial z_1} = K'M^{-1}\left\{[I - (1-k)\alpha H]fBW + \frac{1}{b}KBK'^{-1}[(c+uf)W\right.$$

$$\left. + b_0\frac{\partial R}{\partial z_1} - N\gamma_0 D'\frac{\partial L}{\partial z_1}]\right\} \tag{A.17}$$

The solution of (A.16) and (A.17) for the two vectors of unknowns, $\partial L/\partial z_1$ and $\partial R/\partial z_1$ is as follows:

$$\frac{\partial L}{\partial z_1} = M_0^{-1}\{[c + uf - (b - b_0)f]B + (b - b_0)f(1-k)\alpha HB\}W \tag{A.18}$$

$$\frac{\partial R}{\partial z_1} = K'_\varepsilon M_0^{-1}\left\{\frac{c+uf}{b}KBK_\varepsilon'^{-1} + fB[I - (1-k)\alpha B^{-1}HB]\right\}W \tag{A.19}$$

where $M_0 = b'KB + BK'_\varepsilon$, $\gamma'_0 = N\gamma_0$, $\varepsilon = \gamma - \gamma'_0$, $b' = (b - b_0)/b$, $K_\varepsilon = I - \varepsilon D$.

We are interested in the response of the difference $r_1 - y_1$ to variations in z_1, which requires the solution of

$$\frac{\partial R}{\partial z_1} - \frac{\partial Y}{\partial z_1} = \frac{\partial R}{\partial z_1} - fW = \frac{1}{b}K'_\varepsilon M_0^{-1}\{[c + uf - (b - b_0)f]KBK_\varepsilon'^{-1}$$

$$- bf(1-k)\alpha HB\}W \tag{A.20}$$

In order to solve (A.18) and (A.20) for $\partial l_1/\partial z_1$ and $\partial(r_1 - y_1)/\partial z_1$ we must invert M_0.

A.2 INVERSION OF M_0

The matrix M_0 assumes the following form:

$$\frac{1}{1+b'}(M_0)_{ij} = \begin{cases} -\theta d^{j-i}\beta^{j-1} & , i < j \\ \beta^{i-1} & , i = j \\ -\mu d^{i-j}\beta^{i-1} & , i > j \end{cases}$$

where $\theta = \dfrac{b'\gamma}{1+b'} = \dfrac{\gamma(b - b_0)}{2b - b_0}$, $\mu = \dfrac{\varepsilon}{1+b'} = \dfrac{b(\gamma - \gamma'_0)}{2b - b_0}$.

We will need the following $T \times T$ matrices:

$$A_{ij} = \begin{cases} 1, & i = j \\ -d, & i = j+1 \; ; \\ 0, & \text{otherwise} \end{cases} \qquad (B_D)_{ij} = \begin{cases} \beta^{-(i-1)/2}, & i = j \\ 0 & , i \neq j \end{cases}$$

Pre- and post-multiplying M_0 by $B_D A'$ and AB_D, respectively, gives

$$(B_D A'M_0 AB_D)_{ij} = (B_D)_{ik}(A')_{kl}(M_0)_{lm}A_{mn}(B_D)_{nj} \tag{A.21}$$

where i and j are the identifying, or free, indices, each of which can have values from 1 to T, while k, l, m, and n are the summation, or dummy, indices which can be changed at will. Summing over k, l, m and n gives

$$B_D A'M_0 AB_D = (1 + b')\rho X \tag{A.22}$$

$$X_{ij} = \begin{cases} 1 & , i = j < T \\ \rho^{-1}, i = j = T \\ x_1 & , j = i+1 \\ x_2 & , j = i-1 \\ 0 & , \text{otherwise} \end{cases}$$

where $\rho = [1 + (1 + \mu + \theta)d^2\beta]$, $x_1 = \dfrac{-(1+\theta)d\beta^{1/2}}{\rho}$, $x_2 = \dfrac{-(1+\mu)d\beta^{1/2}}{\rho}$.

Now let us find triangular matrices U_1 and U_2 such that $U_1 X U_2 = P$ is a diagonal matrix, where

$$(U_1)_{ij} = \begin{cases} 0 & , i < j \\ 1 & , i = j \\ \text{unknown}, i > j \end{cases} \quad (i,j = 1, 2, \dots, T)$$

$$(U_2)_{ij} = \begin{cases} \text{unknown}, i < j \\ 1 & , i = j \\ 0 & , i > j \end{cases}$$

Pre-multiplying X by U_1 gives, where U_{ij} is the element in the ith row and jth column of U_1,

$$(U_1 X)_{ij} = \begin{cases} 0 & , i < j-1 \\ x_1 & , i = j-1 \\ 1 & , i = j = 1 \\ U_{i,j-1}x_1 + 1 & , 1 < i = j < T \\ U_{i,j-1}x_1 + \rho^{-1} & , i = j = T \\ U_{ij} + U_{i,j-1}x_1 + U_{i,j+1}x_2, \; i > j \end{cases} \tag{A.23}$$

We want U_1 to be such that the elements of $U_1 X$ below the main diagonal are zero. This requires that the elements in the tth row of U_1 satisfy the following relation:

$$X_t^0 U_t^0 = -X_2 \tag{A.24}$$

where the X_t^0 are square matrices of order $t-1$ such that

$$(X_t^0)_{ij} = \begin{cases} x_2, i = j-1 \\ 1, i = j \\ x_1, i = j+1 \\ 0, \text{otherwise} \end{cases} \quad (t = 2, 3, \dots, T)$$

$(U_t^0)' = [U_{t1} U_{t2} \dots U_{t,t-1}]$ is formed from the elements to the left of the main diagonal of the tth row of U_1 $(t = 2, 3, \dots, T)$ and $X_2' = [0\ 0 \dots 0\ x_2]$ also contains $t-1$ elements.

The determinant of X_t^0 may be expressed as the second-order homogeneous difference equation

$$P_{t-1} = P_{t-2} - x_1 x_2 P_{t-3} = |X_t^0| \tag{A.25}$$

with solution

$$P_{t-1} = \frac{1}{v}\left[\left(\frac{1+v}{2}\right)^t - \left(\frac{1-v}{2}\right)^t\right], \qquad (A.26)$$

where $v = (1 - 4x_1 x_2)^{1/2}$ and the initial conditions are $P_0 = 1$ and $P_{-1} = 0$. The cofactors of X_t^0 may also be expressed as solutions of difference equations. The resulting inverse of X_t^0 is

$$(X_t^0)_{ij}^{-1} = \begin{cases} (-x_2)^{j-i} P_{t-1}^{-1} P_{i-1} P_{t-1-j}, & i \le j \\ (-x_1)^{i-j} P_{t-1}^{-1} P_{j-1} P_{t-1-i}, & i \ge j \end{cases} \quad (t = 2, 3, ..., T) \qquad (A.27)$$

From (A.24) and (A.27),

$$(U_t^0)_i = -(X_t^0)_{ij}^{-1}(X_2)_j = P_{t-1}^{-1} P_{i-1}(-x_2)^{t-i} \quad (i = 1, 2, ..., t-1; t = 2, 3, ..., T) \qquad (A.28)$$

The column vector U_t^0 contains the elements of the tth row ($t = 2, 3, ..., T$) of U_1, which, accordingly, is defined as follows:

$$(U_1)_{ij} = \begin{cases} 0 & i < j \\ (-x_2)^{i-j} P_{i-1}^{-1} P_{j-1}, & i \ge j \end{cases} \qquad (A.29)$$

We can solve for the elements of U_2 by performing the same operation on $U_2'X'$ as for $U_1 X$. The resulting matrix U_2 is the transpose of U_1 except that the x_2's in U_1 are replaced by x_1's in U_2. It will now be shown that $U_1 X U_2 = P$ is a diagonal matrix.

$$(U_1 X U_2)_{ij} = (U_1)_{ik} X_{kl}(U_2)_{lj} = P_{ij} = \begin{cases} P_i/P_{i-1}, & i = j < T \\ p^{-1}, & i = j = T \\ 0, & i \ne j \end{cases} \qquad (A.30)$$

where $p = \dfrac{\rho P_{T-1}}{P_{T-1} - \rho x_1 x_2 P_{T-2}}$.

From (A.22) and (A.30),

$$U_1 B_D A' M_0 A B_D U_2 = (1 + b')\rho P \qquad (A.31)$$

Hence, the inverse of M_0 is

$$M_0^{-1} = \frac{1}{(1 + b')\rho} A B_D U_2 P^{-1} U_1 B_D A' \qquad (A.32)$$

where P^{-1} is obtained by inverting each of the elements in (A.30).

Before using (A.32) in connection with (A.18) and (A.20) to solve for $\partial l_1/\partial z_1$, and $\partial(r_1 - y_1)/\partial z_1$, it will be useful to derive the second-order conditions for a profit maximum.

A.3 SECOND-ORDER CONDITIONS

The second partial derivatives of (A.7) with respect to L, R and Λ form the following bordered Hessian determinant:

$$\Delta_T = \begin{vmatrix} 0 & B & K \\ B & 0 & bI \\ K' & bI & 0 \end{vmatrix} \qquad (A.33)$$

Equation (A.7) was maximized with respect to $2T$ variables (l_t and r_t for $t = 1, 2, ..., T$) subject to T constraints (equation (A.2) for each period). Hence, a profit maximum requires that the last T principal minors of Δ_T alternate in sign, the first principal minor that we use being of sign $(-1)^{T+1}$. In the present case the tth principal minor used (the $(2T + t)$th principal minor of Δ_T) assumes the value

$$(-1)^{T+t} \beta^{[T(T-1)-t(t-1)]} \Delta_t \qquad (t = 1, 2, ..., T)$$

where Δ_t is the determinant of the matrix of order $3t$ corresponding to (A.33). Since $\beta > 0$, the second-order conditions for a maximum require that $\Delta_t > 0$ for $t = 1, 2, ... T$.

Solving for Δ_t, let Δ_t^* be the matrix of which Δ_t is the determinant. Then Δ_t^* may be partitioned as follows:

$$\Delta_t^* = \begin{bmatrix} 0 & B & K \\ B & 0 & bI \\ K' & bI & 0 \end{bmatrix} = \begin{bmatrix} C & K \\ K' & bI & 0 \end{bmatrix} \qquad (A.34)$$

where B, K and I are of order t.

Now write

$$F\Delta_t^* = \begin{bmatrix} I & 0 \\ -[K'\, bI]C^{-1} & I \end{bmatrix} \begin{bmatrix} C & K \\ K' & bI & 0 \end{bmatrix} = \begin{bmatrix} C & K \\ 0 & J \end{bmatrix} \qquad (A.35)$$

where

$$J = -b[B^{-1}K + K'B^{-1}] \qquad (A.36)$$

From a theorem on the determinants of partitioned matrices[1] the determinant of $F\Delta_t^*$ may be written

$$|F\Delta_t^*| = |J|\,|C - \begin{bmatrix} K \\ bI \end{bmatrix} J^{-1} \cdot 0| = |J|\,|C| \qquad (A.37)$$

Since the determinants of C and F are $(-1)^t|B|^2$ and unity, respectively,

$$|F\Delta_t^*| = \Delta_t = (-1)^t|BJB| = b^t|KB + BK'| = b^t|M_t| \qquad (A.38)$$

Given $b > 0$, the second-order conditions are satisfied if $|M_t| > 0$ for all t. Since M_0 reduces to M when $b_0 = \gamma_0' = 0$, $|M_t|$ may be calculated from (A.31):

$$|M_t| = 2^t \rho^{t-1} \beta^{t(t-1)/2} (P_{t-1} - \rho x^2 P_{t-2}) \quad (t = 1, 2, ..., T) \qquad (A.39)$$

where, when $b_0 = \gamma_0' = 0$, we have $\rho = [1 + (1 + \gamma)d^2\beta]$, $x_1 = x_2 = x = -\dfrac{(2 + \gamma)d\beta^{1/2}}{2\rho}$, $v = (1 - 4x^2)^{1/2}$.

Considering only non-negative values of γ, d and β, if $x = -\frac{1}{2}$ we have $v = 0$ so that P_t and (A.39) are undefined. Thus, the second-order conditions for a profit maximum are not satisfied if $x = -\frac{1}{2}$. If $x < -\frac{1}{2}$ we have $4x^2 > 1$ so that v and P_t are complex numbers. Since linear order has no meaning except for real values (A.39) is not satisfied for $x < -\frac{1}{2}$.

Given that (A.39) requires $x > -\frac{1}{2}$, substituting (A.26) into (A.39) and rearranging, we find that (A.39) is positive for all T, including $T \to \infty$, only if

$$(1 + \gamma)\mathrm{d}\beta^{1/2} < 1 \qquad (A.40)$$

The smaller is T the larger are the values of γ, d and β consistent with a profit maximum; examples of second-order conditions ($T = 2, 3$) are given in (2.15) and (2.27) in Chapter 2.

A.4 THE SOLUTION

The derivations of $\partial l_1/\partial z_1$ and $\partial(r_1 - y_1)/\partial z_1$ from (A.18) and (A.20) require only the first row of M_0^{-1} in (A.32), which may be written as follows:

$$(M_0^{-1})_{1t} = \frac{1}{(1 + b')\rho} A_{1i}(B_D)_{il}(U_2)_{lk}(P^{-1})_{km}(U_1)_{mj}(B_D)_{jn}(A')_{nt} \qquad (A.41)$$

Summing over i, j, k, l, m and n from 1 to T yields the elements of the first row of M_0^{-1}, where $p_1 = p/P_{T-1}$:

$$(M_0^{-1})_{1t} = \left(\frac{-x_1}{\beta^{1/2}}\right)^{t-1} \left[\frac{P_{T-t-1} + p_1(x_1 x_2)^{T-t}(P_{t-1} + x_2 \mathrm{d}\beta^{1/2} P_{t-2}) + \delta_t \dfrac{\mathrm{d}\beta^{1/2} P_{T-t}}{x_1}}{(1 + b')\rho P_{T-1}}\right] \qquad (A.42)$$

where $\delta_t = \begin{cases} 0, & t = 1 \\ 1, & t = 2, 3, \ldots, T \end{cases}$

Denoting the $(1, t)$th element of M_0^{-1} by m_t and substituting (A.42) into (A.18) and (A.20) gives

$$\frac{\partial l_1}{\partial z_1} = \frac{[c + uf - (b - b_0)f]}{(1 - w)} \sum_{t=1}^{T} m_t \beta^{t-1}(1 - w^t)$$

$$+ \frac{(b - b_0)(1 - k)\alpha h f}{(1 - w)} \sum_{t=1}^{T} m_t \beta^t \left\{ \frac{[1 - (h\beta)^{T-t}]}{(1 - h\beta)} - \frac{w^{t-1}[1 - (h\beta w)^{T-t}]}{(1 - h\beta w)} \right\} \qquad (A.43)$$

$$\frac{\partial(r_1 - y_1)}{\partial z_1} = \frac{[c + uf - (b - b_0)f]}{(b - b_0)(1 - w)} \left[(1 - w) - \sum_{t=1}^{T} m_t \beta^{t-1}(1 - w^t)\right]$$

$$- \frac{(1 - k)\alpha h f}{(1 - w)} \sum_{t=1}^{T} m_t \beta^t \left\{ \frac{[1 - (h\beta)^{T-t}]}{(1 - h\beta)} - \frac{w^{t-1}[1 - (h\beta w)^{T-t}]}{(1 - h\beta w)} \right\} \qquad (A.44)$$

Performing the indicated summations and letting the bank's horizon become infinitely long, (A.43) and (A.44) reduce to (A.45) and (A.46), respectively:

$$\lim_{T \to \infty} \frac{\partial l_1}{\partial z_1} = \frac{2b}{(2b - b_0)\rho v_1 v_2} \Big[[c + uf - (b - b_0)f][(1 + v)(1 - d\beta w) - d\beta v_2]$$

$$+ \frac{(b - b_0)(1 - k)f\alpha\beta h\{v_2[1 - d\beta(1 + w - h\beta w)] + w(1 + v)(1 - h\beta)(1 - d\beta w)\}}{(1 - h\beta)(1 - h\beta w)} \Big]$$

$$\text{(A.45)}$$

$$\lim_{T \to \infty} \frac{\partial (r_1 - y_1)}{\partial z_1}$$

$$= \frac{2[c + uf - (b - b_0)f][v_3\{(1 + v)[1 - (1 + \gamma)d\beta w] - (1 + \gamma)d\beta v_2\} - (1 + \gamma)d^2 \beta \varepsilon v_1 v_2]}{(2b - b_0)\rho v_1 v_2[1 + v + 2x_1(1 + \varepsilon)d\beta^{1/2}]}$$

$$- \frac{2b(1 - k)f\alpha\beta h\{v_2[1 - d\beta(1 + w - h\beta w)] + w(1 + v)(1 - h\beta)(1 - d\beta w)\}}{(2b - b_0)\rho v_1 v_2(1 - h\beta)(1 - h\beta w)}$$

$$\text{(A.46)}$$

where $v_1 = (1 + v + 2x_1\beta^{1/2})$, $v_2 = (1 + v + 2x_1 w\beta^{1/2})$, $v_3 = (1 + v + 2x_1 d\beta^{1/2})$.

Given β, d, $h > 0$, satisfaction of the second-order conditions for a profit maximum and $0 \le w < 1$, the only additional assumption needed to assure finite limits of (A.43) and (A.44) as $T \to \infty$ is $h\beta < 1$.

A.5 LONG-RUN EQUILIBRIUM

If z and y are constant, l_t and r_t may be expressed as Tth-order difference equations, where l_t and r_t are the values assumed by l_1 and r_1 in the tth period:

$$l_t = [a + cz + (u - b + b_0)y] \sum_{t=1}^{T} m_t \beta^{t-1} + \frac{(b - b_0)(1 - k)\alpha h y}{(1 - h\beta)} \sum_{t=1}^{T} m_t \beta^t [1 - (h\beta)^{T-t}]$$

$$+ \varepsilon \sum_{i=1}^{T} d^i l_{t-i} \sum_{t=1}^{T+1-i} m_t (d\beta)^{t-1}$$

$$\text{(A.47)}$$

$$r_t = \frac{(a + cz + uy)}{(b - b_0)} \Big[1 - \sum_{t=1}^{T} m_t \beta^{t-1} \Big] + y \sum_{t=1}^{T} m_t \beta^{t-1}$$

$$- \frac{(1 - k)\alpha h y}{(1 - h\beta)} \sum_{t=1}^{T} m_t \beta^t [1 - (h\beta)^{T-t}] + \frac{\varepsilon}{(b - b_0)} \sum_{i=1}^{T} d^i l_{t-i} \Big[1 - \sum_{t=1}^{T+1-i} m_t (d\beta)^{t-1} \Big]$$

$$\text{(A.48)}$$

The long-run equilibrium value of l_t, l_e, is derived by setting $l_t = l_{t-1} = \ldots = l_{t-T}$ and solving for $l_t = l_e$. When $T \to \infty$ the solution may be written as follows:

$$\lim_{T \to \infty} l_e = \frac{2b(1 - d)(1 - d\beta)v_3 \Big\{ [a + cz + (u - b + b_0)y] + \dfrac{(b - b_0)(1 - k)\alpha\beta hy}{(1 - h\beta)} \Big\}}{v_1[(2b - b_0)(1 - d)\rho v_3 - 2b\varepsilon d(1 - d^2\beta)]}$$

$$\text{(A.49)}$$

A necessary condition for a finite limit of l_e as $T \to \infty$ is $d < 1$ where we continue to consider only positive values of d. The long-run equilibrium loan rate, r_e, in the infinite-horizon case is obtained by substituting l_e for l_{t-i} ($i = 1, \ldots, T$) in (A.48), performing the indicated summations and letting $T \to \infty$:

$$\lim_{T \to \infty} r_e = \frac{(a + cz + uy)}{(b - b_0)}\left[1 - \frac{2b(1 - d\beta)}{(2b - b_0)\rho v_1}\right] + \frac{2b(1 - d\beta)y}{(2b - b_0)\rho v_1}$$

$$- \frac{(1 - d\beta)(1 - k)\alpha\beta hy}{(1 - h\beta)\rho v_1} + \frac{\varepsilon}{(b - b_0)(1 - d)}\left[1 - \frac{2b(1 - d^2\beta)}{(2b - b_0)\rho v_3}\right] \quad \text{(A.50)}$$

Let us now determine sufficient conditions for the stability of long-run equilibrium in the infinite-horizon case. The difference equation (A.47) reduces to the following when $T \to \infty$:

$$l_t = \frac{2b(1 - d\beta)\left\{[a + cz + (u - b + b_0)y] + \frac{(b - b_0)(1 - k)\alpha\beta hy}{(1 - h\beta)}\right\}}{(2b - b_0)\rho v_1}$$

$$+ \frac{2b\varepsilon(1 - d^2\beta)}{(2b - b_0)\rho v_3} \sum_{i=1}^{\infty} d^i l_{t-i} \quad \text{(A.51)}$$

The solution of (A.51) will involve the following characteristic equation:

$$x^T - Cdx^{T-1} - Cd^2x^{T-2} - \ldots - Cd^{T-1}x. \quad - Cd^T = 0 \quad \text{(A.52)}$$

where $C = 2b\varepsilon(1 - d^2\beta)/(2b - b_0)\rho v_3$ and $T \to \infty$. Since, by assumption, b, ε, $2b - b_0 > 0$ and given the satisfaction of the second-order conditions for a profit maximum and $0 \le d$, $\beta < 1$ so that $\rho,(1 - d^2\beta)$, $v_3 > 0$, we have $C > 0$. The difference equation (A.51) is stable if and only if the absolute values of all of the roots of (A.52) are less than unity. Applying the Schur conditions, the necessary and sufficient conditions that the absolute values of all of these roots be less than unity are that all of the following determinants be positive:[2]

$$\begin{vmatrix} 1 & -Cd^T \\ -Cd^T & 1 \end{vmatrix} \quad ; \quad \begin{vmatrix} 1 & 0 & -Cd^T & -Cd^{T-1} \\ -Cd & 1 & 0 & -Cd^T \\ -Cd^T & 0 & 1 & -Cd \\ -Cd^{T-1} & -Cd^T & 0 & 1 \end{vmatrix}$$

$$\begin{vmatrix} 1 & 0 & \ldots & 0 & -Cd^T & -Cd^{T-1} & \ldots & -Cd \\ -Cd & 1 & \ldots & 0 & 0 & -Cd^T & \ldots & -Cd^2 \\ \multicolumn{8}{c}{\cdots\cdots\cdots\cdots\cdots\cdots} \\ -Cd^{T-1} & -Cd^{T-2} & \ldots & 1 & 0 & 0 & \ldots & -Cd^T \\ -Cd^T & 0 & \ldots & 0 & 1 & -Cd & \ldots & -Cd^{T-1} \\ -Cd^{T-1} & -Cd^T & \ldots & 0 & 0 & 1 & \ldots & -Cd^{T-2} \\ \multicolumn{8}{c}{\cdots\cdots\cdots\cdots\cdots\cdots} \\ -Cd & -Cd^2 & \ldots & -Cd^T & 0 & 0 & \ldots & 1 \end{vmatrix}$$

Note that these determinants contain one's on the main diagonals and non-positive elements elsewhere. Also note that the sum of the elements in each row is $1 - C \sum_{i=1}^{T} d^i$ where $C \sum_{i=1}^{T} d^i$ is the sum of the coefficients of $l_{t-i} (i = 1, \ldots, T)$

in (A.51). If $C \sum_{i=1}^{T} d^i < 1$ these are determinants of simple examples of Ostroski M matrices. 'An M matrix is defined to be a real matrix A such that $a_{ij} \leq 0$, $i \neq j$, possessing one of the following three equivalent properties: (a) There exist N positive numbers x_j such that $\sum_{j=1}^{N} a_{ij}x_j > 0$ $(i = 1, ..., N)$; (b) A is non-singular and all elements of A^{-1} are non-negative; (c) All principal minors of A are positive.' [Bellman, 1960, p. 295]. Hence, a sufficient condition for the stability of (A.51) is that $1 - C \sum_{i=1}^{\infty} d^i$ and, equivalently, the denominator of (A.49) be positive. An example of these stability conditions is shown for $T = 2$ in (2.35) in Chapter 2.4.

NOTES

1. See Theorem 1.50 in Graybill [1961, pp. 8–9].
2. For discussions of these conditions, first derived by Schur, see Chipman [1951, pp. 118–21], Baumol [1959, pp. 246–48] and Chiang [1967, pp. 551–52].

APPENDIX B

Sources and Descriptions of the Data

The data presented in most of the tables and the charts in Chapters 1–6 are discussed in this appendix. Emphasis is placed on those points at which published data have been adjusted by the author. All adjustments were made in response to revisions in published data and are intended to facilitate intertemporal comparison of the data used in this study. Published data were not adjusted except in the instances discussed below; adjustments have not been made in response to numerous minor revisions. Many of the numbers for 1973 are based on preliminary figures from the May 1973 *Federal Reserve Bulletin* (*FRB*) and *Survey of Current Business* (*SCB*). Those tables and charts for which no detailed explanation is necessary or which are explained adequately in the text are not treated below.

Table 1.1. Interest Rates and Bank Portfolios at Postwar Cyclical Peaks and Troughs

Loans (*L*) and *security holdings* (*G*), seasonally adjusted and exclusive of interbank loans, are derived from data reported in the Federal Reserve Board's series 'Loans and Investments at Commercial Banks' reported in the *FRB*. Especially see the *FRB* issues of August 1968, August 1969 and December 1971. The published data are end-of-month figures; the data in Table 1.1 are estimated monthly averages, being simply unweighted averages of end-of-month figures. These data were revised in June 1969, affecting *L* and *G* in two ways: (1) Banks were 'required to submit consolidated reports, including figures for all bank premises subsidiaries and other significant majority-owned domestic subsidiaries; (2) figures for total loans and for individual categories of securities are now reported gross—that is, without deduction of valuation reserves—rather than net of such reserves, as they had been previously'. [*FRB*, August 1969, p. 642]. Both the old and new series were reported for June 1969 and it was seen that the revised value of L was about 102 per cent of that reported on the old basis while G was virtually unaffected. Consequently, values of L in Table 1.1 after June 1969 are based on data equal to 98 per cent of those reported in the *FRB* in order to make this series comparable over time.

The rate on short-term business loans of banks (r) is an estimated monthly average derived from straight-line interpolation of the Federal Reserve Board's 'Quarterly Survey of Interest Rates on Business Loans' reported in the *FRB*. Until 1967 this series was based on a survey of 19 centres for the first fifteen days of March, June, September and December. Since 1967 it has been based on a survey of 35 centres for the first fifteen days of February, May, August and November. The 1967 revision also excluded certain categories of loans, modified the maturities of loans included in the survey and altered the weights used to calculate average rates. The net effect of these changes in February 1967, when data based on both the old and the revised surveys were published, was an increase in the reported r of five basis points. [*FRB*, May 1967, pp. 721–27]. Consequently, five basis points have been subtracted from the published 1967–70 data. This series was revised again in February 1971 when the principal changes were the exclusion of accounts receivable, a shorter assumed maturity of loans and a change in the calculation of effective annual rates on discounted loans using annual rather than quarterly compounding of interest. The 1971 revision reduced the reported average rate by seventeen basis points, twelve basis points below rates based on the pre-1967 method. [*FRB*, June 1971, pp. 468–77]. Therefore, twelve basis points have been added to post-1970 published data. This and other interest rate series contain little or no seasonal variation and have not been seasonally adjusted. A convenient source of interest rate data for 1941–63, with descriptions of the data, is the *Supplement to Banking and Monetary Statistics*, Section 12, published in 1966 by the Federal Reserve Board.

The average yield on securities (y) is a weighted average of the following yields (weights in parentheses): (i) market yield on 3-month Treasury bills (0·105); (ii) average yield on selected 9–12 month U.S. note and bond issues (0·105); (iii) average yield on selected 3–5 year U.S. note and bond issues (0·430); (iv) average yield on selected U.S. long-term issues (0·049); (v) an estimate of the monthly average of yields on 5–10 year prime municipal bonds (0·311). These weights are based on the observation that the average proportions of U.S. 0–1, 1–10 and over-ten year securities and state and local government securities in the security portfolios of commercial banks during 1948–70 were 0·210, 0·430, 0·049 and 0·311, respectively. An unweighted average of (i) and (ii) was used as an estimate of the average yield on U.S. 0–1 year securities; the average yield on U.S. 1–10 year securities is estimated by (iii). Series (i)–(iv) are monthly averages of daily figures as they appear in the *FRB*. Data reported by Robinson [1960, p. 88], Rothwell [1966] and Rabinowitz [1969, pp. 236–37] suggest that the average maturity of state and local government securities held by commercial banks during the period 1956–65 was between six and nine years. An estimate of the yield on this type of security was derived by averaging yields on 5 to 10 year prime municipal bonds as reported in Salomon Brothers and Hutzler [1969, 1971, 1973]. Estimates of monthly averages were obtained by averaging first-of-month data. Since the Salomon Brothers' data (S) begin with 1950, estimates for 1948–49 were extrapolated from the very close relationship existing during 1950–67 between these data and Moody's *Aaa* state and local yields (*M*). A regression estimate of the relationship was $S_t = -0.0037 + 0.962M_t$. This relationship did not appear to be applicable to the period 1968–72 and a line with the same slope but a constant term of -0.0065 was used to estimate *S* for April 1973. Since interest on municipal securities is free of tax and most banks have been in tax brackets near fifty per cent during the postwar period, municipal yields were doubled in order to make them consistent with those on U.S. securities on a before-tax basis.

Table 4.1. Bank Loans as Proportions of Earning Assets and Earning Assets Plus Free Reserves

L and *G* are described above in connection with Table 1.1. *Member bank free reserves* (*E*) are monthly averages of daily figures reported in the *FRB* in the table entitled 'Reserves and Borrowings of Member Banks'. This series contains little or no seasonal variation and has not been seasonally adjusted.

Table 5.1. Published Rates and Expected One-Period Rates of Return

Moody's corporate bond yields (R_A, R_B) 'represent market yields to maturity on long-term, taxable, nonconvertible seasoned corporate bonds as reflected in quotations on selected bonds rated Aaa...and Baa by Moody's Investors Service.' [*Supplement to Banking and Monetary Statistics*, Section 12, p. 15]. For detailed descriptions of these data see the *Supplement* and the references contained therein. R_A and R_B are seasonally unadjusted monthly averages of daily figures reported in the *FRB*.

The market yield on Treasury bills ($\bar{y}$) is a monthly average of daily figures reported in the *FRB*.

The other yields, *y* and *r*, are discussed in connection with Table 1.1.

Chart 5.1 Economic Activity, Interest Rates and Commercial Bank Behaviour, II/1948-I/1973.

The measure of loan risk ($\bar{R}$) and the *average rate on short-term business loans*, adjusted for risk, ($\bar{r}$) are quarterly averages calculated according to the formulae shown in Table 5.1.

The average rate on short-term business loans (*r*) is a quarterly average of the loan rate described in connection with Table 1.1.

The market yield on Treasury bills ($\bar{y}$) is a quarterly average of monthly data reported in the *FRB*.

Commercial Bank loans as a proportion of earning assets plus free reserves

$[l = L/(L + G + E)]$ is based on quarterly averages of L, G and E estimated as discussed in connection with Tables 1.1 and 4.1.

The Federal Reserve Board's Index of Industrial Production (IP; 1957–59 = 100), seasonally adjusted, is a quarterly average of monthly data reported in the *FRB*. The base year was changed to 1969 when this series was revised in 1971. The new series has been adjusted to a basis comparable with pre-1971 data by multiplying 1971–72 data by 1·568, which was the ratio of the old to the new series in the first quarter of 1971.

Gross national product (GNP) in billions of 1958 dollars, seasonally adjusted quarterly totals at annual rates, was taken from *Business Statistics* (Department of Commerce, 1971) and the *SCB*.

All of the data in Chart 5.1 are listed in Table B.1 below.

Table 6.1. Loan Rates by Size of Loan

Short-term business loan rates by size of loan $(r_1, r_2, r_3, r_4, r_5)$ are estimated monthly averages calculated by straight-line interpolation of the Federal Reserve Board's 'Quarterly Survey of Interest Rates on Business Loans' reported in the *FRB*. (See *Supplement to Banking and Monetary Statistics*, Section 12, for 1941–63 data). These data, like r discussed in connection with Table 1.1, were revised in 1967 and 1971. The 1967 revision included changes in the size groupings of loans in addition to the changes discussed with respect to r. Since both the continued and the new size groups were reported for February 1967 for both the earlier and the revised procedures it is possible to observe the effects of that revision on average rates on loans of 1–10, 10–100, 100–500, 500–1000 and over-1000 millions of dollars. Changes in these groups due to the revision were -8, -5, $+1$, $+4$ and $+2$ basis points, respectively. The 1971 revision produced further changes in the same groups of -7, -16, -11, -4 and -6 basis points. These changes have been added or subtracted, as appropriate, to the published data in order to make the data used in this study comparable on a pre-1967 basis.

The prime rate charged by banks (r_6) is a monthly average of data reported in the *FRB*.

The average yield on securities (y) is discussed in connection with Table 1.1.

Table 6.2. Loans and Investments of Commercial Banks by Federal Reserve Class

Loans (L) and *investments* (G) of commercial banks, not seasonally adjusted, are based on those reported in the *FRB* table entitled 'Principal Assets and Liabilities and Number, by Class of Bank'. *Average end-of-year assets* have been calculated from data presented in the same table. Loans and investments are estimated monthly averages, being unweighted averages of end-of-month figures. These data were revised in June 1969 as described in the discussion of L in Table 1.1. The effects of this revision are not known precisely since there was no overlap in the reporting of the old and new series by Federal Reserve class. For purposes of this study the loan data reported since the revision have been adjusted downward 2 per cent on the assumption that all classes of banks were similarly affected. The factor of 2 per cent was discussed in connection with Table 1.1. The loan classes in Table 6.1 do not sum to L in Table 1.1 because the former are not seasonally adjusted and do not exclude interbank loans.

Chart 6.1   The Behaviour of Large and Small Banks, II/1948–I/1973

The rate on small short-term business loans, adjusted for risk, $(\bar{r}_s)$ is a quarterly average of r_1 reported in Table 6.1 adjusted for risk in the manner shown in Table 5.1 except that $\bar{R}$ instead of $0{\cdot}5\bar{R}$ is used in the adjustment.

The rate on large short-term business loans (r_L) is a quarterly average of r_4 reported in Table 6.1 for the period 1948–66. For the period 1967–73 r_L is a weighted average of r_4 and r_5 in Table 6.1, the weights being 3/7 and 4/7, respectively. Average rates on loans between \$500,000 and \$1,000,000 and on loans in excess of \$1,000,000 were not reported prior to February 1967 and the average rate on all loans over \$200,000 was not reported after that date. But the single period of overlap in the reporting of these series has made possible the use of the weighted average defined above as an estimate of the average rate on all loans over \$200,000 during the post-1966 period.

The market yield on Treasury bills $(\bar{y})$ is a quarterly average of monthly data reported in the *FRB*.

Loans as proportions of earning assets of non-member banks (l_s) and of New York City member banks (l_L) are based on quarterly averages of the data shown in Table 6.2. Loans are expressed as proportions of $L + G$ rather than $L + G + E$ as in Chart 5.1 because of the absence of data on excess reserves for non-member banks. Data for classes of member banks were not reported except for call dates prior to October 1948. However, it was seen from 1947 and 1948 call dates that loans and investments of all New York City member banks were on average 101·5 per cent and 102·2 per cent, respectively, of loans and investments of 'Weekly Reporting New York City Member Banks' reported in the *FRB*. These factors were applied to the data for weekly reporting banks to obtain estimates of loans and investments of all New York City member banks for the missing months. $l_s = L_s/(L + G)_s$ and $l_L = L_L/(L + G)_L$ were calculated from data listed in Table B.1; r_s, $\bar{r}_s$, r_L and $\bar{y}$ are also listed in Table B.1.

Table B.1.   Data Used in Chapters 5 and 6

The following data are not seasonally adjusted unless denoted by (S). All series are quarterly averages of published figures except GNP(S), \$GNP and P(S), which are published on a quarterly basis. All dollar figures are in billions; this includes L, $L + G$, E, Q, and \$GNP. All interest rates are percentages. Table (T) and chart (C) numbers indicate where in this appendix sources and descriptions of data may be found. Sources are listed for those series not discussed previously in the appendix.

$L(S)$, L:	Loans of all commercial banks. (T1.1, C5.1)
L_s, L_L:	Loans of non-member banks and New York City member banks. (T6.2, C6.1)
$(L + G)(S)$, $(L + G)$:	Loans and investments of all commercial banks. (T1.1, C5.1)
$(L + G)_s$, $(L + G)_L$:	Loans and investments of non-member banks and New York City member banks. (T6.2, C6.1)
E:	Excess reserves of all member banks. (T4.1, C5.1)
$Q(S)$:	Demand and time deposits of the public plus U.S. Government deposits in commercial banks. U.S. Government deposits are not seasonally adjusted. For descriptions and lists of data see *FRB*, October 1966, December 1970 and November 1971. These deposit series were revised in February 1973 to take account of the change in Regulation *J* governing check-collection procedures, which raised Q in 1972 by approximately 1·7 per cent. [*FRB*, February 1973, pp. 61–79]. The published data for I/73 were adjusted downwards to a level consistent with the old basis by applying the ratio of the old to the new series prevailing in I/72.
$\bar{y}$:	Market yield on three-month Treasury bills. (T5.1, C5.1, C6.1)
R_B, R_A:	Moody's market yields to maturity on selected corporate bonds rated *Baa* and *Aaa*. (T5.1)
$\bar{R}$:	A measure of loan risk. (C5.1)
r, $\bar{r}$:	Average rate on short-term business loans of all sizes, unadjusted and adjusted for risk. (T1.1, C5.1)
r_s, $\bar{r}_S$:	Average rate on small short-term business loans, unadjusted and adjusted for risk; r_s corresponds to r_1 in Table 6.1. (T6.1, C6.1).
r_L:	Average rate on large short-term business loans; r_L is an average of r_4 and r_5 in Table 6.1. (T6.1, C6.1)
IP(S):	Federal Reserve Board's Index of Industrial Production 1957–59 = 100. (C5.1)
GNP(S):	Gross national product in billions of 1958 dollars. (C5.1)
\$GNP:	Dollar GNP, non-seasonally adjusted, appears only in the July issues of the *SCB* for periods ending with the fourth quarter of the preceding year. The 1972–73 data in Table B.1 are estimates based on \$GNP(S) assuming that seasonal factors in 1972–73 were unchanged from those used in 1971.
P(S):	GNP price deflator. Data prior to 1966 are from *The National Income and Product Accounts of the U.S. 1929–65*, Department of Commerce. Subsequent data are from the *SCB*.

Table B.1. Data Used in Chapters 5 and 6

Quarter	$L(S)$	L	L_s	L_L	$(L+G)(S)$	$(L+G)$	$(L+G)_s$	$(L+G)_L$
48–2	39·4	39·1	5·9	7·3	115·2	114·0	18·5	19·3
48–3	40·6	40·2	6·1	7·5	114·5	114·3	18·6	19·3
48–4	41·3	41·8	6·4	7·8	113·1	113·9	18·7	18·6
49–1	41·7	42·1	6·4	8·0	113·3	113·5	18·6	18·6
49–2	41·4	41·0	6·5	7·7	114·0	112·8	18·5	18·6
49–3	41·2	40·8	6·6	7·4	116·2	116·0	18·6	19·3
49–4	41·6	42·1	6·7	7·5	118·4	119·3	18·7	19·5
50–1	42·6	42·9	6·8	7·5	120·1	120·4	18·8	19·4
50–2	44·1	43·8	7·0	7·6	121·8	120·6	19·0	19·3
50–3	47·0	46·4	7·3	8·3	122·8	122·3	19·1	19·6
50–4	49·8	50·4	7·5	9·2	123·7	124·8	19·1	20·1
51–1	52·5	52·8	7·8	10·0	124·6	125·0	19·5	20·1
51–2	54·4	54·1	7·9	10·1	126·1	125·1	19·4	20·3
51–3	55·1	54·6	8·0	10·2	126·5	126·3	19·7	20·2
51–4	55·9	56·4	8·1	10·9	129·2	130·4	20·3	20·8
52–1	56·9	57·0	8·2	11·2	131·4	131·9	20·5	21·2
52–2	58·3	58·0	8·5	11·1	133·7	132·4	20·7	21·3
52–3	60·1	59·6	8·8	11·2	136·3	135·9	21·3	21·5
52–4	61·9	62·4	9·1	11·8	138·3	140·3	21·9	21·6
53–1	63·5	63·7	9·2	12·2	139·5	140·0	22·1	21·3
53–2	64·8	64·6	9·4	12·3	139·1	138·0	22·1	20·7
53–3	65·7	65·3	9·5	12·0	142·3	141·8	22·6	21·4
53–4	66·1	66·6	9·7	12·3	142·7	144·1	23·0	21·9
54–1	66·3	66·4	9·8	11·8	144·1	144·3	23·1	21·7
54–2	66·7	66·5	10·0	11·8	145·7	144·3	23·0	22·0
54–3	66·7	66·5	10·1	11·5	148·3	147·9	23·4	22·8
54–4	67·5	68·2	10·2	11·8	152·3	153·8	24·1	23·7
55–1	70·3	70·3	10·5	12·2	154·3	154·5	24·3	23·5
55–2	72·7	72·5	10·7	12·9	155·4	154·1	24·4	23·4
55–3	76·0	75·9	11·0	13·5	156·2	155·7	24·7	23·1
55–4	79·0	79·5	11·4	14·2	156·9	158·2	25·3	23·2
56–1	81·8	81·6	11·7	14·5	158·3	158·3	25·4	23·1
56–2	84·6	84·5	12·0	15·2	159·4	158·7	25·5	23·2
56–3	86·2	86·2	12·1	15·4	159·8	159·4	25·7	23·1
56–4	87·7	88·1	12·2	15·9	161·0	162·2	26·2	23·4
57–1	88·7	88·3	12·2	15·9	162·0	161·9	26·2	23·3
57–2	90·2	90·1	12·5	16·2	164·0	163·5	26·6	23·5
57–3	91·3	91·5	12·7	16·2	164·8	164·5	26·9	23·3
57–4	91·6	91·9	12·8	16·1	165·5	166·5	27·4	23·3
58–1	91·6	91·2	12·9	15·9	167·7	167·6	27·5	23·9
58–2	92·1	91·9	13·1	16·3	174·5	174·0	28·1	25·8
58–3	92·3	92·5	13·4	15·6	177·8	177·5	28·5	25·9
58–4	94·0	94·4	13·7	15·7	180·2	182·4	29·8	25·5
59–1	97·0	96·5	14·2	16·0	183·0	182·8	30·4	25·8
59–2	100·1	100·0	14·7	16·4	184·5	183·5	30·6	25·7
59–3	104·3	104·6	15·4	17·1	185·9	185·7	31·4	25·7
59–4	106·9	107·3	15·9	17·7	185·8	186·9	32·1	25·1
60–1	108·9	108·4	16·1	17·7	185·8	185·5	32·2	24·7
60–2	110·9	110·7	16·6	17·9	186·7	185·7	32·2	25·1

Table B.1. Continued

Quarter	$L(S)$	L	L_s	L_L	$(L+G)(S)$	$(L+G)$	$(L+G)_s$	$(L+G)_L$
60–3	112·2	112·3	17·1	17·6	189·1	188·9	32·6	25·6
60–4	113·3	113·8	17·4	17·6	192·9	194·2	33·5	26·4
61–1	114·7	114·7	17·3	18·0	196·7	196·6	33·5	27·4
61–2	115·7	115·4	17·5	18·3	199·2	198·2	33·5	27·8
61–3	116·7	116·7	18·0	18·0	204·1	203·5	34·3	28·7
61–4	119·0	119·7	18·4	18·4	208·0	209·5	35·3	29·2
62–1	121·5	121·3	18·6	19·1	211·7	212·0	35·8	29·8
62–2	125·0	124·7	19·4	19·3	216·2	215·3	36·6	29·8
62–3	127·6	127·5	20·1	19·4	220·8	219·3	37·7	30·0
62–4	131·8	132·7	20·9	20·6	221·8	227·0	39·4	31·1
63–1	135·7	135·3	21·3	21·0	230·4	230·8	39·9	32·3
63–2	138·8	138·5	22·1	20·8	234·5	233·9	40·6	32·2
63–3	142·9	143·1	23·1	21·4	239·2	238·5	41·7	32·4
63–4	147·5	148·2	23·8	22·6	243·4	244·9	43·0	33·5
64–1	151·8	151·2	24·1	23·1	247·8	248·2	43·8	34·0
64–2	156·1	156·2	25·0	24·4	252·4	251·9	44·4	35·3
64–3	160·6	160·8	25·9	25·2	257·8	256·7	45·3	36·4
64–4	165·0	165·5	26·9	25·9	264·2	266·2	47·5	37·6
65–1	171·5	170·8	27·8	27·4	271·1	271·3	48·7	39·0
65–2	178·1	178·2	28·9	29·6	278·0	277·3	49·6	40·5
65–3	183·8	184·2	29·9	30·1	284·3	283·3	50·6	41·4
65–4	189·7	189·9	30·9	31·1	291·0	292·3	52·7	42·6
66–1	196·5	194·5	31·6	32·8	297·6	297·6	54·3	43·7
66–2	201·2	201·3	32·8	34·2	302·9	302·6	55·4	44·6
66–3	204·8	206·0	33·8	35·1	308·4	307·9	56·7	45·6
66–4	207·2	207·4	34·4	34·7	309·1	310·1	57·8	45·0
67–1	210·4	209·6	34·8	35·0	316·0	315·7	58·9	45·9
67–2	213·1	213·3	36·2	35·5	323·8	323·6	60·6	46·7
67–3	217·2	218·3	37·3	36·6	333·9	333·4	62·6	48·5
67–4	222·3	222·3	38·0	37·1	343·0	344·1	65·1	50·1
68–1	228·0	227·0	38·9	37·9	351·1	351·5	66·9	50·7
68–2	231·8	231·8	40·3	38·0	356·7	355·5	68·6	50·5
68–3	239·4	240·9	42·2	40·2	370·3	367·3	70·8	53·2
68–4	248·3	248·4	44·1	41·3	381·9	381·4	73·9	55·3
69–1	255·5	253·8	44·7	42·5	386·5	386·2	75·8	55·3
69–2	262·0	262·3	47·3	43·3	391·8	390·9	78·2	55·3
69–3	265·3	266·0	49·1	44·7	392·6	392·3	79·6	56·4
69–4	270·0	270·0	50·6	45·4	394·4	395·6	81·4	57·1
70–1	272·6	270·6	51·7	45·1	394·9	394·5	82·6	56·6
70–2	272·4	272·4	53·3	44·2	399·4	399·1	84·5	56·6
70–3	277·5	278·7	55·1	44·7	410·4	409·8	87·6	57·6
70–4	284·3	284·4	56·5	45·4	423·2	424·7	90·9	59·2
71–1	289·2	287·8	57·7	45·5	437·8	437·6	94·2	60·1
71–2	294·0	293·7	60·2	44·9	449·1	448·1	98·1	59·0
71–3	302·2	303·3	62·1	46·4	460·6	460·2	101·5	59·9
71–4	312·3	312·4	65·2	47·2	472·9	474·6	105·8	61·1
72–1	321·2	319·5	67·5	47·8	488·5	488·0	109·8	61·8
72–2	332·7	332·7	71·5	49·4	505·4	504·4	115·3	63·9
72–3	345·3	346·5	75·8	51·9	519·3	518·8	120·3	67·1
72–4	362·9	363·5	79·7	54·0	539·0	541·1	125·7	69·8
73–1	384·0	382·5	83·4	59·0	562·6	562·8	130·8	73·8

Table B.1. Continued

Quarter	E	Q(S)	$\bar{y}$	R_B	R_A	$\bar{R}$	r	$\bar{r}$	r_s	$\bar{r}_s$
48–2	0·7	124·2	1·00	3·40	2·77	0·63	2·45	2·14	4·41	3·77
48–3	0·7	124·4	1·05	3·42	2·83	0·59	2·56	2·27	4·52	3·92
48–4	0·7	124·1	1·14	3·52	2·82	0·70	2·63	2·28	4·51	3·80
49–1	0·6	124·0	1·17	3·46	2·71	0·74	2·68	2·31	4·59	3·84
49–2	0·6	124·0	1·17	3·46	2·71	0·74	2·73	2·36	4·63	3·88
49–3	0·9	124·5	1·04	3·41	2·63	0·77	2·66	2·27	4·62	3·84
49–4	0·7	125·4	1·08	3·34	2·60	0·74	2·64	2·27	4·55	3·80
50–1	0·7	126·7	1·10	3·24	2·58	0·66	2·62	2·29	4·47	3·80
50–2	0·6	128·4	1·15	3·25	2·61	0·64	2·66	2·34	4·49	3·84
50–3	0·6	130·1	1·22	3·25	2·63	0·62	2·65	2·34	4·51	3·88
50–4	0·7	130·7	1·34	3·21	2·67	0·54	2·79	2·52	4·58	4·03
51–1	0·3	131·9	1·37	3·19	2·70	0·49	2·97	2·73	4·66	4·16
51–2	0·5	134·9	1·49	3·41	2·90	0·51	3·06	2·81	4·72	4·20
51–3	0·5	135·5	1·60	3·50	2·89	0·61	3·07	2·77	4·74	4·12
51–4	0·5	137·0	1·61	3·56	2·95	0·61	3·22	2·92	4·77	4·15
52–1	0·5	139·0	1·57	3·51	2·96	0·55	3·40	3·13	4·83	4·27
52–2	0·2	141·7	1·65	3·50	2·93	0·57	3·49	3·21	4·89	4·31
52–3	−0·3	145·4	1·78	3·51	2·95	0·56	3·50	3·22	4·91	4·34
52–4	−0·7	145·9	1·89	3·53	2·99	0·54	3·51	3·24	4·89	4·34
53–1	−0·6	145·9	1·98	3·54	3·07	0·47	3·53	3·30	4·89	4·41
53–2	−0·2	146·1	2·15	3·76	3·32	0·44	3·68	3·46	4·96	4·51
53–3	−0·2	149·9	1·95	3·86	3·27	0·59	3·74	3·45	5·00	4·40
53–4	0·3	148·5	1·47	3·77	3·13	0·64	3·75	3·43	4·99	4·34
54–1	0·6	150·3	1·06	3·61	2·96	0·65	3·73	3·41	4·99	4·33
54–2	0·6	152·2	0·79	3·48	2·88	0·60	3·63	3·33	4·98	4·37
54–3	0·7	155·3	0·88	3·49	2·88	0·61	3·57	3·27	4·98	4·36
54–4	0·6	158·6	1·02	3·45	2·89	0·56	3·55	3·27	4·94	4·37
55–1	0·3	158·2	1·23	3·47	2·96	0·51	3·54	3·29	4·93	4·41
55–2	0·2	160·4	1·48	3·50	3·03	0·47	3·56	3·33	4·92	4·44
55–3	−0·1	161·1	1·86	3·56	3·10	0·46	3·72	3·49	4·96	4·49
55–4	−0·4	161·3	2·34	3·60	3·12	0·48	3·89	3·65	5·00	4·51
56–1	−0·3	160·7	2·33	3·59	3·10	0·49	3·94	3·70	5·04	4·54
56–2	−0·4	163·0	2·57	3·72	3·26	0·46	4·09	3·86	5·15	4·68
56–3	−0·2	163·4	2·58	3·93	3·42	0·51	4·29	4·04	5·27	4·75
56–4	−0·1	164·0	3·01	4·26	3·68	0·57	4·37	4·08	5·32	4·74
57–1	−0·2	164·0	3·10	4·46	3·70	0·75	4·38	4·00	5·36	4·60
57–2	−0·5	167·3	3·14	4·53	3·77	0·75	4·41	4·03	5·38	4·62
57–3	−0·4	167·8	3·35	4·83	4·07	0·75	4·71	4·33	5·59	4·83
57–4	−0·3	168·5	3·30	5·04	4·00	1·03	4·83	4·32	5·66	4·62
58–1	0·3	169·6	1·76	4·72	3·61	1·10	4·58	4·03	5·58	4·47
58–2	0·5	176·8	0·95	4·61	3·58	1·02	4·26	3·75	5·48	4·45
58–3	0·3	180·2	1·68	4·69	3·87	0·81	4·21	3·80	5·45	4·63
58–4	0	187·8	2·69	4·88	4·09	0·78	4·42	4·03	5·48	4·69
59–1	−0·1	183·3	2·77	4·87	4·13	0·73	4·52	4·15	5·52	4·78
59–2	−0·4	185·9	3·00	4·95	4·35	0·59	4·78	4·48	5·65	5·05
59–3	−0·5	187·5	3·54	5·12	4·47	0·64	5·16	4·84	5·86	5·21
59–4	−0·4	186·3	4·23	5·27	4·57	0·69	5·33	4·98	5·97	5·27
60–1	−0·3	184·2	3·87	5·31	4·55	0·75	5·35	4·97	6·00	5·24
60–2	−0·1	185·1	2·99	5·25	4·45	0·79	5·34	4·94	6·00	5·20

Table B.1.   Continued

Quarter	E	Q(S)	$\bar{y}$	R_B	R_A	$\bar{R}$	r	$\bar{r}$	r_s	$\bar{r}_s$
60–3	0·3	188·3	2·36	5·10	4·31	0·78	5·08	4·69	5·96	5·17
60–4	0·6	190·2	2·31	5·10	4·32	0·77	4·98	4·59	5·91	5·13
61–1	0·6	192·7	2·35	5·06	4·27	0·78	4·98	4·59	5·89	5·10
61–2	0·5	195·7	2·30	5·02	4·28	0·73	4·97	4·60	5·89	5·15
61–3	0·5	200·0	2·31	5·11	4·44	0·66	4·98	4·65	5·87	5·20
61–4	0·5	204·0	2·46	5·11	4·41	0·69	4·97	4·62	5·85	5·15
62–1	0·5	207·2	2·72	5·06	4·41	0·64	4·98	4·66	5·88	5·23
62–2	0·4	212·8	2·71	5·01	4·30	0·70	5·00	4·65	5·88	5·17
62–3	0·4	216·6	2·84	5·05	4·34	0·70	5·00	4·65	5·87	5·16
62–4	0·4	219·8	2·81	4·96	4·26	0·69	5·01	4·66	5·87	5·17
63–1	0·3	224·0	2·91	4·89	4·20	0·68	5·01	4·67	5·89	5·20
63–2	0·2	229·3	2·94	4·85	4·22	0·62	5·01	4·70	5·87	5·24
63–3	0·1	234·3	3·29	4·84	4·29	0·54	5·01	4·74	5·86	5·31
63–4	0·1	237·1	3·50	4·84	4·33	0·50	5·00	4·75	5·86	5·35
64–1	0·1	241·2	3·53	4·83	4·37	0·46	4·99	4·76	5·84	5·37
64–2	0·1	246·4	3·48	4·85	4·41	0·44	4·99	4·77	5·84	5·39
64–3	0·1	251·9	3·50	4·82	4·41	0·41	4·98	4·78	5·85	5·43
64–4	0·1	256·6	3·68	4·81	4·43	0·38	4·99	4·80	5·85	5·46
65–1	0	262·8	3·89	4·79	4·42	0·37	4·98	4·80	5·88	5·50
65–2	−0·2	270·4	3·87	4·82	4·44	0·38	4·98	4·79	5·88	5·49
65–3	−0·2	275·8	3·86	4·89	4·50	0·39	5·00	4·81	5·90	5·50
65–4	−0·1	280·8	4·16	4·97	4·61	0·36	5·20	5·02	5·95 ·	5·58
66–1	−0·1	286·3	4·60	5·17	4·81	0·36	5·48	5·30	6·09	5·72
66–2	−0·3	293·1	4·58	5·49	5·00	0·48	5·76	5·52	6·33	5·84
66–3	−0·4	296·1	5·03	5·87	5·32	0·54	6·17	5·90	6·34	6·09
66–4	−0·3	294·6	5·20	6·14	5·38	0·75	6·30	5·92	6·77	6·01
67–1	0·1	303·0	4·51	5·88	5·12	0·75	6·14	5·75	6·79	6·03
67–2	0·2	312·5	3·66	5·98	5·26	0·71	5·92	5·56	6·70	5·98
67–3	0·3	322·3	4·29	6·33	5·62	0·70	5·90	5·55	6·67	5·96
67–4	0·2	329·6	4·74	6·72	6·03	0·68	6·01	5·67	6·72	6·03
68–1	0	336·3	5·04	6·83	6·13	0·69	6·40	6·05	6·94	6·24
68–2	−0·4	340·8	5·51	7·02	6·25	0·76	6·76	6·37	7·26	6·49
68–3	−0·2	350·0	5·20	6·86	6·08	0·77	6·77	6·38	7·40	6·62
68–4	−0·2	359·8	5·58	7·03	6·24	0·78	6·76	6·36	7·43	6·64
69–1	−0·6	364·1	6·09	7·38	6·70	0·67	7·34	7·00	7·85	7·17
69–2	−1·0	365·6	6·19	7·59	6·89	0·69	8·00	7·65	8·39	7·69
69–3	−1·0	358·7	7·01	7·92	7·06	0·85	8·69	8·26	9·02	8·15
69–4	−0·9	356·7	7·35	8·37	7·47	0·88	8·78	8·33	9·15	8·25
70–1	−0·8	359·5	7·22	8·76	7·89	0·85	8·75	8·31	9·22	8·35
70–2	−0·7	368·0	6·67	8·98	8·14	0·82	8·47	8·05	9·16	8·32
70–3	−0·7	383·5	6·33	9·41	8·22	1·17	8·38	7·79	9·18	7·99
70–4	−0·2	396·4	5·35	9·28	7·91	1·34	7·84	7·16	8·86	7·49
71–1	−0·1	414·8	3·84	8·53	7·22	1·29	6·71	6·06	8·17	6·86
71–2	−0·1	430·2	4·24	8·61	7·47	1·12	6·25	5·68	7·69	6·55
71–3	−0·5	440·7	5·00	8·70	7·56	1·12	6·53	5·96	7·72	6·58
71–4	−0·1	447·1	4·23	8·41	7·30	1·09	6·22	5·66	7·60	6·49
72–1	0·1	462·9	3·44	8·23	7·23	0·98	5·71	5·21	7·26	6·26
72–2	0	476·5	3·77	8·22	7·28	0·92	5·75	5·28	7·25	6·31
72–3	−0·2	488·6	4·22	8·17	7·21	0·94	6·02	5·54	7·45	6·49
72–4	−0·5	501·3	4·86	8·00	7·14	0·84	6·44	6·01	7·67	6·82
73–1	−1·3	522·1	5·70	7·97	7·22	0·74	6·76	6·38	7·84	7·09

Table B.1. Continued

Quarter	r_L	IP(S)	GNP(S)	$ GNP	P(S)
48–2	2·15	68·5	322·9	62·1	0·792
48–3	2·26	69·5	325·8	65·3	0·806
48–4	2·33	68·5	328·7	70·7	0·803
49–1	2·40	66·2	324·5	61·8	0·797
49–2	2·43	64·5	322·5	62·2	0·791
49–3	2·35	64·3	326·1	64·5	0·788
49–4	2·34	64·0	323·3	68·0	0·789
50–1	2·32	67·4	339·6	64·0	0·783
50–2	2·37	73·1	348·5	66·8	0·790
50–3	2·36	79·0	362·8	73·5	0·808
50–4	2·51	80·3	370·1	80·5	0·823
51–1	2·71	81·9	374·8	76·6	0·848
51–2	2·80	82·2	381·5	79·9	0·854
51–3	2·78	80·3	388·7	83·2	0·856
51–4	2·97	80·8	388·7	88·7	0·867
52–1	3·18	82·6	391·4	82·0	0·867
52–2	3·28	81·4	389·6	83·3	0·871
52–3	3·28	83·6	393·9	85·7	0·877
52–4	3·29	89·7	405·3	94·4	0·883
53–1	3·32	91·6	412·1	87·4	0·884
53–2	3·47	95·4	416·4	91·3	0·883
53–3	3·54	92·8	413·7	90·3	0·884
53–4	3·56	87·8	408·8	95·6	0·884
54–1	3·53	84·9	402·9	86·5	0·895
54–2	3·41	85·2	402·1	89·7	0·896
54–3	3·33	85·6	407·2	90·0	0·895
54–4	3·31	87·5	415·7	98·6	0·898
55–1	3·30	92·1	428·0	92·6	0·902
55–2	3·33	96·0	435·4	97·4	0·906
55–3	3·50	98·2	442·1	100·4	0·910
55–4	3·70	100·0	446·4	107·6	0·916
56–1	3·74	99·3	443·6	98·6	0·926
56–2	3·91	99·7	445·6	102·9	0·934
56–3	4·13	98·7	444·5	104·1	0·946
56–4	4·20	101·8	450·3	113·7	0·954
57–1	4·21	102·3	453·4	104·4	0·964
57–2	4·24	101·8	453·2	109·1	0·971
57–3	4·56	101·8	455·2	110·6	0·980
57–4	4·70	97·0	448·2	117·0	0·985
58–1	4·40	90·4	437·5	103·9	0·993
58–2	4·05	89·9	439·5	108·8	0·997
58–3	4·00	95·3	450·7	111·7	1·001
58–4	4·24	99·0	461·6	123·0	1·006
59–1	4·33	103·0	468·6	113·1	1·011
59–2	4·62	108·8	479·9	121·4	1·015
59–3	5·03	105·2	475·0	119·3	1·019
59–4	5·21	105·2	480·4	129·9	1·021
60–1	5·22	111·1	490·2	120·5	1·026
60–2	5·21	109·7	489·7	125·6	1·031
60–3	4·90	108·5	487·3	124·6	1·035

Table B.1. Continued

Quarter	r_L	IP(S)	GNP(S)	$ GNP	P(S)
60–4	4·81	105·3	483·7	133·1	1·040
61–1	4·81	103·7	482·6	120·6	1·043
61–2	4·80	108·6	492·8	128·2	1·045
61–3	4·81	112·0	501·5	129·1	1·045
61–4	4·79	114·7	511·7	142·2	1·051
62–1	4·80	116·3	519·5	131·3	1·055
62–2	4·83	118·1	527·7	139·6	1·056
62–3	4·83	119·2	533·4	138·1	1·058
62–4	4·84	119·4	538·3	151·5	1·063
63–1	4·84	120·8	541·2	137·8	1·067
63–2	4·84	124·2	546·0	146·1	1·070
63–3	4·85	125·6	554·7	146·5	1·072
63–4	4·83	126·4	562·1	160·2	1·078
64–1	4·82	128·7	571·1	148·5	1·082
64–2	4·81	131·8	578·6	157·1	1·085
64–3	4·80	133·8	585·8	156·3	1·091
64–4	4·81	135·0	588·5	170·6	1·096
65–1	4·79	139·8	601·6	158·2	1·102
65–2	4·79	142·0	610·4	169·1	1·107
65–3	4·81	144·4	622·5	168·9	1·110
65–4	5·06	147·1	636·6	188·7	1·115
66–1	5·36	152·3	649·1	176·2	1·124
66–2	5·62	155·3	655·0	187·4	1·135
66–3	6·04	157·7	660·2	186·3	1·145
66–4	6·18	159·3	668·1	199·8	1·154
67–1	5·97	157·2	666·6	186·5	1·162
67–2	5·79	156·0	671·6	197·2	1·168
67–3	5·76	157·2	678·9	198·4	1·180
67–4	5·84	159·7	683·6	211·7	1·194
68–1	6·26	162·1	692·6	199·2	1·203
68–2	6·68	164·2	705·3	216·8	1·215
68–3	6·69	165·2	712·3	215·6	1·228
68–4	6·59	167·4	716·5	232·7	1·241
69–1	7·22	170·2	722·4	216·7	1·256
69–2	7·85	172·6	725·8	233·3	1·272
69–3	8·63	174·3	729·2	232·9	1·288
69–4	8·71	171·9	725·1	247·3	1·301
70–1	8·66	170·7	720·4	229·5	1·324
70–2	8·34	169·3	723·2	245·3	1·340
70–3	8·23	167·9	726·8	242·9	1·356
70–4	7·67	162·6	718·0	258·7	1·374
71–1	6·48	165·4	731·9	244·6	1·398
71–2	6·08	167·5	737·9	264·1	1·413
71–3	6·61	167·0	742·5	260·8	1·423
71–4	6·03	168·4	754·5	280·8	1·429
72–1	5·46	172·5	766·5	265·1	1·447
72–2	5·50	177·3	783·9	288·3	1·454
72–3	5·80	180·3	796·1	287·5	1·462
72–4	6·20	185·7	811·6	310·7	1·472
73–1	6·54	189·6	827·1	295·9	1·496

APPENDIX C

The Stability of Equilibrium

If we assume that the market which is suppressed in the analysis of comparative statics in Chapter 7, the securities market, is continuously in equilibrium our dynamic analysis may be restricted to the remaining markets. Suppressing the market for securities by dropping equations (7.1), (7.2), (7.4), (7.7) and (7.10) in Chapter 7.2.1 and substituting (7.11)–(7.13) into (7.3), (7.5), (7.6), (7.8), (7.9), (7.14) and an equilibrium condition for the labour market gives the following system of seven equations in seven jointly dependent variables—y, W, P, r, q, L, Q.

$$E_1 = PR(y, Q/P) - R = 0 \tag{C.1}$$

$$E_2 = N^d(W/P) - N^s(W/P) = 0 \tag{C.2}$$

$$E_3 = X(y, r, q, Z(N^d(W/P))) - Z(N^d(W/P)) = 0 \tag{C.3}$$

$$E_4 = r(y, Z(N^d(W/P))) - r = 0 \tag{C.4}$$

$$E_5 = q(y, Z(N^d(W/P))) - q = 0 \tag{C.5}$$

$$E_6 = PL(y, r, q, Z(N^d(W/P))) - L = 0 \tag{C.6}$$

$$E_7 = PQ(y, r, q, Z(N^d(W/P))) - Q = 0 \tag{C.7}$$

E_1, E_2, E_3, E_6, and E_7 denote excess demands for bank reserves, labour, commodities, loans and deposits, respectively, while E_4 and E_5 indicate the excess of profit maximizing loan and deposit rates over their actual values. All of the E_i are zero in equilibrium. For economy of notation define $p_1 = y$, $p_2 = W$, $p_3 = P$, $p_4 = r$, $p_5 = q$, $p_6 = L$, $p_7 = Q$. Let the adjustment processes of the jointly dependent variables in disequilibrium be governed by (C.8).

$$dp/dt = KE \tag{C.8}$$

where $p = [p_1 \ldots p_7]'$, $E = [E_1 \ldots E_7]'$ and K is a matrix of constants K_{ij}, i, $j = 1, \ldots, 7$.

Consider the meaning of the K_{ij}, $i = j$. Positive values of K_{22} and K_{33}, for example, indicate that excess demands for labour and commodities induce increases in W and P, respectively. The principal means by which banks adjust their reserve positions in the presence of an excess demand or supply of reserves is to sell or purchase securities[1], thereby causing increases or decreases in y. This implies $K_{11} > 0$.

Adjustments of r, q, L and Q are treated differently from y, W and P because, unlike the markets for securities, labour and commodities, the loan and deposit markets are assumed to be imperfectly competitive. This is consistent with our microeconomic model and equations (7.8) and (7.9) in the macroeconomic model. It is assumed that banks adjust loan and deposit rates toward their optimal values continuously and as proportions of the differences between profit maximizing and actual rates; thus, K_{44}, $K_{55} > 0$. Banks set the rates r and q and extend loans and accept deposits at these rates in the amounts determined by the public's preferences for loans and deposits. The last two rows of (C.8) indicate that the public adjusts their loans and deposits as constant proportions of the differences between desired and actual quantities; thus, K_{66}, $K_{77} > 0$.

The K_{ij}, $i \neq j$, take account of the possibility that price and quantity adjustments in one market may be influenced by disequilibria in other markets. For example, an excess demand for commodities may result in pressure on the prices of securities as well as commodity prices so that $K_{13} < 0$.

We obtain a linear approximation of the system in the neighbourhood of equilibrium by differentiating equations (C.1)–(C.7). Substituting this approximation into (C.8) gives

$$dp/dt = KE_p(p - p_e) \tag{C.9}$$

where p_e is a vector of equilibrium values of p and E_p is a matrix of partial derivatives of E with respect to p:

$$E_p = \begin{vmatrix} \dfrac{\partial E_1}{\partial p_1} & \cdots & \dfrac{\partial E_1}{\partial p_7} \\ \cdots\cdots\cdots\cdots\cdots \\ \dfrac{\partial E_7}{\partial p_1} & \cdots & \dfrac{\partial E_7}{\partial p_7} \end{vmatrix}$$

Our system is stable if $\lim_{t \to \infty} p = p_e$, which will be the case if the real roots of the characteristic equation (C.10) are all negative.[2]

$$|KE_p - \lambda I| = 0 \tag{C.10}$$

But the determinant $|KE_p| = |K||E_p|$ is equal to the product of the roots of equation (C.10). Hence, a necessary condition for stability is $|K||E_p| < 0$.

If we assume that price and quantity adjustments in a given market are dominated by the extent of disequilibrium in that market—i.e. the K_{ij}, $i = j$, are much larger than the K_{ij}, $i \neq j$–then, since all of the K_{ij}, $i = j$, are positive, a necessary condition for stability is $|E_p| < 0$. It can be shown that $|E_p| = -\Delta$

as defined following equation (7.24). Therefore, under our assumptions regarding dynamic adjustment processes, a necessary condition for stability is $\Delta > 0$ as asserted in Chapter 7.2.2.

NOTES

1. See equation (4.3) in Chapter 4.1.
2. This approach is based on Samuelson [1947, pp. 269–83]. Also see Patinkin [1965, pp. 484–94].

The Macroeconomic Effects of the Customer Relationship and a Variable Deposit Rate

D.1 THE CUSTOMER RELATIONSHIP

D.1.1 Shifts in Commodity Demand

This section lists the derivatives discussed in Chapter 7.3.1, i.e. the effects of variations in the strength of the customer relationship as reflected in r_z on the responses of the loan rate, r, the yield on securities, y, the commodity price index, P, and output, Z, to shifts, dS, in the demand for commodities. The notation is the same as in Chapter 7.

The results in (7.38) and (7.39) are based on the derivatives of (7.16)–(7.19) with respect to r_z. These derivatives may be written as follows:

$$\frac{\partial(dr/dS)}{\partial r_z} = X_s A[R_y + R_\varrho(Q_y + Q_r r_y + Q_q q_y)] \cdot$$
$$\cdot [B(X_y + X_q q_y) + A\{(1 - X_z)[R_y + R_\varrho(Q_y + Q_q q_y)]$$
$$+ R_\varrho Q_z(X_y + X_q q_y)\}] \tag{D.1}$$

$$\frac{\partial(dy/dS)}{\partial r_z} = - X_s A[R_y + R_\varrho(Q_y + Q_r r_y + Q_q q_y)]\{BX_r + AR_\varrho[X_r Q_z + Q_r(1 - X_z)]\} \tag{D.2}$$

$$\frac{\partial(dP/dS)}{\partial r_z} = \frac{X_s P^2}{R}[R_y + R_\varrho(Q_y + Q_r r_y + Q_q q_y)] ABC \tag{D.3}$$

$$\frac{\partial(dZ/dS)}{\partial r_z} = X_s[R_y + R_\varrho(Q_y + Q_r r_y + Q_q q_y)] A^2 C \tag{D.4}$$

In the *classical case* $(A = 0)$, (D.1)–(D.4) are zero. In the *Keynesian case* $(X_y = X_r = X_q = 0)$, (D.3)–(D.4) are zero and (D.1)–(D.2) become

$$\frac{\partial(dr/dS)}{\partial r_z} = \frac{X_s[R_y + R_\varrho(Q_y + Q_q q_y)]}{(1 - X_z)[R_y + R_\varrho(Q_y + Q_r r_y + Q_q q_y)]} \tag{D.1.1}$$

$$\frac{\partial(dy/dS)}{\partial r_z} = \frac{- X_s R_\varrho Q_r}{(1 - X_z)[R_y + R_\varrho(Q_y + Q_r r_y + Q_q q_y)]} \tag{D.2.1}$$

D.1.2 Federal Reserve Credit

The following derivatives, the signs of which are given in equations (7.43) and (7.44), are discussed in Chapter 7.3.2.

$$\frac{\partial(dr/dR)}{\partial r_z} = \frac{A}{P}(X_y + X_r r_y + X_q q_y) \cdot$$
$$\cdot [B(X_y + X_q q_y) + A\{(1 - X_z)[R_y + R_Q(Q_y + Q_q q_y)]$$
$$+ R_Q Q_z(X_y + X_q q_y)\}] \tag{D.5}$$

$$\frac{\partial(dy/dR)}{\partial r_z} = -\frac{A}{P}(X_y + X_r r_y + X_q q_y)\{BX_r + AR_Q[X_r Q_z + Q_r(1 - X_z)]\} \tag{D.6}$$

$$\frac{\partial(dP/dR)}{\partial r_z} = \frac{P}{R}(X_y + X_r r_y + X_q q_y) ABC \tag{D.7}$$

$$\frac{\partial(dZ/dR)}{\partial r_z} = \frac{A^2}{P}(X_y + X_r r_y + X_q q_y) C \tag{D.8}$$

The derivatives (D.5)–(D.8) are zero in the *classical* and *Keynesian cases*.

D.2   VARIABLE DEPOSIT RATES

D.2.1   Shifts in Commodity Demand

The derivatives of (7.15)–(7.19) with respect to q_y, the signs of which are shown in (7.47)–(7.49) in Chapter 7.4.1, may be written as follows:

$$\frac{\partial(dq/dS)}{\partial q_y} = -X_s[B + AR_Q(Q_r r_z + Q_z)] \cdot$$
$$\cdot [B(X_y + X_r r_y) + A\{[R_y + R_Q(Q_y + Q_r r_y)](1 - X_z - X_r r_z)$$
$$+ R_Q(X_y + X_r r_y)(Q_r r_z + Q_z)\}] \tag{D.9}$$

$$\frac{\partial(dr/dS)}{\partial q_y} = X_s[B + AR_Q(Q_r r_z + Q_z)] \cdot$$
$$\cdot \left[BX_q r_y + A\{r_y R_Q[X_q Q_z + Q_q(1 - X_z)]\right.$$
$$\left. + r_z[R_Q Q_q X_y - X_q(R_y + R_Q Q_y)]\} \right] \tag{D.10}$$

$$\frac{\partial(dy/dS)}{\partial q_y} = X_s[B + AR_Q(Q_r r_z + Q_z)] \cdot$$
$$\cdot \{BX_q + AR_Q[X_q(Q_r r_z + Q_z) + Q_q(1 - X_z - X_r r_z)]\} \tag{D.11}$$

$$\frac{\partial(dP/dS)}{\partial q_y} = \frac{-X_s P^2}{R}[B + AR_Q(Q_r r_z + Q_z)] BD \tag{D.12}$$

$$\frac{\partial(dZ/dS)}{\partial q_y} = -X_s[B + AR_Q(Q_r r_z + Q_z)] AD \tag{D.13}$$

where $D = X_q[R_y + R_Q(Q_y + Q_r r_y + Q_q q_y)] - R_Q Q_q(X_y + X_r r_y + X_q q_y) > 0$
In the *classical case* (D.13) is zero and the remaining derivatives become

$$\frac{\partial(dq/dS)}{\partial q_y} = \frac{-X_s(X_y + X_r r_y)}{(X_y + X_r r_y + X_q q_y)^2} \tag{D.9.1}$$

$$\frac{\partial(dr/dS)}{\partial q_y} = \frac{X_s X_q r_y}{(X_y + X_r r_y + X_q q_y)^2} \tag{D.10.1}$$

$$\frac{\partial(dy/dS)}{\partial q_y} = \frac{X_s X_q}{(X_y + X_r r_y + X_q q_y)^2} \tag{D.11.1}$$

$$\frac{\partial(dP/dS)}{\partial q_y} = \frac{-X_s P^2 D}{R(X_y + X_r r_y + X_q q_y)^2} \tag{D.12.1}$$

In the *Keynesian case*, equations (D.12)–(D.13) are zero and (D.9)–(D.11) reduce to

$$\frac{\partial(dq/dS)}{\partial q_y} = \frac{-X_s[B + AR_Q(Q_r r_z + Q_z)][R_y + R_Q(Q_y + Q_r r_y)]}{A(1 - X_z)[R_y + R_Q(Q_y + Q_r r_y + Q_q q_y)]^2} \tag{D.9.2}$$

$$\frac{\partial(dr/dS)}{\partial q_y} = \frac{X_s R_Q Q_q r_y[B + AR_Q(Q_r r_z + Q_z)]}{A(1 - X_z)[R_y + R_Q(Q_y + Q_r r_y + Q_q q_y)]^2} \tag{D.10.2}$$

$$\frac{\partial(dy/dS)}{\partial q_y} = \frac{X_s R_Q Q_q[B + AR_Q(Q_r r_z + Q_z)]}{A(1 - X_z)[R_y + R_Q(Q_y + Q_r r_y + Q_q q_y)]^2} \tag{D.11.2}$$

D.2.2 Federal Reserve Credit

The partial derivatives of (7.20)–(7.24) with respect to q_y are listed in this section. The signs of these derivatives are shown in (7.50)–(7.52) in Chapter 7.4.2.

$$\frac{\partial(dq/dR)}{\partial q_y} = \frac{A}{P}(1 - X_z - X_r r_z) \cdot$$
$$\cdot [B(X_y + X_r r_y) + A\{[R_y + R_Q(Q_y + Q_r r_y)](1 - X_z - X_r r_z)$$
$$+ R_Q(X_y + X_r r_y)(Q_r r_z + Q_z)\}] \tag{D.14}$$

$$\frac{\partial(dr/dR)}{\partial q_y} = \frac{-A}{P}(1 - X_z - X_r r_z) \cdot$$
$$\cdot \left[BX_q r_y + A\{r_y R_Q[X_q Q_z + Q_q(1 - X_z)] \right.$$
$$\left. + r_z[R_Q Q_q X_y - X_q(R_y + R_Q Q_y)]\} \right] \tag{D.15}$$

$$\frac{\partial(dy/dR)}{\partial q_y} = \frac{-A}{P}(1 - X_z - X_r r_z)\{BX_q + AR_Q[X_q(Q_r r_z + Q_z)$$
$$+ Q_q(1 - X_z - X_r r_z)]\} \tag{D.16}$$

$$\frac{\partial(dP/dR)}{\partial q_y} = \frac{P}{R}(1 - X_z - X_r r_z)ABD \tag{D.17}$$

$$\frac{\partial(dZ/dR)}{\partial q_y} = \frac{A^2}{P}(1 - X_z - X_r r_z)D \tag{D.18}$$

In the *classical case*, (D.14)–(D.18) are zero. In the *Keynesian case*, (D.17)–(D.18) are zero and (D.14)–(D.16) reduce to

$$\frac{\partial(dq/dR)}{\partial q_y} = \frac{[R_y + R_Q(Q_y + Q_r r_y)]}{P[R_y + R_Q(Q_y + Q_r r_y + Q_q q_y)]^2} \qquad (D.14.1)$$

$$\frac{\partial(dr/dR)}{\partial q_y} = \frac{- R_Q Q_q r_y}{P[R_y + R_Q(Q_y + Q_r r_y + Q_q q_y)]^2} \qquad (D.15.1)$$

$$\frac{\partial(dy/dR)}{\partial q_y} = \frac{- R_Q Q_q}{P[R_y + R_Q(Q_y + Q_r r_y + Q_q q_y)]^2} \qquad (D.16.1)$$

References

Alhadeff, D. A., *Monopoly and Competition in Banking*, Berkeley, University of California Press, 1954.

Andersen, L. A. and Burger, A. E., 'Asset Management and Commercial Bank Portfolio Behavior: Theory and Practice', *Journal of Finance*, May 1969, 207–22.

Baumol, W. J., *Economic Dynamics*, 2nd ed., New York, Macmillan, 1959.

Bellman, R., *Introduction to Matrix Analysis*, New York, McGraw-Hill, 1960.

Benston, G. J., 'Economies of Scale and Marginal Costs in Banking Operations', *The National Banking Review*, June 1965, 507–49. Reprinted in K. J. Cohen and F. S. Hammer, eds., *Analytical Methods in Banking*, Homewood, Ill., Irwin, 1966, pp. 545–74.

Bowers, R. D., 'Businesses, Households and Their Banks', Federal Reserve Bank of Philadelphia *Business Review*, March 1969, 14–19.

Cagan, P., 'Interest Rates and Bank Reserves—A Reinterpretation of the Statistical Association', in J. M. Guttentag and P. Cagan, eds., *Essays on Interest Rates*, New York, National Bureau of Economic Research, 1969, pp. 223–71.

Chamberlin, E. H., *The Theory of Monopolistic Competition*, 7th ed., Cambridge, Mass., Harvard University Press, 1956.

Chambers, D. and Charnes, A., 'Intertemporal Analysis and Optimization of Bank Portfolios', *Management Science*, July 1961, 393–410. Reprinted in K. J. Cohen and F. S. Hammer, eds., *Analytical Methods in Banking*, Homewood, Ill., Irwin, 1966, pp. 67–86.

Charnes, A. and Littlechild, S. C., 'Intertemporal Bank Asset Choice with Customer Relationships', July 1970. Revised version of 'Intertemporal Bank Asset Choice with Stochastic Dependence', *Systems Research Memorandum No. 188*, Northwestern University, April 1968.

Chase, S. B., 'Bank Reactions to Securities Losses', in D. R. Cawthorne *et. al.*, eds., *Essays on Commercial Banking*, Federal Reserve Bank of Kansas City, 1962, pp. 87–98.

Chiang, A. C., *Fundamental Methods of Mathematical Economics*, New York, McGraw-Hill, 1967.

Chipman, J. S., *The Theory of Inter-Sectoral Money Flows and Income Formation*, Baltimore, The Johns Hopkins Press, 1951.

Clemens, E. W., 'Price Discrimination and the Multiple-Product Firm', *The Review of Economic Studies*, 1951, 1–11. Reprinted in R. B. Heflebower and G. W. Stocking, eds., *Readings in Industrial Organization and Public Policy*, Homewood, Ill., Irwin, 1958, pp. 262–76.

141

Cohen, K. J., and Hodgman, D. R., 'A Macro–Econometric Model of the Commercial Banking Sector', presented to the Econometric Society, Pittsburgh, December 27, 1962.

Dhrymes, P. J., *Distributed Lags: Problems of Estimation and Formulation*, San Francisco, Holden–Day, 1971.

Durbin, J., 'Testing for Serial Correlation in Least–Squares Regression when Some of the Regressors are Lagged Dependent Variables', *Econometrica*, May 1970, 410–21.

Enthoven, A. C., 'Monetary Disequilibrium and the Dynamics of Inflation', *Economic Journal*, June 1956, 256–70.

Fabricant, S., 'Recent Economic Changes and the Agenda of Business-Cycle Research', *National Bureau of Economic Research Report* (Supplement), May 1971.

Federal Reserve Bank of Cleveland, 'Continuous Borrowing Through 'Short-Term' Bank Loans', *Monthly Business Review*, September 1956, 6–18. Partially reprinted in L. S. Ritter, ed., *Money and Economic Activity*, 3rd edition, Houghton Mifflin Co., Boston, 1967, pp. 98–109.

Freimer, M. and Gordon, M. J., 'Why Bankers Ration Credit', *Quarterly Journal of Economics*, August 1965, 397–416.

Galbraith, J. A., *The Economics of Banking Operations: A Canadian Study*, Montreal, McGill University Press, 1963.

Garvy, G., 'Structural Aspects of Money Velocity', *Quarterly Journal of Economics*, August 1959, 429–47.

Gilbart, J. W., *A Practical Treatise on Banking*, 2 vols., London, Bell and Daldy, 1865.

Gillespie, R. W., Hodgman, D. R. and Yancey, T. A., 'Commercial Bank Asset Selection: A Micro-Econometric Study', *Mimeographed Report of the Department of Economics*, University of Illinois, June 1969.

Gramley, L. E. and Chase, S. B., 'Time Deposits in Monetary Analysis', *Federal Reserve Bulletin*, October 1965, 1380–1406. Reprinted in K. Brunner, ed., *Targets and Indicators of Monetary Policy*, San Francisco, Chandler Publishing Co., 1969, pp. 219–49.

Graybill, F. A., *An Introduction to Linear Statistical Models*, I, New York McGraw-Hill, 1961.

Griliches, Z., 'Distributed Lags: A Survey', *Econometrica*, January 1967, 16–49.

Gurley, J. G. and Shaw, E. S., *Money in a Theory of Finance*, Washington, The Brookings Institution, 1960.

Guttentag, J., 'Credit Availability, Interest Rates and Monetary Policy', *Southern Economic Journal*, January 1960, 219–29.

Guttentag, J. M. and Herman, E. S., *Banking Structure and Performance*, New York University Graduate School of Business Administration, Institute of Finance, Bulletin No. 41/43, February 1967.

Hammond, B., *Banks and Politics in America from the Revolution to the Civil War*, Princeton, Princeton University Press, 1957.

Harris, D. G., 'Rationing Credit to Business: More Than Interest Rates', *Federal Reserve Bank of Philadelphia Business Review*, August 1970, 3–14.

Harris, D. G., 'Credit Rationing at Commercial Banks: Some Empirical Results', *Journal of Money, Credit and Banking*, May 1974, 227–40.

Hendershott, P. H., 'Open Market Operations, the Money Stock, and Various Policy Issues', in K. Brunner, ed., *Targets and Indicators of Monetary Policy*, San Francisco, Chandler Publishing Co., 1969, pp. 283–99.

Hendry, D. F., 'Stochastic Specification of an Aggregate Demand Model of the United Kingdom', unpub. paper, London School of Economics, 1971.

Hendry, D. F. and Trivedi, P. K., 'Maximum Likelihood Estimation of Difference Equations with Moving Average Errors: A Simulation Study', *Review of Economic Studies*, April 1972, 117–45.

Hester, D. D., 'An Empirical Examination of a Commercial Bank Loan Offer Function', *Yale Economic Essays*, Spring 1962, pp. 3–57. Reprinted in K. J. Cohen and F. S. Hammer, eds., *Analytical Methods in Banking*, Homewood, Ill., Irwin, 1966, pp. 178–215.

Hicks, J. R., 'Mr. Keynes and the "Classics"', *Econometrica*, April 1937. 147–59. Reprinted in W. Fellner and B. F. Haley, eds., *Readings in the Theory of Income Distribution*, Philadelphia, The Blakiston Co., 1951, pp. 461–76.

Hodgman, D. R., 'Credit Risk and Credit Rationing', *Quarterly Journal of Economics*, May 1960, 258–78.

Hodgman, D. R., 'The Deposit Relationship and Commercial Bank Investment Behavior', *Review of Economics and Statistics*, August 1961, 257–68.

Hodgman, D. R., *Commercial Bank Loan and Investment Policy*, Champaign, Ill., Bureau of Economic and Business Research, University of Illinois, 1963.

Houthakker, H. S. and Taylor, L. D., *Consumer Demand in the United States, 1929–1970*, Cambridge, Mass., Harvard University Press, 1966.

Jacobs, D. P., *Business Loan Costs and Bank Market Structure*, National Bureau of Economic Research, Occasional Paper 115, New York, Columbia University Press, 1971.

Jaffee, D. M., *Credit Rationing and the Commercial Loan Market*, New York, John Wiley and Sons, 1971.

Jaffee, D. M. and Modigliani, F., 'A Theory and Test of Credit Rationing', *American Economic Review*, December 1969, 850–72.

Johnston, J., *Econometric Methods*, 2nd ed., New York, McGraw-Hill, 1972.

Kane, E. J., 'Is There a Predilected Lock-In Effect?', *National Tax Journal*, December 1968, 365–85.

Kane, E. J. and Malkiel, B. G., 'Bank Portfolio Allocation, Deposit Variability, and the Availability Doctrine', *Quarterly Journal of Economics*, February 1965, 113–34.

Laidler, D. E. W., *The Demand for Money: Theories and Evidence*, Scranton, Pa., International Textbook Co., 1969.

Mayne, L. S., 'Supervisory Influence on Bank Capital', *Journal of Finance*, June 1972, 637–52.

Metzler, L. A., The Nature and Stability of Inventory Cycles', *Review of Economics and Statistics*, August 1941, 113–29. Reprinted in R. A. Gordon and L. R. Klein, eds., *Readings in Business Cycles*, Homewood Ill., Irwin, 1965, pp. 100–129.

Mints, L. W., *A History of Banking Theory in Great Britain and the United States*, Chicago, University of Chicago Press, 1945.

Modigliani, F., 'Liquidity Preference and the Theory of Interest and Money', *Econometrica*, January 1944, 45–88. Reprinted in F. A. Lutz and L. W. Mints, eds., *Readings in Monetary Theory*, Homewood, Ill., Irwin, 1951, pp. 186–240.

Modigliani, F., 'The Monetary Mechanism and its Interaction with Real Phenomena', *Review of Economics and Statistics*, February 1963 (Supplement), 79–107.

Monti, M., 'A Theoretical Model of Bank Behavior and Its Implications for Monetary Policy', *L'Industria Revista di Economia Politica*, No. 2, 1971, pp. 165–91.

Moore, B. J., *An Introduction to the Theory of Finance*, New York, The Free Press, 1968.

Moore, G. H., ed., *Business Cycle Indicators*, I, Princeton, Princeton University Press, 1961.

Moore, G. H. and Shiskin, J., *Indicators of Business Expansions and Contractions*, New York, National Bureau of Economic Research, 1967.

Murphy, N., 'A Test of the Deposit Relationship Hypothesis', *Journal of Financial and Quantitative Analysis*, March 1967, 53–59.

Nerlove, M., 'The Market Demand for Durable Goods: A Comment', *Econometrica*, January 1960, 132–42.

Patinkin, D., *Money, Interest and Prices*, 2nd ed., New York, Harper and Row, 1965.

Payne, P. L. and Davis, L. E., *The Savings Bank of Baltimore, 1818–1866*, Baltimore, The Johns Hopkins Press, 1956.

Peltzman, S., 'Capital Investment in Commercial Banking and Its Relationship to Portfolio Regulation', *Journal of Political Economy*, January–February 1970, 1–26.

Phelps, E. S. and Winter, S. G., 'Optimal Price Policy under Atomistic Competition', in E. S. Phelps *et. al.*, eds., *Microeconomic Foundations of Employment and Inflation Theory*, New York, W. W. Norton and Co., 1970, pp. 309–37.

Pollak, R. A., 'Habit Formation and Dynamic Demand Functions', *Journal of Political Economy*, July–August 1970, 745–63.

Powell, M. J. D., 'A Method for Minimizing a Sum of Squares of Non-Linear Functions without Calculating Derivatives', *Computer Journal*, January 1965, 303–307.

Pye, G. and Young, I., 'The Effect of Deposit Rate Ceilings on Aggregate Income', *Journal of Finance*, December 1972, 1023–34.

Rabinowitz, A., *Municipal Bond Finance and Administration*, New York, Wiley, 1969.

Rae, G., *The Country Banker: His Clients, Cares, and Work. From an Experience of Forty Years*, London, John Murray, 1885.

Robinson, R., *Postwar Market for State and Local Government Securities*, New York, National Bureau of Economic Research, 1960.

Roosa, R. V., 'Interest Rates and the Central Bank', in *Money, Trade and Economic Growth; in Honor of John Henry Williams*, New York, Macmillan, 1951, pp. 270–95.

Rothwell, J. C., 'The Move to Municipals', *Federal Reserve Bank of Philadelphia Business Review*, September 1966, 3–7.

Salomon Brothers and Hutzler, *An Analytical Record of Yields and Yield Spreads*, 1950–1968, New York, 1969. ('Supplements' published in 1971 and 1973).

Samuelson, P. A., *Foundations of Economic Analysis*, Cambridge, Mass., Harvard University Press, 1947.

Schumpeter, J. A., *Business Cycles: A Theoretical, Historical, and Statistical Analysis of the Capitalist Process*, New York, McGraw–Hill, 1939.

Scott, I. O., 'The Availability Doctrine: Theoretical Underpinnings', *Review of Economic Studies*, October 1957, 41–48.

Shull, B., 'Commercial Banks as Multiple-Product Price-Discriminating Firms', in D. Carson, ed., *Banking and Monetary Studies*, Homewood, Ill., Irwin, 1963, pp. 351–68.

Smith, P. F., 'Measuring Risk on Instalment Credit', *Management Science*, November 1964. Rep. in K. J. Cohen and F. S. Hammer, eds., *Analytical Methods in Banking*, Homewood, Ill., Irwin, 1966, pp. 136–51.

Staats, W. F., 'Corporate Treasuries and Their Depositories', *Federal Reserve Bank of Philadelphia Business Review*, March 1969, 9–13.

Stigler, G. J., *The Theory of Price*, rev. ed., New York, Macmillan, 1952.

Sutherland, R. J., 'Commercial Bank Portfolio Analysis', unpublished Ph.D. dissertation, University of Oregon, 1971.

Telser, L. G., 'A Critique of Some Recent Empircal Research on the Explanation of the Term Structure of Interest Rates', *Journal of Political Economy*, August 1967 (Supplement), 546–61.

Theil, H., *Economic Forecasts and Policy*, 2nd ed., Amsterdam, North-Holland Publishing Co., 1961.

Thornton, H., *An Enquiry into the Nature and Effects of the Paper Credit of Great Britain* (1802). Rep. with other writings of Thornton and with an Introduction by F. A. v. Hayek, New York, Augustus M. Kelley, 1965.

Tobin, J. and Brainard, W. C., 'Financial Intermediaries and the Effectiveness of Monetary Controls', *American Economic Review*, May 1963, 383–400. Reprinted in D. D. Hester and J. Tobin, eds., *Financial Markets and Economic Activity*, New York, John Wiley and Sons, 1967, pp. 55–93.

Wallis, K. F., 'Some Recent Developments in Applied Econometrics: Dynamic Models and Simultaneous Equation Systems', *Journal of Economic Literature*, September 1969, 771–96.

Wallis, K. F., 'Testing for Fourth Order Autocorrelation in Quarterly Regression Equations', *Econometrica*, July 1972, 617–36.

Wood, J. H., 'A Model of Federal Reserve Behavior', in G. Horwich, ed., *Monetary Process and Policy*, Homewood, Ill., Irwin, 1967, pp. 135–66.

Wood, J. H., 'A Model of Commercial Bank Loan and Investment Behaviour', in H. G.

Johnson and A. R. Nobay, eds., *Issues in Monetary Economics*, Oxford, Oxford University Press, 1974, pp. 402–53.

Zellner, A. and Geisel, M. S., 'Analysis of Distributed Lag Models with Applications to Consumption Function Estimation', paper presented to the European Meeting of the Econometric Society, 1968.

Index of Names

147

Index of Subjects

150